MILLENNIUM

A LATIN READER

A.D. 374–1374

*'Plurimi pertransibunt, et multiplex
erit scientia'*

F. E. HARRISON

Published by Bristol Classical Press (U.K.)
General Editor: John H. Betts
and by
Bolchazy-Carducci Publishers (U.S.A.)
(By arrangement with Oxford University Press)

Printed in Great Britain
First published by Oxford University Press, 1968.
Reprinted, with permission, 1987 by
Antony Rowe Ltd, Chippenham, Wiltshire

U.K.	U.S.A.
Bristol Classical Press	Bolchazy-Carducci Publishers
Wills Memorial Building	44 Lake Street
Queens Road	OAK PARK
BRISTOL BS8 1RJ	IL 60302
ISBN 0-86292-245-3	ISBN 0-86516-191-7

© Oxford University Press, 1968.

PREFACE

This book is intended for all who are interested in exploring the range of Latin literature well beyond the confines of the 'classical' period. There is, perhaps fortunately, no single label to cover this thousand years, but the two dates are significant. In 374 Aurelius Ambrosius, governor of Liguria, with his seat at Milan, by now an administrative capital of the Western Empire, a layman and an unbaptized Christian, was acclaimed by the populace bishop of Milan—and sixteen years later he excommunicated the Christian emperor Theodosius for his part in authorizing a massacre: an exaltation of the Church, and fusion or confusion of Church and State, which would have been inconceivable a century earlier, on the eve of the last and most violent persecutions. In 1374 Petrarch died—and if the modern world is to be dated from the fifteenth-century Renaissance, he, more than most in the field of scholarship, heralded and helped to shape the coming age. Between these two dates many forces were at work. This book concentrates on two of them: the leaven of Christianity, and the persistence and vitality of classical thought and literature—revolution and conservatism side by side. If its theme can be summed up in a few words, it is continuity in spite of unceasing change: an adventurous, exploring continuity.

Its limitations are conspicuous. It leaves on one side the major problems of politics, and in particular the central issue of Church and State; it is concerned with literature, not documents, with highlights rather than with shadows, and with monks and clerics more than with laymen, since it was they who for most of these centuries wielded the pen.

Of twenty-one known authors only one seems to be a layman—the author of the *Gesta Francorum*—and he is nameless. Even within these limits the omissions are glaring both in time and space: for example, the Carolingians have been crowded out, and, apart from the First Crusade, there is no reference to the world that lay outside western Christendom. The compiler can only suggest that longer selections from fewer authors, in spite of the resulting lack of balance, are more valuable than snippets from a wider field.

Passages are grouped under seven main headings, each of which spills over into the others, the first two in particular colouring all the rest.

1. The Bible;
2. The Christian Life;
3. History and Biography;
4. The World of Learning;
5. Wine, Woman, and Song;
6. Satire and Complaint;
7. Ghosts and Marvels.

Selections vary greatly in difficulty, but they have one thing in common: the *ipsissima verba* of a wide range of writers, with all the flavour and difficulty that involves— the walking and climbing pace, compared with the chairborne ease of a translation. A small dictionary is taken for granted (*Langenscheidt's Pocket Latin Dictionary—Latin– English*, by S. A. Handford (Methuen, London, 1962) has been used as a basis), and words and meanings not contained there are explained in the commentary.

The historical and biographical introductions are deliberately full, on the assumption that most readers leave the Middle Ages behind at the age of twelve or so, and only return to them a good deal later. But at least this gives the period the charm of unfamiliarity, while at the same time one sees the Latin classics in yet another light, through the eyes of an Augustine, a William of Malmesbury, a Petrarch.

The Notes on Language sketch in outline its evolution, and provide a framework of reference for the Commentary. The texts, according to their sources and period, exhibit different styles of orthography, but these changes are generally indicated, and after a preliminary dip this will not cause much trouble.

Where passages are shortened, summaries are sometimes given in English. With prose passages these may be included in the text but, with verse, in the commentary, so as not to spoil the appearance of the page.

ACKNOWLEDGEMENTS

I AM deeply indebted all round. First to the authors and editors who are listed in the Bibliography; but in addition to them to a wide range of scholars without whom this book could not have been written by a latecomer from the classics to medieval studies.

Beyond them I owe special thanks to two societies: to the Benedictines of Quarr Abbey, and to Brasenose College, Oxford, where I have long enjoyed the double freedom of a library and a home; and to these I should add the British Museum Reading Room, and that venerable institution, the Bodleian Library. Among individual scholars I am especially grateful to Dr. R. W. Hunt, Keeper of Western Manuscripts in the Bodleian, to Professor Sir Roger Mynors, to Mr. L. D. Reynolds of Brasenose College, and to Professor R. W. Southern, for light in dark places, and for much personal kindness. I must not shelter unduly behind such names, and the proportions (or lack of proportion) and errors are all my own. I am most grateful to the Press for their patience and skill. Above and beyond all, to my wife, without whom . . .

I am also indebted to the following editors and publishers for permission to use copyright texts: to Messrs. Nelson & Sons for *Gesta Francorum*, edited by Rosalind Hill (Nos. 34–36), and *The Chronicle of Jocelin of Brakelond*, edited by H. E. Butler (Nos. 37–38); to Sansoni, Florence, for Francesco Petrarca, *Le Familiari*, edited by Vittorio Rossi (Nos. 46–49); to Ricciardi, Milan, for Francesco Petrarca, *Prose*, edited by G. Martellotti (No. 45); to Fiorentino, Naples, for Riccardo da Bury, *Philobiblon*, edited by A. Altamura (No. 44); to the Oxford University Press for *The Oxford Book of Medieval Latin Verse*, edited by F. J. E. Raby (Nos. 25, 51, 55–57, 65–66); to the University of California Press for *Speculum Stultorum*, edited by J. H. Mozley and R. H. Raymo (No. 60); and to the Manchester University Press and V. H. Galbraith for No. 70, reprinted from the introduction to *The Anonimalle Chronicle*. (It has not proved possible to trace the present ownership of the Ingilby MS.)

The motto on the title-page will be found in Daniel, 12. 4: 'Many shall run to and fro, and knowledge shall be increased.'

F. E. H.

CONTENTS

LIST OF AUTHORS	xvii
SOME NOTES ON LANGUAGE	xix
SOME NOTES ON VERSE	xxvii

PART ONE. THE BIBLE

INTRODUCTION	1
1. Trust in God: Psalm 90 (St. Jerome's Vulgate)	3
2. Wisdom: Proverbs 8. 22–36 (Vulgate)	4

PART TWO. THE CHRISTIAN LIFE

INTRODUCTION	6
ST. JEROME (*c.* 345–420): *Letters*	
3. Cicero or Christ? (XXII. 30)	7
4. Wars, and Rumours of Wars (CXXVII. 12)	8
ST. AUGUSTINE (354–430): *The Confessions*	10
5. Introduction (I. 1)	13
6. Childhood and Schooldays (I. 9)	13
7. Adolescence (II. 2, 10)	15
8. Conversion (VIII. 11–12)	16
9. Looking Back (X. 27)	18
ST. BENEDICT (*c.* 480–547): *The Rule*	18
10. Introduction (from The Prologue)	20
11. The Abbot (ch. 64)	20
12. The Cellarer (ch. 31)	21
ST. ANSELM (*c.* 1033–1109): *Proslogion*	22
13. Faith seeks Understanding (ch. 1)	23

CONTENTS

EADMER (c. 1055–c. 1124): *The Life of Anselm*

14. Monastic Life under Difficulties (II. 8–9) — 26
15. St. Anselm and the Hare (II. 18) — 28

ST. BERNARD (1090–1153): *Letters* — 29

16. Come to Clairvaux! (Letter 106) — 31
17. Jerusalem Found (Letter 64) — 33

THE PAPACY: St. Bernard, *De Consideratione* (treatise for Pope Eugenius III) — 35

18. Your Greatness (II. 15, 16) — 35
19. Your Wretchedness (II. 18) — 37
20. Your Perils (I. 4, 13) — 38

VIRTUE AND VICE: Caesarius of Heisterbach (c. 1180–c. 1240), *Dialogus Miraculorum* — 39

21. Introductory (IV, concl.) — 39
22. Avarice (IV. 68) — 40
23. Simplicity (II. 1, 2) — 41

THE FOUR LAST THINGS — 44

24. The Death of Gerard: St. Bernard, Sermon 26, *On the Song of Songs* — 46
25. The Day of Judgement (*Dies irae*): Thomas of Celano (c. 1190–1260) — 49
26. The World to Come: Hildebert of Lavardin (1056–1133) — 51

PART THREE. HISTORY AND BIOGRAPHY

INTRODUCTION — 54

THE CONVERSION OF NORTHUMBRIA (625–64): Bede (c. 671–735), *Historia Ecclesiastica Gentis Anglorum* — 56

27. Edwin, 625–32 (II. 13) — 58
28. Oswin and Aidan, 641–51 (III. 14) — 61
29. The Synod of Whitby, 664 (III. 25) — 63

CONTENTS

WILLIAM RUFUS (1087–1100): William of Malmesbury (*c.* 1080– *c.* 1143), *De Gestis Regum Anglorum*

30. The Siege of Mont-Saint-Michel, 1091 (IV, §§ 309–10)	65
31. Back to Normandy, 1099 (IV, §§ 320–1)	67
32. His End, 1100 (IV, §§ 331–3)	68

THE FIRST CRUSADE (1095–9) 71

33. The Council of Clermont: Robert the Monk (*fl.* 1100), *Historia Hierosolomitana* (chs. 1, 2)	73
34. Bohemond takes the Cross: Anon., *Gesta Francorum* (I. iv)	75
35. The Battle of Dorylaeum: *Gesta Francorum* (III. ix)	77
36. Antioch: *Gesta Francorum* (IX. xxvi, xxvii)	80
Postscript	82

ABBOT SAMSON (1135–1211): Jocelin of Brakelond (*fl.* 1200), *Cronica de rebus gestis Samsonis Abbatis Monasterii Sancti Edmundi* 84

37. Who would be an Abbot! (ed. H. E. Butler, p. 36)	86
38. Portrait of Abbot Samson (pp. 39–40)	86

PART FOUR. THE WORLD OF LEARNING

INTRODUCTION 89

ST. AUGUSTINE: *De Doctrina Christiana*

39. Spoiling the Egyptians (II. 60–61)	93

AELFRIC (*c.* 950–*c.* 1020): *Colloquia*

40. The Latin Lesson	95

EADMER: *The Life of Anselm*

41. St. Anselm: Thoughts on Education (I. 22)	98

WILLIAM OF MALMESBURY: Cambridge University Library, MS. Dd. 13. 2

42. A Defence of the Classics	100

CONTENTS

MATTHEW PARIS (c. 1200–59): *Chronica Majora*
43. Trouble at Oxford, 1238 (Rolls Series, vol. 3, pp. 481–4) — 102

RICHARD DE BURY (1287–1345): *Philobiblon*
44. In Praise of Books (ch. 1) — 105

PETRARCH: (1304–74): *Letters* — 108
45. Student Days at Bologna (*Senilium Rerum*, X. 2) — 111
46. The Ascent of Mont Ventoux (*Familiarium Rerum*, IV. 1) — 112
47. Come to Vaucluse! (1) (*Fam.* VI. 3) — 116
48. Come to Vaucluse! (2) (*Fam.* XVI. 6) — 117
49. To Cicero (*Fam.* XXIV. 3, 4) — 119

PART FIVE. WINE, WOMAN, AND SONG

INTRODUCTION — 122
(50–59 are by anonymous twelfth-century poets)
50. Begone, dull Care! (*Carmina Burana*) — 126
51. The Archpoet's Confession — 127
52. A Drinking Song (*Carmina Burana*) — 128
53. The Debate between Wine and Water — 129
54. Phyllis and Flora (*Carmina Burana*) — 131
55. In Praise of his Mistress (*Ripoll Collection*) — 135
56. Love's Companion (*Carmina Burana*) — 137
57. Love and Reason (*Arundel Collection*) — 138
58. Reluctant Celibates — 140
59. A Cursing Song (*Carmina Burana*) — 141

PART SIX. SATIRE AND COMPLAINT

INTRODUCTION — 143
60. Money Talks: Nigel de Longchamps (*fl.* 1170), *Speculum Stultorum* — 145
61. Money is King (*Carmina Burana*) — 147
62. O Most Pernicious Woman! (1) Anon., *De Vita Monachorum* — 148

CONTENTS

63. O Most Pernicious Woman! (2) Anon. 149
64. The Gospel according to the Mark of Silver (*Carmina Burana*) 150
65. The Roman Curia: Walter of Châtillon (*fl.* 1170) 151
66. The Poor Scholar: Walter of Châtillon 154

PART SEVEN. GHOSTS AND MARVELS

INTRODUCTION 156

67. The Witch of Berkeley: William of Malmesbury, *De Gestis Regum Anglorum*, II, § 204. 156
68. The Two Clerks of Nantes (III, § 237) 158
69. Buried Treasure (II, § 169) 161
70. Warning to Slanderers: Anon., The Ingilby MS. 163

COMMENTARY 165

SELECT BIBLIOGRAPHY 250

LIST OF AUTHORS
CHRONOLOGICALLY ARRANGED

(The numbers refer to passages in this book)

The Bible	1, 2
St. Jerome (*c.* 345–420)	3, 4
St. Augustine (354–430)	5–9, 39
St. Benedict (*c.* 480–547)	10–12
Bede (*c.* 671–735)	27–29
Aelfric (*c.* 950–*c.* 1020)	40
St. Anselm (*c.* 1033–1109)	13
Eadmer (*c.* 1055–*c.* 1124)	14, 15, 41
Hildebert of Lavardin (1056–1133)	26
Robert the Monk (*fl.* 1100)	33
Anon.—*Gesta Francorum* (*fl.* 1100)	34–36
William of Malmesbury (*c.* 1080–*c.* 1143)	30–32, 42, 67–69
St. Bernard of Clairvaux (1090–1153)	16–20, 24
'The Archpoet' (*fl.* 1170)	51
Nigel de Longchamps (*fl.* 1170)	60
Walter of Châtillon (*fl.* 1170)	65, 66
Anon.—Twelfth-century poets and satirists	50, 52–59, 61–64
Jocelin of Brakelond (*fl.* 1200)	37, 38
Caesarius of Heisterbach (*c.* 1180–*c.* 1240)	21–23, 70
Thomas of Celano (*c.* 1190–1260)	25
Matthew Paris (*c.* 1200–59)	43
Richard de Bury (1287–1345)	44
Petrarch (1304–74)	45–49

SOME NOTES ON LANGUAGE

Four phases concern us here, which to some extent succeed one another, but still more overlap and combine to form what can loosely be called MEDIEVAL LATIN (ML).

1. CLASSICAL LATIN (CL) can be broadly defined as that used by the outstanding writers of the late Republic and early Empire for some two hundred years, from Cicero (106–43 B.C.) to Suetonius (c. A.D. 69–c. 140), from Lucretius (c. 99–55 B.C.) and Virgil (70–19 B.C.) to Juvenal (c. A.D. 50–130). All were versed in Greek literature, but applied their knowledge and skill to enrich Latin largely from its own resources, and increase its flexibility and range while importing little of an alien vocabulary or syntax: Cicero, for example, and Lucretius coined new Latin terms when they naturalized Greek philosophy. By surviving as classics, or at worst as school-books, they served as a permanent background at all periods, offering standards of correctness, models for imitation, maxims for living, or tags for quotation, and in some cases friends for life. Petrarch looked to Cicero, as Dante did to Virgil, as father, master, and friend. Two more points: they reach us in an elaborately written, rather than spoken, language; and the frontiers are not so rigid as grammarians tend to suggest, but the language emerges from an earlier pre-classical period, and passes almost insensibly into

2. LATE LATIN (LL). The term is used to describe the next three hundred years or more (J. F. Niermeyer suggests c. A.D. 200–550). Within this large time-span and in the wide area of the Empire there was room for great differences; but, broadly speaking, old standards of

accuracy were slipping, and declensions, conjugations, and sentence construction in general began to be confused, while debased vocabulary and hybrid Graeco-Latin and barbarous words increased (cf. 'cheeseburgers', 'beatniks'). In short, the language began to break down into the various Romance languages that were to succeed it. But there were positive developments too, such as the great increase in abstract nouns (e.g. *iussio, impossibilitas*); and the process as a whole—linguistic decay and growth side by side—is a familiar one in the evolution of a living language. (Twentieth-century English is both richer and poorer than that of the sixteenth.) Meanwhile literary traditions persisted, and the language could still be used with mastery, whether to uphold the old ways or to create new effects. This period too experienced a new and vitalizing influence, that of

3. CHRISTIAN, OR ECCLESIASTICAL, LATIN (EL). This brought a flood of new ideas, new vocabulary (largely Greek in origin), and a new way of writing into the language—in the first instance from the Bible in its Greek and early Latin versions. They were exploited by men of genius such as Tertullian (*c.* 160–220) and the Latin Fathers Ambrose (*c.* 339–97), Jerome (*c.* 342–420), and Augustine (354–430), who between them bequeathed to the West an immense legacy of Christian 'classics' to set beside the pagan ones. As the tide of barbarism advanced, and literacy came to rest largely with the clergy, this thought and language seeped into every form of literature and written records, secular as well as religious, poetry as well as prose. By the fourth century too, emerging from its earlier isolation, the Church in such notable figures as Augustine drew on the pagan classics, in spite of reservations, to enrich Christian culture, thereby

establishing a precedent which was to persist throughout the Middle Ages.

One more factor is to be reckoned with, not so much succeeding as underlying the other three—a powerful current which emerged in the later centuries in full flood:

4. POPULAR, OR VULGAR, LATIN, i.e. the conversational language of daily life. It can be traced from the pre-classical comedies of Plautus (*c.* 254–184 B.C.), through Cicero's letters, the poems of Catullus, and the picaresque novel of Petronius to epitaphs and illiterate scribbles on the walls of Pompeii. It used diminutives extensively to express familiarity or affection or a mild contempt, till the practice became habitual, and often drove out the basic word. So French *oreille* from *auricula*, *soleil* from *soliculus* (the same tendency is found in the popular speech of south Germany and Russia). It showed a growing preference for longer words: e.g. *vado* and *ambulo* for *eo* (Fr. *aller* combines the three); *longo tempore* for *diu*; for frequentative verbs such as *cantare*, *pensare*, and elaborate compounds over simple ones: e.g. *Torrentem pertransivit anima mea* (Ps. 123. 5). It adopted popular slang: e.g. *bucca* ('cheek') for 'mouth', *bellus* for *pulcher*, *testa* ('tile', then 'earthenware pot', and so 'skull') for 'head', till they often drove out their classical predecessors; and, along with Late Latin, it increasingly incorporated new words from the semi-Romanized West, particularly in the field of political and social institutions.

To sum up, it was chiefly the pervasive influence of the Church, drawing on the Bible, the liturgy, and the Christian classics, while remaining rooted linguistically both in popular speech and pagan literature, which maintained the language as a highway across the centuries, falling into disrepair in places, but opening up new territory as it went; while on either side tracks led off into a tangled undergrowth, out of which were to emerge eventually the Romance languages. (So the Norse sagas of the eleventh century preserved the Icelandic language with its elaborate inflexions, while the parent Norwegian, without their stabilizing influence, fell into linguistic decay.)

Something of a turning-point was reached at the end of the eighth century with the Carolingian 'Renaissance' and its schools; and from then on the educational system in general purged the language to a fair extent; while in yet another 'Renaissance' twelfth-century Latin literature reached new levels of achievement. For administrative purposes too, for a Europe with fluid frontiers and a multitude of local dialects, some kind of international language, however crudely adapted, was invaluable. But for much of this period almost all administration from government downwards was in the hands of ecclesiastics of one kind or another, so that once more we are carried back to the Church and to this common language as the main source of such cultural unity as existed.

There is another side to the story:[1] the gross illiteracy of many of the clergy, whose howlers added to the gaiety of scholars, while they caused alarm and despondency at Diocesan Visitations; the drawbacks of a written rather than a spoken language; and the rooted strength all over Europe of men's mother-tongue. Bede, as he lay dying, sang Anglo-Saxon verses alongside Latin antiphons; and Ailred of Rievaulx (1109–67) crying '*Festinate, festinate*' 'often drove the word home by calling on the name of Christ in English, a word of one syllable in this tongue and easier to utter, and in some ways sweeter to hear: "*Festinate*, for crist luve."'[2] But beside their

[1] See G. G. Coulton, *Europe's Apprenticeship*, Nelson, 1940.
[2] *Vita Ailredi*, by Walter Daniel, trans. F. M. Powicke, Nelson, 1950.

mother-tongue, educated men had a second *patria lingua*,[1] rooted in a lifetime of liturgy and study; and this book is concerned with its successes, not its failures. Petrarch, at the end of the period, pinned his hopes of immortality not on his Italian poems, his *nugae vulgares*, but on his major Latin works and letters. He was proved wrong by history; and the humanists of the next two centuries helped to kill by devotion the language they loved; but for them, as for the thousand years represented here, it was, as it still is, a living tradition.

5. These changes can now be traced in some detail.

VOCABULARY. (*a*) *New Words* (largely Greek) flooded in from the Bible and the evolving life of the Church: e.g. *ecclesia, diaconus, presbyter, episcopus, abba(s)* (Hebrew by origin, but already naturalized in the N.T.), *monachus* (monk), *eremita* (a man of the desert, hermit), *clerus* (the clerical order) and its adjective *clericus* (the sing. gives cleric and clerk, the pl. clergy), *elemosine* (alms), etc.

(*b*) *Old Words* acquired new meanings: e.g. *gentes* (Gentiles, or pagans), *virtutes* (mighty works, miracles), *sacramentum* (the soldier's oath of loyalty; then something to be kept sacred: hence the Christian 'mysteries'), *conversatio* (the Christian, and especially the monastic, way of life—the former meaning is retained in the A.V.), *peregrinus* (a stranger and pilgrim on earth seeking his *patria* in heaven, or—more specifically—some Christian shrine), *villa* (village or town), *civitas* (city—already appearing in CL), *comes* (king's companion, holding land in return for services; so 'count'—Eng. 'earl'. A similar usage had developed in the late Empire).

---

[1] 'From the civil law was borrowed the maxim, *Roma est patria omnium*': A. L. Smith, *Church and State in the Middle Ages*, Oxford, 1913.

(c) *Celtic and Germanic languages* contributed largely: e.g. *caballus* (a nag, cob) ultimately tended to supplant *equus*; *bannus* (a proclamation or command, with penalties attached; so *bannire*, etc.); *werra* (war), with its collateral forms *gerra* and *guerra*, which have replaced *bellum* in the Romance languages; *marca* (1) (a weight of silver, a coin, etc.); *marca* (2) (boundary, border-land, hence 'marches'); and *marchisus* (defending the frontiers—'marquis)'.

6. ORTHOGRAPHY. There was a general fluidity in spelling, especially in Germanic words. In particular:

(a) By the eleventh and twelfth centuries the diphthongs *ae* and *oe* were almost completely replaced by *e* (reflecting a change in pronunciation), and did not appear again until they were reintroduced by the Humanists: e.g. *preparo*, *pena* (*poena*), *penitet* (*paenitet*). This can lead to confusion: e.g. *cepit* (from *capio* or *coepi*), *equus* (*equus* or *aequus*), *queritur* (from *queror* or *quaero*). Texts exhibiting these changes will be noted when they occur.

(b) *t* between vowels became *c*, and was pronounced *ts*: e.g. *eciam*, *nacio* (cf. Italian *nazione*. English and French keep the *t*, but pronounce it as *s*; Spanish keeps the *c*).

(c) *michi* and *nichil* are commonly found for *mihi* and *nihil*; *charus* for *carus* (cf. Fr. *cher*; charity).

(d) *i* and *y* are often confused. The latter was introduced to represent Gk. *u*; e.g. *presbyter*, *mysterium*, etc., but *presbiter*, *misterium* are equally common; and conversely the *y* invades Latin words: e.g. *lacryma*, *hyems*. (English and French keep the Greek *y*; Italian uses *i* throughout.)

7. SYNTAX (one or two changes in word-formation are also included here). (a) *Nouns*. Cases are still further reinforced by prepositions, and the feeling for case weakens: e.g. *ad eum dicit*; *fatigati de vigiliis*. The preposition *de*

takes on a good deal of extra work, as a substitute for the genitive: e.g. *abbacia de Oseneie* (Oseney abbey); and eventually in the Romance languages the case-system practically disappears.

Neut. pl. nouns and adjectives (ending in *-a*) have a way of becoming fem. sing. nouns: e.g. *montana*, n.pl. adj. (Fr. *la montagne*).

(*b*) *Pronoun-Adjectives*: *Hic, ille, iste, ipse* lose their distinctive meanings and become largely interchangeable. *Ille* and *unus* are gradually reduced to a definite and indefinite article respectively. Reflexive *se, suus* are confused with *eum*, etc., *aliquis* with *quisquam* and *ullus, nullus* with *nemo*.

(*c*) *Adverbs and Prepositions* tend to fuse and produce new compounds: e.g. *abante* (*avant*), *depost* (*depuis*), *amodo* (from now on). Notice *ad/ab/pro invicem*, (to/from/for each other); an extension of CL *in vicem* (mutually).

(*d*) *Verbs*

(i) The subjunctive loses ground in some directions (e.g. in Reported Questions and Result Clauses), but tends to replace the indicative without adequate reason in many subordinate clauses, being thought of as a typically subordinate mood.

(ii) The distinction between *ne* and *non* tends to disappear: e.g. *non confundar in aeternum*: 'Let me not be confounded . . .' (Vulgate).

(iii) The present participle is used loosely, as in English; and a gerund in the ablative tends to take its place: e.g. *pertransiit benefaciendo et sanando* (Vulgate)—a usage that has persisted in Italian, and in French, where the two become confused (*allant* and *en allant*).

(iv) 'Double' perfect passives are common: e.g. *captus fui*.

(v) Other periphrastic tenses develop: e.g. *Turci iam undique erant circumcingentes nos* (*Gesta Francorum*).

(vi) The infinitive can be governed by a preposition (as in Greek): e.g. *pro posse, ultra posse*.

(*e*) *Some Common Constructions*

(i) *Reported Statements*: *dico quod, quia,* or *quoniam,* followed almost indifferently by indic. or subj., is common from the fourth century onwards; but this has roots in popular language as far back as Plautus, and may have been influenced too by Greek usage. (The accusative and infinitive persists, and the two are often found side by side.)

(ii) *Reported Questions* can use subj. or indic., e.g. in two successive sentences St. Augustine uses one of each: *Da talem, et scit quid dicam. Si autem frigido loquor, nescit quid loquor.*

(iii) *Reported Commands* can be expressed by the infinitive (as in Greek, and often in CL verse).

(iv) *Purpose* can be expressed by the infinitive—or at times by the indicative. *Quatenus* (*quatinus*) is frequently used to introduce Purpose Clauses.

(v) *Dum* often replaces *cum*, and tends to take the subjunctive automatically.

(vi) *Quod* tends to become a universal conjunction, largely replacing *ut* (Fr. and It., *que, che.*)

(vii) *Si* can introduce a Direct or Indirect Question. *Siquidem* (CL 'if/since indeed') is commonly no more than a connecting particle (= *quidem* or *autem*).

(viii) *Time*: the distinction between Time 'when' and 'how long' is blurred, and the Ablative is commonly used for both, reinforced at times by a preposition: e.g. *in illa die*.

(ix) *Place*: Where and Whither are confused; and *ad*+ acc. does duty for Locative: e.g. *fui ad ecclesiam* (cf. two meanings of *à Paris*).

SOME NOTES ON VERSE

THE following notes offer only a bird's-eye view of a wide field. It is examined in more detail by F. Brittain in *The Penguin Book of Latin Verse*, and fully surveyed by F. J. E. Raby in *A History of Christian-Latin Poetry*, and *A History of Secular Latin Poetry in the Middle Ages* (see the Bibliography).

One can distinguish at least four stages or factors in the evolution of medieval verse.

1. *The Classical Tradition* persisted for some centuries, with its quantitative verse and familiar metres, sometimes practised with real freshness, sometimes with mechanical skill. It was revived, too, successfully at various periods; e.g. by Alcuin (735–804) and the Carolingians, and again in the eleventh–twelfth centuries, and on a large scale by Petrarch, in his epic, and in his metrical epistles. All these felt they were treading in the steps of the masters, and maintaining a great tradition: e.g. Nos. 60 and 62, in elegiac couplets.

2. *Stress-Accent*. By the seventh–eighth centuries, though the same verse-patterns persisted, the notion of quantity had weakened, and stress-accent began to take its place. This had played a major part in the earliest Latin verse; and after the adoption of Greek quantitative metres it had provided, in the hands of the masters, a subtle tension between the natural accent and the metrical pattern; but now the medieval poets were reverting to older and simpler principles.

3. *Rhyme* began to appear as a fairly regular feature by the fourth century. This too was a characteristic of the

earliest Latin verse, as well as of rhetorical prose; and is easily come by in an inflected language. It was not unknown in the classical period: e.g. 'Cicero certainly made no attempt to avoid jingle, assonance or even rhyme in the endings of consecutive hexameters.' Ultimately, along with stress-accent, it became a normal element, and passed from Latin into the vernacular verse of Europe. Rhyme may be between unstressed syllables: e.g. *ostium:auxilium*, where it is hardly more than assonance, or between stressed ones: e.g. *angelorum:viatorum*. Internal (Leonine) rhymes in the hexameter were particularly popular in the tenth–eleventh centuries: e.g.

In terra summus rex est hoc tempore Nummus

(No. 61), and No. 63.

4. *New Rhythms* began to appear for lyric verse, chiefly on an iambic (∪ –) or trochaic (– ∪) basis. (It is convenient to use these traditional terms, but they are to be understood here as denoting stress-accent, not quantity.) These were frequently used in a four-foot, or octosyllabic, line (in Greek metrical terms, a 'dimeter'), and subtle effects could be obtained by varying the stanza pattern, and by elaborate rhyming schemes. 'Catalectic' lines (i.e. dropping the final syllable) could be interspersed to supply a rhythmic comma or full stop. These are familiar in English verse, and particularly in hymns, which took over medieval Latin rhythms.

It is worth listing a few of the most familiar and successful schemes.

(*a*) The 'Ambrosian' hymn: iambic dimeters (originally quantitative and unrhymed) are used in a four-line stanza: e.g. *Iam lucis orto sidere* (No. 52).

[1] L. P. Wilkinson, *Golden Latin Artistry*, Cambridge, 1963.

(*b*) A series of trochaic rhythms, based on the dimeter: e.g.

  (i) *Reus mortis non despero* (No. 26): rhyming couplets.
  (ii) *Dies irae, dies illa* (No. 25): a three-line stanza, rhyming a a a.
  (iii) *Propter Sion non tacebo* (No. 65): a six-line stanza (lines 3 and 6 catalectic), rhyming a a b c c b. There are many variations on this pattern: e.g.
  (iv) *O comes amoris, dolor* (No. 57): a nine-line stanza;
  (v) *Sidus clarum puellarum* (No. 55), where internal rhymes are employed.

(*c*) The Goliardic stanza may take its name from Goliath (*Golias*) the Philistine giant who discomfited the Israelites. He supplied a nickname, or an eponymous hero and patron, for the twelfth-century satirists and their more disreputable followers, who were known as *Goliardi* by the respectable. (An alternative derivation is from *gula*, 'gluttony'.) It is basically trochaic, and has a clearly marked caesura, sometimes indicated by a break in the line: e.g. *Aestuans intrinsecus ira vehementi* (No. 51), and Nos. 53, 54, 58, 59, 66; cf.

'(Come), landlord, fill the flowing bowl   Till it doth run over'
'Good King Wenceslas looked out   On the feast of Stephen'

With its vigorous rhythm and quadruple rhyme it became immensely popular for drinking-songs and the like, and in the two-way traffic of the times was borrowed for hymns.

(*d*) *The Sequence*. The practice grew up in the eighth century of prolonging the notes of the *Alleluia* which follows the Gradual in the Mass, and fitting words to them. During the eleventh century this semi-rhythmical 'prose' developed a life of its own, with a firmer metrical structure and rhyme; emerging as hymns in the liturgy, e.g. the *Dies irae* (No. 25), while suggesting new and more spontaneous lyric forms in secular verse: e.g.

Vacillantis trutine (No. 57).

The lyrics as they stand are incomplete without their music. 'In the Sequences there is no mistaking the fact that Music is the mistress and Poetry the handmaid';[1] and Heloise, speaking of the love-songs that Abelard had written for her, adds that even the illiterate are haunted by the sweetness of their melody. Yet the words alone have a plangent quality which might well have appealed to the early Roman poets—and equally have horrified their classical successors.

[1] J. S. Phillimore.

PART ONE

THE BIBLE

Divinus etenim sermo sicut mysteriis prudentes exercet, sic plerumque superficie simplices refovet. Habet in publico unde parvulos nutriat, servat in secreto unde mentes sublimium in admiratione suspendat. Quasi quidam quippe est fluvius, ut ita dixerim, planus et altus, in quo et agnus ambulet et elephas natet.

Gregory the Great, *Letter* V. 53

THE Bible must come first, for it is not only the foundation-document of the Christian life, but, in so far as a book can be, a cornerstone of the Middle Ages. 'Book'—but it is a misleading title for a whole collection of books,[1] ranging in composition over a thousand years, in imagination from the creation of this world to the last trump and the inauguration of the next; in subject-matter from history in its most primitive form to the very different drama and daylight-world of the New Testament; from the poetry of the Psalms and the speculations of the Wisdom books to the commands and promises of the Gospels, the ethics and theology of the Epistles, and the visionary consummation of the Apocalypse. A book, too, credited with an authority which no other has ever possessed; and all this was offered to a world in some ways simpler than our own, but just as subtle, and intellectually far less dissipated, in so far as its range of thought and reading were more restricted.

No wonder then that its story fascinated them, its demands and denunciations haunted them, and its obscurities teased them—teased practical people like Charlemagne, with wars to wage and an empire to govern, so that Alcuin can write him a three-thousand-word letter unravelling the meaning, literal and symbolic, of the sword in the gospels.[2] (It is difficult to imagine a modern ruler asking such a question, or receiving such an answer from one of his ministers.) For not only had the Scriptures height and breadth, so to speak, but they

[1] *Biblia Sacra* is n. pl., not fem. sing.
[2] See N. F. Cantor, *The Medieval World*, pp. 146-8.

possessed hidden depths; and it is this exploration that dominated men's search from the Fathers onwards for the next thousand years and more. Space forbids any adequate illustration here, but some mention is called for, or the whole picture will be oversimplified. They distinguished, then, four levels of interpretation, of which the literal or surface meaning (*sensus historicus*, or *littera*) was often considered the least important. For beneath it lay the spiritual meaning, which Bede likens to the honey concealed in the comb. Here were to be found the truths of 'allegory', by which persons, places, and events in the Old Testament foreshadowed or 'typified' their fulfilment in the New. For example, the escape of the Israelites from Egypt was a 'type' of the deliverance of the whole human race from the bondage of sin; and every just man was, in his measure, a forerunner (*typice*, or *per figuram*) of Christ. Even apparently trifling details—the number of fish taken in a net, the measurements of a wall, the place and moment of an encounter—are significant: *omnia ista innuunt aliquid, indicare volunt aliquid, intentos nos faciunt, ad pulsandum hortantur*. They yielded up secrets hidden from the human author himself (so that 'allegory' in this technical sense is thus distinguished from the conscious allegories of prophecy and parable). Beyond this again was the 'moral' meaning, to be applied to the individual here and now; and an 'anagogical' meaning, pointing onwards to the fulfilment of heaven.

A familiar instance, often quoted from Bede onwards, is the fourfold meaning of 'Jerusalem'. In the literal sense, it is the historical city; allegorically, it represents the Church of Christ dispersed throughout the world; morally, each Christian soul 'militant here upon earth'; and lastly, the Holy City, the New Jerusalem.

By the close of the sixth century a vast body of commentary had been built up for the West by the four Latin Fathers, Ambrose, Jerome, Augustine, and Gregory; a world of thought and imagination which discovered new patterns in, or imposed its own on, the original text, and offered rich quarries for their successors. Meanwhile, on a more familiar level, its phrases and imagery passed into men's daily speech and their letters to friends, as they did in the England of Cromwell and Bunyan, Fox and Wesley. Passed too into the speech of jesters and rebels, colouring their protests, or transformed into parody—and the point of parody is lost if there is no audience equally familiar with the original. So at one end of the scale monks meditate their *lectio divina*, and scholars write their commentaries: at the other is the cheerful bandying of scriptural authorities, as in *the Debate between Wine and Water*. Somewhere between the two, when Richard de Bury wishes to rise to the height of his subject in praise of books, he flings down twenty-two successive images from Scripture to encompass the full range of their splendour and power.

1   *Trust in God*

1 Qui habitat in adiutorio Altissimi,
    in protectione Dei caeli commorabitur.
2 Dicet Domino: Susceptor meus es tu et refugium meum;
    Deus meus, sperabo in eum.
3 Quoniam ipse liberavit me de laqueo venantium,
    et a verbo aspero.
4 Scapulis suis obumbrabit tibi,
    et sub pennis eius sperabis.
5 Scuto circumdabit te veritas eius;
    non timebis a timore nocturno;
6 a sagitta volante in die, a negotio perambulante in tenebris,
    ab incursu, et daemonio meridiano.
7 Cadent a latere tuo mille, et decem millia a dextris tuis;
    ad te autem non appropinquabit.
8 Verumtamen oculis tuis considerabis,
    et retributionem peccatorum videbis.
9 Quoniam tu es, Domine, spes mea;
    Altissimum posuisti refugium tuum.
10 Non accedet ad te malum,
    et flagellum non appropinquabit tabernaculo tuo.
11 Quoniam angelis suis mandavit de te,
    ut custodiant te in omnibus viis tuis.
12 In manibus portabunt te,
    ne forte offendas ad lapidem pedem tuum.

13 Super aspidem et basiliscum ambulabis,
   et conculcabis leonem et draconem.
14 Quoniam in me speravit, liberabo eum;
   protegam eum, quoniam cognovit nomen meum.
15 Clamabit ad me, et ego exaudiam eum;
   cum ipso sum in tribulatione;
   eripiam eum, et glorificabo eum.
16 Longitudine dierum replebo eum,
   et ostendam illi salutare meum.

Psalm 90 (91)

2 *Wisdom*

22 Dominus possedit me in initio viarum suarum,
   antequam quidquam faceret a principio.
23 Ab aeterno ordinata sum,
   et ex antiquis, antequam terra fieret.
24 Nondum erant abyssi, et ego iam concepta eram,
   necdum fontes aquarum eruperant;
25 necdum montes gravi mole constiterant:
   ante colles ego parturiebar.
26 Adhuc terram non fecerat, et flumina,
   et cardines orbis terrae.
27 Quando praeparabat caelos, aderam;
   quando certa lege et gyro vallabat abyssos;
28 quando aethera firmabat sursum,
   et librabat fontes aquarum;
29 quando circumdabat mari terminum suum,
   et legem ponebat aquis, ne transirent fines suos;
   quando appendebat fundamenta terrae;
30 cum eo eram, cuncta componens.
   Et delectabar per singulos dies,
   ludens coram eo omni tempore,

31 ludens in orbe terrarum;
   et deliciae meae esse cum filiis hominum.
32 Nunc ergo, filii, audite me:
   Beati qui custodiunt vias meas.
33 Audite disciplinam, et estote sapientes,
   et nolite abiicere eam.
34 Beatus homo qui audit me,
   et qui vigilat ad fores meas quotidie,
   et observat ad postes ostii mei.
35 Qui me invenerit inveniet vitam,
   et hauriet salutem a Domino.
36 Qui autem in me peccaverit, laedet animam suam;
   omnes qui me oderunt diligunt mortem.

Proverbs, 8. 22–36

PART TWO

THE CHRISTIAN LIFE

Porro si poetae dicere licuit: Trahit sua quemque voluptas,[1] *non necessitas sed voluptas, non obligatio sed delectatio, quanto fortius nos dicere debemus trahi hominem ad Christum, qui delectatur veritate, delectatur beatitudine, delectatur iustitia, delectatur sempiterna vita, quod totum Christus est. An vero habent corporis sensus voluptates suas, et animus deseritur a voluptatibus suis? Si animus non habet voluptates suas, unde dicitur:* Filii autem hominum sub tegmine alarum tuarum sperabunt; inebriabuntur ab ubertate domus tuae, et torrente voluptatis tuae potabis eos; quoniam apud te est fons vitae, et in lumine tuo videbimus lumen?[2] *Da amantem, et sentit quod dico. Da desiderantem, da esurientem, da in ista solitudine peregrinantem atque sitientem, et fontem aeternae patriae suspirantem, da talem, et scit quid dicam. Si autem frigido loquor, nescit quid loquor.*

Augustine, *Tractatus in Iohannem*, 26. 4 (on ch. 6. 44)

MOST of the authors represented in this section have their own introductions, and only a few points need be added here. The omissions are conspicuous: for example, the Benedictines and Cistercians are well represented; but the friars who began to overshadow them in the thirteenth century are almost entirely absent for lack of space. The darker side too is chiefly dealt with in the section on Satire; and the controversies between the secular and regular clergy, and among the regulars themselves, between cleric and layman, and between powerful individuals such as Bernard and Abelard—all this is crowded out.

Yet the complexity remains, and must be allowed for. In short, no simple picture of the religious life of the Middle Ages can do justice to the facts. Faith and unfaith, the world and the flesh as well as the spirit, credulity and criticism, and much learning—Scripture, the Fathers, the classics—are to be found side by side with ignorance, greed, and superstition, and clash or correct one another. The familiar

[1] Virgil, *Eclogue* II. 65.   [2] Ps. 35. 8–10 (36. 7–9).

metaphor of the sea of this world, *mare huius saeculi,* dear to Augustine and Bernard among others, which a man crosses on the bark of the Church, is as apt as any to describe the situation. If the vessel is thought of as Peter's bark, then Peter's successors again and again fall asleep at the helm, storms spring up, and the crew fall out with one another. St. Augustine pictures it in a sermon on John 6. 16–18. 'When evening came, his disciples went down to the sea; and they entered into a boat, and were going over the sea to Capernaum. And it was now dark, and Jesus had not yet come to them. And the sea was rising by reason of a great wind that blew.' 'Navicula illa ecclesiam significabat. . . . Tenebrae iam factae erant, et non venerat ad eos Iesus. Quantum accedit finis mundi, crescunt errores, crebrescunt terrores, crescit iniquitas, crescit infidelitas. . . . Crescunt istae tenebrae odiorum fraternorum, quotidie crescunt: et nondum venit Iesus. . . . Etenim quia abundavit iniquitas, et refrigescit caritas multorum, crescunt fluctus, augentur tenebrae, saevit ventus: sed tamen navis ambulat.'

ST. JEROME (*c.* 345–420)

St. Jerome was born in Dalmatia, but after studying rhetoric at Rome—a process which set its mark on him for life—he shortly afterwards went east, where he spent five years of penance and study, living with a group of hermits in the desert. (This form of monasticism had begun before the end of the third century in Egypt, and had rapidly spread in the surrounding regions.)

Ordained priest at Antioch in 379, he came to Rome with his bishop and became an intimate friend of Pope Damasus, who commissioned him to produce a revised Latin version of the New Testament and the Psalms, to replace several already in existence. So began his labours of some twenty years; for on the death of the pope (having made, too, a number of enemies in Rome) he returned to Palestine with a party of friends, and settled at Bethlehem, where he founded and presided over two monastic communities, one for men and one for women. He learnt Hebrew in order to study the Old Testament in the original (most scholars were content with the Greek version, the Septuagint), and finally completed his translation of the Bible, which became known as the Vulgate, or 'Current Version' of the Roman Church; adding commentaries which helped to fill the nine folio volumes edited by Erasmus in 1516.

He is a complex figure. A rigorous ascetic, who could not bear to part with his Plautus and Cicero; a satirist who served up the familiar Roman dishes, and some newer Christian ones, with the traditional sauce of rhetoric. *Nulla erit rhetorici pompa sermonis*, he remarks in a letter; but it had become second nature. In particular, an anti-feminist who was to supply plenty of ammunition for the Middle Ages—yet he drew noble Roman ladies after him, not only to adopt his ascetic practices but to follow him to Bethlehem and give themselves up to the religious life. A tireless scholar; a tireless controversialist too, quarrelling with his bishop and with all who disagreed with him, scourging his fellow monks and, still more, the secular clergy—and putting it all down on paper. But his Vulgate was a unique contribution to the West, influencing not only thought (here he was simply the spokesman) but language, in spheres that lay far outside the Bible. Moreover, thanks to this Latinized Bible, biblical thought could intermarry over the centuries with that of Roman law. So these two legacies of the late Roman world, so different, and yet complementary, reinforced each other in shaping the structure of the Europe that was to come.[1]

3   *Cicero or Christ?*

To Eustochium   Rome, 384

Cum ante annos plurimos domo, parentibus, sorore, cognatis et, quod his difficilius est, consuetudine lautioris cibi propter caelorum me regna castrassem et Hierosolymam militaturus pergerem, bibliotheca, quam mihi
5 Romae summo studio ac labore confeceram, carere non poteram. Itaque miser ego lecturus Tullium ieiunabam; post noctium crebras vigilias, post lacrimas, quas mihi praeteritorum recordatio peccatorum ex imis visceribus eruebat, Plautus sumebatur in manibus. Si quando in
10 memet reversus prophetam legere coepissem, sermo horrebat incultus, et quia lumen caecis oculis non videbam, non oculorum putabam culpam esse, sed solis. Dum

[1] See W. Ullmann, *The Relevance of Medieval Ecclesiastical History*, Cambridge, 1966.

ita me antiquus serpens inluderet, in media ferme quadragesima medullis infusa febris corpus invasit exhaustum et sine ulla requie—quod dictu quoque incredibile sit—sic infelicia membra depasta est, ut ossibus vix haererem.

Interim parabantur exsequiae et vitalis animae calor toto frigente iam corpore in solo tantum tepente pectusculo palpitabat, cum subito raptus in spiritu ad tribunal iudicis pertrahor, ubi tantum luminis et tantum erat ex circumstantium claritate fulgoris, ut proiectus in terram sursum aspicere non auderem. Interrogatus condicionem Christianum me esse respondi: et ille qui residebat, 'Mentiris', ait, 'Ciceronianus es, non Christianus; *ubi thesaurus tuus, ibi et cor tuum.*' Ilico obmutui et inter verbera—nam caedi me iusserat—conscientiae magis igne torquebar illum mecum versiculum reputans: *In inferno autem quis confitebitur tibi?* Clamare tamen coepi et eiulans dicere: 'Miserere mei, domine, miserere mei.' Haec vox inter flagella resonabat. Tandem ad praesidentibus genua provoluti qui adstiterant, precabantur ut veniam tribueret adulescentiae, ut errori locum paenitentiae commodaret exacturus deinde cruciatum, si gentilium litterarum libros aliquando legissem. Ego, qui tanto constrictus articulo vellem etiam maiora promittere, deiurare coepi et nomen eius obtestans dicere: 'Domine, si umquam habuero codices saeculares, si legero, te negavi.'

Letter XXII. 30

4 *Wars, and Rumours of Wars*

To Principia   Bethlehem, 412

Dum haec aguntur in Iebus, terribilis de occidente rumor adfertur obsideri Romam et auro salutem civium redimi spoliatosque rursum circumdari, ut post substantiam vitam quoque amitterent. Haeret vox et singultus intercipiunt verba dictantis. Capitur urbs quae totum cepit orbem, immo fame perit ante quam gladio et vix pauci, qui caperentur, inventi sunt. Ad nefandos cibos erupit esurientium rabies et sua invicem membra laniarunt, dum mater non parcit lactanti infantiae et recipit utero, quem paulo ante effuderat. *Nocte Moab capta est, nocte cecidit murus eius. Deus, venerunt gentes in hereditatem tuam, polluerunt templum sanctum tuum, posuerunt Hierusalem in pomorum custodia, posuerunt cadavera servorum tuorum escas volatilibus caeli, carnes sanctorum tuorum bestiis terrae. Effuderunt sanguinem ipsorum sicut aquam in circuitu Hierusalem et non erat, qui sepeliret.*

> Quis cladem illius noctis, quis funera fando
> Explicet aut possit lacrimis aequare dolorem?
> Urbs antiqua ruit multos dominata per annos,
> Plurima perque vias sparguntur inertia passim
> Corpora perque domos, et plurima mortis imago.

Letter CXXVII. 12

ST. AUGUSTINE (354–430)

St. Augustine, like many other figures in this book, but to an exceptional degree, looks before and after. Living in an age of crisis, 'he was no mere passive spectator of the crisis. He was, to a far greater degree than any emperor or general or barbarian war-lord, a maker of history and a builder of the bridge which was to lead from the old world to the new.'[1]

The son of a pagan father and a Christian mother, he was born at Tagaste in North Africa. A gifted schoolboy, he naturally took to rhetoric, that mastery of the spoken and written word, which for

---

[1] C. Dawson, in *A Monument to St. Augustine*, 1930.

THE CHRISTIAN LIFE

centuries had been the goal, and in some ways the bane, of Roman education. He studied at Carthage to such effect that after practising there as a rhetorician he went on to Rome, and then to Milan, where events finally caught up with him.

Between the ages of 19 and 32 his restless spirit underwent four 'conversions'. The first he owed to Cicero's *Hortensius*, a lost dialogue in praise of philosophy, which fired him to a pursuit of 'wisdom' which he never abandoned, though its perspectives shifted as he advanced. His second conversion was to Manicheism, a rival of Christianity in Africa. This held him for ten years, though increasingly disillusioned, till he was delivered intellectually by discovering Platonism in its latest flowering, in the writings of Plotinus (*c.* 205–70) and the Neoplatonists (see No. 39). But he was still morally enslaved to his past. His busy mother had got rid of his first mistress, pending the marriage she was trying to arrange, but meanwhile he had taken a second—till the undertow of his Christian background, and the troubles and encounters of his foreground (among them, Ambrose, bishop of Milan) carried him into the Catholic Church, and within a few years had committed him to the unending tasks of bishop in his native Africa, preacher, controversialist, correspondent, philosopher-historian, and theologian.

His presence was felt throughout the thousand years of this book, and beyond. His theology was taken over *en bloc* by Gregory the Great (pope, 590–604), the most universally read of the Western Fathers. His intellectual explorations, grounded in faith (*crede ut intelligas*), were carried forward by Anselm to new conclusions in his *fides quaerens intellectum* (see No. 13). His *De Civitate Dei*, a defence of Christianity against the charge that it had undermined the Roman Empire and led to the sack of Rome by Alaric in 410, occupied him some thirteen years, as he attempted to build a philosophy of man in society, where from the dawn of history 'two loves built two cities'—self-love, the warring communities summed up under the name of 'Babylon' and culminating in the Roman Empire, while the love of God built up 'Jerusalem', a city already present in time, but only to be fulfilled in eternity. Here, more than in any other work, he spread before the Middle Ages a panorama of world events as he knew them, interpreted in the light of the Christian scheme of salvation: a full circle of thought and imagination which led to consequences undreamed of in Church and State, and broken arcs of quotations for whose continuation scholars such as William of Malmesbury and Roger Bacon searched in vain.

Most intimate of all his writings (though everywhere he gives himself away) are his *Confessions*, a spiritual autobiography down to the time of his conversion, the first of a new genre in European literature. It is written in the form of a dialogue with God, but is addressed in fact to the human race (*Cui narro haec? neque enim tibi, deus meus, sed apud te narro haec generi meo, generi humano*), analysing with a subtlety unknown till now the experiences of childhood, adolescence, and manhood, his thoughts and temptations, his relations with his mother, his friendships. It is echoed by Anselm and by Ailred of Rievaulx, to whom the writer is *Augustinus meus*; it was the lifelong companion of Petrarch, till he could no longer read its tiny script; owing its appeal not only to his convictions, but to the power and beauty of his language.

Both language and style owe much to the fourth century, and are coloured in turn by the audience he is addressing. (The sermons in particular are aimed at a simple congregation, and are vibrant with the spoken word.) Though he professes allegiance to the rhetorical principles of Cicero, and commends them to Christian preachers, he and his age had travelled far. The period, for example, had gone out of fashion, giving place to short pithy sentences or long and rambling ones. There was an increasing emphasis on the familiar devices of antithesis, and repetition, and an assonance which readily passed into rhyme. And apart from these influences, which can be observed in his pagan contemporary Apuleius, the Scriptures which at first he had despised—*visa est mihi indigna, quam Tullianae dignitati compararem*—acted like a blood transfusion. (Apart from the general colouring, there are something like a thousand quotations in the *Confessions*.) Juvenal's gibe was even truer than when he wrote in the first century:

Iam pridem Syrus in Tiberim defluxit Orontes;

the rivers of Jewish and Greek thought and imagery had flooded into the Latin West.

Many forces then were at work; but among fourth-century African Christians there was only one Augustine, whose experiences and convictions and artistic genius together forged this unique expression of a personality summed up unconsciously in a few lines of self-portrait: *Da amantem, et sentit quod dico* . . . .[1]

[1] See the passage quoted on p. 6 above.

THE CONFESSIONS

5 *Introduction*

Magnus es, domine, et laudabilis valde: magna virtus tua et sapientiae tuae non est numerus. Et laudare te vult homo, aliqua portio creaturae tuae, et homo circumferens mortalitatem suam, circumferens testimonium peccati sui et testimonium quia *superbis resistis*. Et tamen laudare te vult homo, aliqua portio creaturae tuae. Tu excitas, ut laudare te delectet, quia fecisti nos ad te et inquietum est cor nostrum, donec requiescat in te.

Confessions, I. 1

6 *Childhood and Schooldays*

(*a*) Inde in scholam datus sum, ut discerem litteras, in quibus quid utilitatis esset ignorabam miser. Et tamen, si segnis in discendo essem, vapulabam. Laudabatur enim hoc a maioribus, et multi ante nos vitam istam agentes praestruxerant aerumnosas vias, per quas transire cogebamur multiplicato labore et dolore filiis Adam.

Invenimus autem, domine, homines rogantes te et didicimus ab eis, sentientes te, ut poteramus, esse magnum aliquem, qui posses etiam non adparens sensibus nostris exaudire nos et subvenire nobis. Nam puer coepi rogare te, auxilium et refugium meum ... et rogabam te parvus non parvo affectu, ne in schola vapularem. Et cum me non exaudiebas, ridebantur a maioribus hominibus usque ab ipsis parentibus, qui mihi accidere mali nihil volebant, plagae meae, magnum tunc et grave malum meum ...

Confessions, I. 9

(*b*) In ipsa tamen pueritia ... non amabam litteras et me in eas urgeri oderam; et urgebar tamen et bene mihi fiebat, nec faciebam ego bene: non enim discerem, nisi cogerer. Nemo enim invitus bene facit, etiamsi bonum est quod facit. Nec qui me urgebant, bene faciebant, sed bene mihi fiebat abs te, deus meus. Illi enim non intuebantur, quo referrem quod me discere cogebant praeterquam ad satiandas insatiabiles cupiditates copiosae inopiae et ignominiosae gloriae. ...

Quid autem erat causae, cur graecas litteras oderam, quibus puerulus imbuebar, ne nunc quidem mihi satis exploratum est. Adamaveram enim latinas, non quas primi magistri, sed quas docent qui grammatici vocantur. Nam illas primas, ubi legere et scribere et numerare discitur, non minus onerosas poenalesque habebam quam omnes graecas. Unde tamen et hoc nisi de peccato et vanitate vitae ...? Nam utique meliores, quia certiores, erant primae illae litterae, quibus fiebat in me et factum est et habeo illud, ut et legam, si quid scriptum invenio, et scribam ipse, si quid volo, quam illae, quibus tenere cogebar Aeneae nescio cuius errores oblitus errorum meorum et plorare Didonem mortuam, quia se occidit ab amore, cum interea me ipsum in his a te morientem, deus, vita mea, siccis oculis ferrem miserrimus.

Quid enim miserius misero non miserante se ipsum et flente Didonis mortem, quae fiebat amando Aenean, non flente autem mortem suam, quae fiebat non amando te, deus, lumen cordis mei et panis intus animae meae et virtus maritans mentem meam et sinum cogitationis meae?

Confessions, I. 12–13

7 *Adolescence*

(*a*) Et quid erat, quod me delectabat, nisi amare et amari? Sed non tenebatur modus ab animo usque ad animum, quatenus est luminosus limes amicitiae, sed exhalabantur nebulae de limosa concupiscentia carnis et scatebra pubertatis et obnubilabant atque obfuscabant cor meum, ut non discerneretur serenitas dilectionis a caligine libidinis. Utrumque in confuso aestuabat et rapiebat inbecillam aetatem per abrupta cupiditatum atque mersabat gurgite flagitiorum.

Invaluerat super me ira tua, et nesciebam. Obsurdueram stridore catenae mortalitatis meae, poena superbiae animae meae, et ibam longius a te, et sinebas, et iactabar et effundebar et diffluebam et ebulliebam per fornicationes meas, et tacebas.

O tardum gaudium meum! Tacebas tunc, et ego ibam porro longe a te in plura et plura sterilia semina dolorum superba deiectione et inquieta lassitudine.

Confessions, II. 2

(*b*) Quis exaperit istam tortuosissimam et inplicatissimam nodositatem? Foeda est; nolo in eam intendere, nolo eam videre. Te volo, iustitia et innocentia, pulchra et decora honestis luminibus et insatiabili satietate. Quies est apud te valde et vita inperturbabilis. Qui intrat in te, intrat in gaudium domini sui et non timebit et habebit se optime in optimo. Defluxi abs te ego et erravi, deus meus, nimis devius ab stabilitate tua in adulescentia et factus sum mihi regio egestatis.

Confessions, II. 10

8 *Conversion*

Sic aegrotabam et excruciabar accusans memet ipsum
solito acerbius nimis ac volvens et versans me in vinculo
meo, donec abrumperetur totum, quo iam exiguo tenebar.
Sed tenebar tamen. Et instabas tu in occultis meis,
5 domine, severa misericordia flagella ingeminans timoris
et pudoris, ne rursus cessarem et non abrumperetur id
ipsum exiguum et tenue, quod remanserat, et revalesceret
iterum et me robustius alligaret. Dicebam enim apud me
intus: 'Ecce modo fiat, modo fiat', et cum verbo iam ibam
10 in placitum. Iam paene faciebam et non faciebam nec
relabebar tamen in pristina, sed de proximo stabam et
respirabam. Et item conabar et paulo minus ibi eram et
paulo minus, iam iamque adtingebam et tenebam: et non
ibi eram nec adtingebam nec tenebam, haesitans mori
15 morti et vitae vivere, plusque in me valebat deterius
inolitum, quam melius insolitum, punctumque ipsum
temporis, quo aliud futurus eram, quanto propius admove-
batur, tanto ampliorem incutiebat horrorem; sed non
recutiebat retro nec avertebat, sed suspendebat.

20 Retinebant nugae nugarum et vanitates vanitantium,
antiquae amicae meae, et succutiebant vestem meam
carneam et submurmurabant: 'Dimittisne nos?' et 'A
momento isto non erimus tecum ultra in aeternum' et
'A momento isto non tibi licebit hoc et illud ultra in
25 aeternum'. . . . Et audiebam eas iam longe minus quam
dimidius, non tamquam libere contradicentes eundo in
obviam, sed velut a dorso mussitantes et discedentem
quasi furtim vellicantes, ut respicerem. Retardabant
tamen cunctantem me abripere atque excutere ab eis et
30 transilire quo vocabar, cum diceret mihi consuetudo
violenta: 'Putasne sine istis poteris?' . . . Ubi vero a fundo

arcano alta consideratio traxit et congessit totam miseriam meam in conspectu cordis mei, oborta est procella ingens ferens ingentem imbrem lacrimarum. Et ut totum effunderem cum vocibus suis, surrexi ab Alypio—solitudo mihi ad negotium flendi aptior suggerebatur—et secessi remotius, quam ut posset mihi onerosa esse etiam eius praesentia . . . . Mansit ergo ille ubi sedebamus nimie stupens. Ego sub quadam fici arbore stravi me nescio quomodo et dimisi habenas lacrimis, et proruperunt flumina oculorum meorum, acceptabile sacrificium tuum, et non quidem his verbis, sed in hac sententia multa dixi tibi: '*Et tu, domine, usquequo? Usquequo, domine, irasceris in finem? Ne memor fueris iniquitatum nostrarum antiquarum.*' Sentiebam enim eis me teneri. Iactabam voces miserabiles: 'Quamdiu, quamdiu cras et cras? Quare non modo? Quare non hac hora finis turpitudinis meae?'

Dicebam haec et flebam amarissima contritione cordis mei. Et ecce audio vocem de vicina domo cum cantu dicentis et crebro repetentis quasi pueri an puellae, nescio: 'Tolle lege, tolle lege.' Statimque mutato vultu intentissimus cogitare coepi, utrumnam solerent pueri in aliquo genere ludendi cantitare tale aliquid, nec occurrebat omnino audisse me uspiam, repressoque impetu lacrimarum surrexi, nihil aliud interpretans divinitus mihi iuberi, nisi ut aperirem codicem et legerem quod primum caput invenissem. Audieram enim de Antonio, quod ex evangelica lectione, cui forte supervenerat, admonitus fuerit, tamquam sibi diceretur quod legebatur: '*Vade, vende omnia, quae habes, da pauperibus et habebis thesaurum in caelis; et veni, sequere me,*' et tali oraculo confestim ad te esse conversum. Itaque concitus redii in eum locum, ubi sedebat Alypius: ibi enim posueram codicem apostoli, cum inde surrexeram. Arripui, aperui et legi in silentio capitulum, quo primum coniecti sunt oculi mei: '*Non in*

comissationibus et ebrietatibus, non in cubilibus et inpudicitiis, non in contentione et aemulatione, sed induite dominum Iesum Christum et carnis providentiam ne feceritis in concupiscentiis.' Nec ultra volui legere nec opus erat. Statim quippe cum fine huiusce
70 sententiae quasi luce securitatis infusa cordi meo omnes dubitationis tenebrae diffugerunt.

Confessions, VIII. 11–12

9   *Looking Back*

Sero te amavi, pulchritudo tam antiqua et tam nova, sero te amavi! Et ecce intus eras et ego foris, et ibi te quaerebam, et in ista formosa, quae fecisti, deformis inruebam. Mecum eras, et tecum non eram. Ea me tenebant longe a te, quae
5 si in te non essent, non essent. Vocasti et clamasti et rupisti surditatem meam, coruscasti, splenduisti et fugasti caecitatem meam, fragrasti, et duxi spiritum et anhelo tibi, gustavi et esurio et sitio, tetigisti me, et exarsi in pacem tuam.

Confessions, X. 27

ST. BENEDICT (*c.* 480–547)

St. Benedict was destined to have as much influence on the West as any single figure in the early Christian centuries. Monasticism was already two hundred years old, and was widespread, particularly in the Greek-speaking world, in both forms—the solitary and the communal life. (The two were sometimes combined by groups of hermits living in what might be called colonies: this seems to have been the form that Irish monasticism took in the beginning.) Nor was the idea of a Rule entirely new: several had grown up in the previous century, e.g. that of St. Basil (*c.* 360), still largely followed by the Eastern Church, and that of Cassian (*c.* 360–435) who founded two monasteries near Marseilles.

What was new was the sobriety—its demands exacting, but not superhuman—and the comprehensiveness of the Rule that St. Benedict drew up after years of living the monastic life in both its forms, and familiarizing himself with the practices of his predecessors; the family spirit that it instilled, and the 'stability' that it demanded, that is, faithfulness to one House (this was one of the vows taken by the monks) in a period when wandering monks (*vagi*) were a common feature of the religious landscape.

There emerged an institution sufficiently firm and flexible to fit western Europe as a whole (there is hardly a country where it did not take deep root) and one which moulded in many ways, both religious and social, the life of the 'Benedictine centuries' (broadly speaking, the seventh to the twelfth century), while persisting beyond them to the present day. In fact the vitality of the Benedictine idea and Order is one of its remarkable characteristics. Monte Cassino, St. Benedict's own monastery was destroyed by the Lombards in 585, by the Saracens in 884, by the Normans, by earthquake, and by the Allies in 1944, and each time has risen from the ruins.

The monasteries served many purposes: a place of retreat where a man might save his soul in licentious and troubled times—though Gregory the Great (*c.* 540–604) like many others left his monastery to save the world as well; a home of prayer, where the Divine Office of the West gradually took shape (the Book of Common Prayer is one of its descendants); and a focus of civilization where much of the literature of the old world was preserved, and contemporary history was recorded (some of these monastic historians appear in this book). Thus they naturally became centres of education, alongside the cathedral school; centres too of agricultural activity and reclamation, where, for example, the Cistercians in the twelfth century had much to contribute to England. Last, and most surprising, they could be outgoing centres of missionary work, preaching the faith in the pagan countries of England, Germany, Holland, Denmark, and Sweden.

To sum up, a school of perfection which found room for the ordinary man, including the illiterate (in the early days they were groups of laymen with only one or two priests in the community), or in St. Benedict's own inclusive words, 'a school of the Lord's service', which indirectly proved to be of service to men in ways which St. Benedict can never have guessed.

One last point. A rule is a norm, or ideal; and human nature has a way of defying, ignoring, or giving an individual twist to every rule yet made. So St. Benedict's portrait of the ideal Cellarer may be compared with the situation at St. Edmund's Abbey, when 'Cellarer succeeded Cellarer, one after the other, and at the end of the year every one of them was burdened with debt. ... Murmurings became more and more frequent, lies were fabricated, blame heaped on blame, nor was there a corner of the house that did not resound with venomous hissings' (Jocelin of Brakelond's *Chronicle*, tr. H. E. Butler, pp. 79–80. See Nos. 37, 38).

THE RULE OF ST. BENEDICT

10 *From the Prologue*

Constituenda est ergo a nobis Dominici schola servitii; in qua institutione nihil asperum, nihil grave nos constituturos speramus. Sed et si quid paululum restrictius, dictante aequitatis ratione, propter emendationem viti-
5 orum vel conservationem caritatis processerit, non illico pavore perterritus refugias viam salutis, quae non est nisi angusto initio incipienda. Processu vero conversationis et fidei, dilatato corde, inenarrabili dilectionis dulcedine curritur via mandatorum Dei; ut ab ipsius nunquam
10 magisterio discedentes, in eius doctrina usque ad mortem in monasterio perseverantes, passionibus Christi per patientiam participemus, ut regni eius mereamur esse consortes.

11 *The Abbot*

Ordinatus autem abbas cogitet semper quale onus suscepit, et cui redditurus est rationem villicationis suae; sciatque sibi oportere prodesse magis quam praeesse. Oportet ergo eum esse doctum lege divina, ut sciat et sit unde proferat nova et vetera, castum, sobrium, misericordem; et semper *superexaltet misericordiam iudicio*, ut idem ipse consequatur. Oderit vitia, diligat fratres.

In ipsa autem correptione prudenter agat, et ne quid nimis, ne dum nimis eradere cupit aeruginem, frangatur vas; suamque fragilitatem semper suspectus sit, meminerítque calamum quassatum non conterendum. In quibus non dicimus ut permittat nutriri vitia, sed prudenter et cum caritate ea amputet, ut viderit cuique expedire, sicut iam diximus; et studeat plus amari, quam timeri. Non sit turbulentus et anxius, non sit nimius et obstinatus, non sit zelotypus et nimis suspiciosus, quia numquam requiescit; in ipsis imperiis suis providus et consideratus; et sive secundum Deum, sive secundum seculum sit opera quam iniungit, discernat ac temperet, cogitans discretionem sancti Jacob, dicentis: '*Si greges meos plus in ambulando fecero laborare, morientur cuncti una die.*' Haec ergo aliaque testimonia discretionis, matris virtutum, sumens, sic omnia temperet, ut sit et fortes quod cupiant, et infirmi non refugiant. Et praecipue, ut praesentem Regulam in omnibus conservet; ut, dum bene ministraverit, audiat a Domino, quod servus bonus, qui erogavit triticum conservis suis in tempore suo: '*Amen dico vobis, super omnia bona sua constituet eum.*'

Ch. 64

12 *The Cellarer*

Cellerarius Monasterii eligatur de congregatione sapiens, maturus moribus, sobrius, non multum edax, non elatus, non turbulentus, non iniuriosus, non tardus, non prodigus, sed timens Deum, qui omni congregationi sit sicut pater. Curam gerat de omnibus; sine iussionem abbatis nihil faciat; quae iubentur, custodiat; fratres non contristet. Si

quis frater ab eo forte aliqua irrationabiliter postulat, non
spernendo eum contristet, sed rationabiliter cum humili-
tate male petenti deneget.

Animam suam custodiat, memor semper illud apostoli-
cum, quia *qui bene ministraverit, gradum bonum sibi acquirit.*
Infirmorum, infantum, hospitum pauperumque cum
omni sollicitudine curam gerat, sciens sine dubio quia pro
his omnibus in die iudicii rationem redditurus est. Omnia
vasa Monasterii cunctamque substantiam ac si altaris
vasa sacrata conspiciat. Nihil ducat negligendum. Neque
avaritiae studeat, neque prodigus sit, et stirpator substan-
tiae monasterii; sed omnia mensurate faciat, et secundum
iussionem abbatis.

Humilitatem ante omnia habeat, et cui substantia non
est quae tribuatur, sermo responsionis porrigatur bonus,
ut scriptum est: *Sermo bonus super datum optimum.* Omnia
quae ei iniunxerit abbas, ipse habeat sub cura sua; a quibus
eum prohibuerit, non praesumat. Fratribus constitutam
annonam sine aliquo typho vel mora offerat, ut non
scandalizentur, memor divini eloquii, quid mereatur *qui
scandalizaverit unum de pusillis.* Si congregatio maior fuerit,
solatia ei dentur, a quibus adiutus et ipse aequo animo
impleat officium sibi commissum. Horis competentibus et
dentur quae danda sunt, et petantur quae petenda sunt,
ut nemo perturbetur, neque contristetur in domo Dei.

Ch. 31

ST. ANSELM (1033–1109)

No short account can do justice to this great man. Born at Aosta in
the Italian Alps, he made his way north to the abbey of Bec in
Normandy, then a centre of vigorous monastic and (within the limits
of the time) intellectual life under another Italian, Lanfranc, whom
Anselm was to succeed as abbot and, in 1093, to follow at Canterbury.

THE CHRISTIAN LIFE 23

The trials and difficulties of such a post for one who was essentially a monk and theologian, under kings such as William Rufus and Henry I, when a prelate was also a great feudal lord, appear in his biography, and in his exile for six of these sixteen years for daring to oppose the claims of Church and papacy to those of the kings.

The impression he made on some of his contemporaries, and the affection he evoked, can be seen in Eadmer's life of him. But his searching mind ranged beyond Eadmer's, and took up problems more or less where Augustine had left them six hundred years earlier. In the intervening centuries most men had been content to go over familiar ground, and cite authorities, rather than seek new answers. Not that Anselm rejected authority: his own thought and style are steeped in those of Augustine, as well as in the Scriptures. His faith is unquestioned, but not unquestioning: that God became man he had no doubt, but 'Cur *Deus homo?*' 'Le cœur a ses raisons que la raison ne connaît pas.' So Pascal, as a counterpoise to the strict rationalism of the seventeenth century; but Anselm in a very different context needed to reassert the claims of the reason, which for him could not conflict with those of the 'heart'; and he set out afresh (the first of the 'Schoolmen' as he is sometimes called) on an exploration which was going to dominate theology and philosophy during the High Middle Ages.

13 *Faith seeks Understanding*

Eia nunc, homuncio, fuge paululum occupationes tuas, absconde te modicum a tumultuosis cogitationibus tuis. Abice nunc onerosas curas, et postpone laboriosas distentiones tuas. Vaca aliquantulum deo, et requiesce aliquantulum in eo. *Intra in cubiculum* mentis tuae, exclude omnia praeter deum et quae te iuvent ad quaerendum eum, et clauso ostio quaere eum. Dic nunc, totum cor meum, dic nunc deo: *Quaero vultum tuum, vultum tuum, domine, requiro.*

Eia nunc ergo tu, domine deus meus, doce cor meum, ubi et quomodo te quaerat, ubi et quomodo te inveniat. Domine, si hic non es, ubi te quaeram absentem? Si autem ubique es, cur non video praesentem? Sed certe habitas *lucem inaccessibilem.* Et ubi est lux inaccessibilis? Aut quomodo accedam ad lucem inaccessibilem? Aut quis me ducet et inducet in illam, ut videam te in illa? Deinde quibus signis, qua facie te quaeram? Numquam te vidi, domine deus meus, non novi faciem tuam. Quid faciet, altissime domine, quid faciet iste tuus longinquus exsul? Quid faciet servus tuus anxius amore tui et longe proiectus a facie tua? Anhelat videre te, et nimis abest illi facies tua. Accedere ad te desiderat, et inaccessibilis est habitatio tua. Invenire te cupit, et nescit locum tuum. Quaerere te affectat, et ignorat vultum tuum. Domine, deus meus es, et dominus meus es, et numquam te vidi. Tu me fecisti et refecisti, et omnia mea bona tu mihi contulisti, et nondum novi te. Denique ad te videndum factus sum, et nondum feci, propter quod factus sum.

O misera sors hominis, cum hoc perdidit, ad quod factus est. O durus et dirus casus ille! Heu! quid perdidit et quid invenit, quid abscessit et quid remansit! Perdidit beatitudinem, ad quam factus est, et invenit miseriam, propter quam factus non est. . . . Heu publicus luctus hominum, universalis planctus filiorum Adae. . . . Ille abundabat, nos mendicamus. Ille feliciter tenebat et misere deseruit, nos infeliciter egemus et miserabiliter desideramus, et heu! vacui remanemus. Cur non nobis custodivit, cum facile posset, quo tam graviter careremus? Quare sic nobis obseravit lucem et obduxit nos tenebris? Ut quid nobis abstulit vitam et inflixit mortem? Aerumnosi, unde sumus expulsi, quo sumus impulsi! Unde praecipitati, quo obruti! A patria in exsilium, a visione dei in caecitatem nostram. A iucunditate immortalitatis in amaritudinem et horrorem mortis. Misera mutatio! De quanto bono in quantum malum! Grave damnum, gravis dolor, grave totum. . . .

Et o *tu, domine, usquequo? Usquequo, domine, oblivisceris nos, usquequo avertis faciem tuam a nobis?* Quando respicies et exaudies nos? Quando illuminabis oculos nostros et ostendes nobis faciem tuam? Quando restitues te nobis? Respice, domine, exaudi, illumina nos, ostende nobis teipsum. Restitue te nobis, ut bene sit nobis, sine quo tam male est nobis. Miserare labores et conatus nostros ad te, qui nihil valemus sine te. Invitas nos, adiuva nos. Obsecro, domine, ne desperem suspirando, sed respirem sperando. Obsecro, domine, amaricatum est cor meum sua desolatione, indulca illud tua consolatione. Obsecro, domine, esuriens incepi quaerere te, ne desinam ieiunus de te. Famelicus accessi; ne recedam impastus. Pauper veni ad divitem, miser ad misericordem; ne redeam vacuus et contemptus.... Liceat mihi suspicere lucem tuam, vel de longe, vel de profundo. Doce me quaerere te, et ostende te quaerenti; quia nec quaerere te possum, nisi tu doceas, nec invenire, nisi te ostendas. Quaeram te desiderando, desiderem quaerendo. Inveniam amando, amem inveniendo.

Fateor, domine, et gratias ago, quia creasti in me hanc imaginem tuam, ut tui memor te cogitem, te amem. Sed sic est abolita attritione vitiorum, sic est offuscata fumo peccatorum, ut non possit facere, ad quod facta est, nisi tu renoves et reformes eam. Non tento, domine, penetrare altitudinem tuam, quia nullatenus comparo illi intellectum meum; sed desidero aliquatenus intelligere veritatem tuam, quam credit et amat cor meum. Neque enim quaero intelligere, ut credam, sed credo, ut intelligam. Nam et hoc credo: quia, nisi credidero, non intelligam.

Proslogion, ch. 1

EADMER (c. 1055–c. 1124)

THE LIFE OF ANSELM

14   *Monastic Life under Difficulties*

Considerans Anselmus post haec quid quietis perdiderit, quid laboris invenerit, anxiatus est spiritu et vehementi dolore attritus. Ducebat enim ante oculos mentis suae qualem in prioratu et abbatia positus vitam agere solebat,
5 quam scilicet iocunde in Dei et proximi caritate quiescebat ac delectabatur, quam devote verba vitae loquens ab omnibus audiebatur, quam devotius ad suae ut sperabat cumulum retributionis quae dicebat opere exercebantur, et nunc e converso, cum in melius per episcopatum pro-
10 ficere debuerit, ecce die ac nocte in saecularibus laborans videbat se nec Deo nec proximo secundum Deum iuxta pristinum morem intendere posse, nec adeo quemquam ex ore suo verbum vitae quod facto impleret ad suae, ut reputabat, detrimentum mercedis audire velle. Accesserant
15 istis in augmentum mali sui crudeles suorum hominum oppressiones quotidie auribus eius insonantes, et minae malignantium deteriora in posterum pollicentium circumquaque detonantes. Sciebatur nempe regiam mentem contra eum in furorem concitatam esse, et ob hoc quisque
20 malus beatum se fore credebat si quod illum exasperaret ullo ingenio facere posset. Multis itaque ac diversis iniuriarum procellis fatigabatur, et nulla terreni honoris vel commodi suavitate unde consolationem haberet fovebatur. Verum salva in omnibus et ad omnes inno-
25 centia conscientiae suae, modicum respirabat ab his et magnopere consolabatur siquando se monachorum claustro inferre, et quae institutio vitae ipsorum expetebat coram eis effari valebat. Quod ipse quadam vice capitulo

THE CHRISTIAN LIFE

eorum praesidens, et ex more de huiusmodi liberius agens, dicendi fine completo, iocunda hilaritate alludens iocosa comparatione innotuit dicens, 'Sicut bubo dum in caverna cum pullis suis est laetatur et suo sibi modo bene est; dum vero inter corvos aut corniculas seu alias aves est, incursatur ac dilaniatur, omninoque sibi male est, ita et mihi. Quando enim vobiscum sum, bene mihi est, et grata ac singularis vitae meae consolatio. Quando vero remotus a vobis inter saeculares conversor, hinc inde variarum me causarum incursus dilacerant, et quae non amo saecularia negotia vexant. Male igitur mihi est quando sic sum, ac tremens pertimesco ne meum huiuscemodi esse procreet immane dispendium animae meae.' Ad quod verbum licet alludens, ut dixi, coeperit, amarissime flens subinferens ait, *Sed, quaeso, miseremini mei, miseremini mei, saltem vos amici mei, quia manus Domini tetigit me.* Quia igitur in tali conversatione magnopere respirabat, ea sibi deficiente graviter suspirabat. Deum testor me saepe illum sub veritatis testimonio audisse protestantem, quod libentius vellet in congregatione monachorum loco pueri inter pueros sub virga magistri pavere quam per pastoralem curam toti Britanniae praelatus in conventu populorum cathedrae pontificali praesidere. Forte dicet aliquis, 'Si tam bonum, tam iocundum erat illi habitare cum monachis, cur non continue habitabat Cantuariae cum suis?' Ad quod ego, 'Si hoc solum sibi possibile esset, magno se consolatum reputaret. Sed et hoc partim remotio villarum suarum, partim usus et institutio antecessorum suorum, partim numerositas hominum sine quibus eum esse pro more terrae pontificalis honor non sinebat, illi adimebat, eumque per villas suas ire ac inibi degere compellebat. Praeterea, si Cantuariam assidue incoleret, homines sui ex advectione victualium oppido gravarentur, et insuper a praepositis, ut saepe contingebat, multis ex causis oppressi, si quem interpellarent nunquam praesentem haberent, magis ac magis oppressi in destructionem funditus irent.'

Nullo tamen loco vel tempore sine suis monachis et clericis erat, iis duntaxat exceptis qui ad eum ex diversis locis confluentes raro deerant. Omnes etenim ad se venientes dulci alacritate suscipiebat, et cuique pro sui negotii qualitate efficaciter respondebat. Videres siquidem istos scripturarum sententiis ac quaestionibus involutos mox ratione proposita ab eo evolvi; istos in morum discretione nutantes non segnius informari; illos necessariarum rerum tenuitate laborantes, datis quibus opus habebant, ab inopia relevari. Nec ista largitas solummodo monachorum seu clericorum penuriam sublevabat, sed et in quosque laicos ea indigentes, ea sibi subveniri petentes, pro posse et nonnunquam ultra posse pii patris redundabat.

De Vita et Conversatione Anselmi Archiepiscopi Cantuariensis,
II. 8, 9

15   *St. Anselm and the Hare*

Discedente autem Anselmo a curia, et ad villam suam nomine Heisam properante, pueri quos nutriebat leporem sibi occursantem in via canibus insecuti sunt, et fugientem infra pedes equi quem pater ipse sedebat subsidentem consecuti sunt. Ille sciens miseram bestiam sibi sub se refugio consuluisse, retentis habenis equum loco fixit, nec cupitum bestiae voluit praesidium denegare. Quam canes circumdantes, et haud grato obsequio hinc inde lingentes, nec de sub equo poterant eiicere, nec in aliquo laedere. Quod videntes admirati sumus. At Anselmus ubi quosdam ex equitibus aspexit ridere, et quasi pro capta bestia laetitiae frena laxare, solutus in lacrimas ait, 'Ridetis? Et utique infelici huic nullus risus, laetitia nulla est. Hostes eius circa eam sunt, et ipsa de vita sollicita confugit ad nos praesidium flagitans. Hoc plane est et animae hominis. Nam cum de corpore exit, mox inimici sui maligni, scilicet spiritus qui eam in corpore degentem per anfractus vitiorum multis modis persecuti sunt, crudeliter assunt, parati eam rapere et in mortem aeternam praecipitare. At ipsa nimis anxia huc illucque circumspicit, et quae tueatur defensionis et auxilii manum sibi porrigi ineffabili desiderio concupiscit. Demones autem e contrario rident, et magno gaudio gaudent si illam nullo fultam adminiculo inveniunt.' Quibus dictis laxato freno in iter rediit, bestiam ultra persequi clara voce canibus interdicens. Tunc illa ab omni laesione immunis exsultans praepeti cursu campos silvasque revisit. Nos vero, depositis iocis, sed non modice alacres effecti de tam pia liberatione pavidi animalis, coepto itinere patrem secuti sumus.

De Vita Anselmi, II. 18

A third passage from the Life of Anselm: Thoughts on Education, *is included in Part Four:* The World of Learning; *No. 41.*

ST. BERNARD (1090–1153)

In 1098 a group of Benedictine monks from the abbey of Molesme in Burgundy (among them an Englishman, Stephen Harding), conscious that the primitive observance of the Rule had been gradually overlaid by the growth of riches and the increasing elaboration of the religious services, broke away and founded a small community at a wild spot in the forest called Cîteaux, determined to observe the Rule in its most literal sense, cutting out liturgical elaborations and rich vestments and furniture, simplifying church architecture, and proposing to live by the labour of their hands, as St. Benedict had laid down.

The experiment still hung in the balance, when in 1112 a young Burgundian nobleman arrived, with twenty-nine others, including four out of his five brothers, and other kinsmen and friends whom he had won over to his point of view—his whole story shows a magnetic personality, with great powers of leadership. From that moment Cîteaux never looked back. Within a few years postulants were flocking in, and Cîteaux began to send out 'colonies', among them Clairvaux in 1115, with Bernard accompanied by twelve others as abbot-elect, at the age of 25. At his death in 1153 Clairvaux itself had 68 daughter-houses, and 167 lineal descendants, while the whole Order numbered 339, and by the end of the century had reached a total of 525.

The whole conception of a monastic 'Order' was something new. In the earlier centuries each Benedictine house had been independent, and only linked in spirit by sharing a common Rule;[1] but here each new foundation was linked with its mother-house, whose abbot was bound to visit it once a year, while the Order as a whole was bound together by a charter, prescribing in detail their observances, and governed by an annual meeting of all the abbots of the Order, meeting in 'General Chapter', at Cîteaux, so that a closely integrated monastic order stretched from Poland to Spain, and from Italy to Scotland. (There were almost 100 houses in England and Scotland, including Rievaulx (1132), Fountains (1132), Tintern (1131), Melrose (1136); and Rievaulx itself had nineteen descendants, almost all founded before 1200.)

The moving spirit for over thirty years was the abbot of Clairvaux, Bernard himself. Letters, sermons, treatises poured from his pen in a Latin formed by the classics, but still more steeped in the Bible, and with an eloquence and passion all his own. And not only from his pen: the spoken word, with the full force of his personality and purpose behind it, had the power to move men's hearts and draw them after him—a terrifyingly successful fisher of men.

Many of the practical cares of a great house (at times there were up to 800 monks and lay-brothers) were taken off his hands by his prior and his brother Gerard; yet as abbot he was compelled by the Constitution to travel far and wide, visiting daughter-houses, and through sheer force of personality and ability he became involved in many of the major controversies of Europe, where church and state

---

[1] Cluny and its Congregation are omitted here; but constitutionally they do not challenge the originality of Cîteaux.

were still inextricably bound together, though each was struggling for the mastery, at least within its own house, and so far as possible in the other. His eloquence helped to launch the Second Crusade in 1145, and he wrote a manual for the Knights Templars, this new order of warrior-monks: *De Laudibus Novae Militiae*. When one of his own monks became pope as Eugenius III (1145–53), he wrote a long treatise for him, *De Consideratione*, a mixture of exhortation and solemn warning—a stiff dose for the head of Christendom, such as no one had ever ventured to mix before.

He drove himself hard, as he drove others; and at times they could not stand it. He writes to a deserter from Clairvaux to Cluny: 'Fuerit certe meae culpae quod discessisti. Delicato quippe adulescentulo austerus exstiteram, et tenerum durus nimis inhumane tractavi' (Ep. I. 2). For much of his life he was himself a sick man, reduced in the end to eat the delicacies he had despised, but there still blazed in him this compound of charity and indignation, compassion and ruthlessness where he believed himself to be right. A life of mortification had not deadened his feelings (as the Stoics had taught men to do), but intensified them, and he shows them nakedly—love of God and his brethren, sympathy, anger, and desolation. He was not a philosopher, like Augustine or Anselm, or his contemporary, Abelard, and had little sympathy with the growing tendency of applying reason to revealed religion, but a monk and a man of prayer, who found himself forced by his gifts and circumstances into a life of action.

'Bernard's death marked the end of an epoch. Eugenius III died only a few days before and with that double loss the great age of Cistercian intervention, and indeed the great monastic age of the Church, the 'Benedictine centuries', came to an end. The future lay outside the monasteries, with the schools, with the universities, with the friars.'[1]

16   *Come to Clairvaux!*

BERNARD TO MASTER HENRY MURDAC

Quid mirum si inter prospera fluctuas et adversa, qui necdum statuisti supra petram pedes tuos? At si iures et

[1] David Knowles, *The Historian and Character*, 1963, p. 49.

statuas custodire iudicia iustitiae Domini, quid horum te poterit separare a caritate Christi? O si scires et quid dicam! *Oculus, Deus, non vidit absque te, quae praeparasti diligentibus te.* Sed tu, frater, qui, ut audivi, Prophetas legis, putas intelligis quae legis? Nam si intelligis, sentis utique sensum propheticae lectionis esse Christum. Quem videlicet si apprehendere cupis, citius illum sequendo, quam legendo consequi potes. Quid quaeris verbum in Verbo, quod iam caro factum praesto est oculis? Iam enim de latibulo Prophetarum egressus est ad oculos Piscatorum: iam de monte umbroso et condenso, tamquam sponsus de thalamo suo, prosilivit in campum Evangelii. Iam qui habet aures audiendi, audiat illum clamantem in templo: *Qui sitit, veniat ad me, et bibat,* et *Venite ad me omnes qui laboratis et onerati estis, et ego reficiam vos.* Tu ergo times deficere, ubi se Veritas reficere te promittit? Certe si tantum te delectat tenebrosa aqua de nubibus aeris, quanto iucundius haurias de serenissimis fontibus Salvatoris?

O si semel paululum quid de adipe frumenti, unde satiatur Ierusalem, degustares! Quam libenter suas crustas rodendas litteratoribus Iudaeis relinqueres! O si te unquam in schola pietatis sub magistro Iesu merear habere sodalem! O si mihi liceat purificatum prius tui pectoris vasculum supponere unctioni quae docet de omnibus! O quam libens tibi pariter calidos panes, quos utique adhuc fumigantes, et quasi modo de furno, ut aiunt, recens tractos, de caelesti largitate crebro Christus suis pauperibus frangit! . . . Experto crede: aliquid amplius invenies in silvis, quam in libris. Ligna et lapides docebunt te, quod a magistris audire non possis. An non putas posse te sugere mel de petra, oleumque de saxo durissimo? An non montes stillant dulcedinem, et colles fluunt lac et mel, et valles abundant frumento? Multis occurrentibus mihi dicendis tibi, vix me teneo. Sed quia non lectionem, sed orationem petis; adaperiat Dominus cor tuum in lege sua et in praeceptis suis. Vale.

Idipsum ipsi Willelmus et Ivo. Quid super hoc vobis dicemus? Quod vos videre, et ad quid desideremus, scitis: quantum vero, nec nos dicere, nec vos scire potestis. Oramus ergo Deum, ut vobis quo nos praeisse debueratis, tribuat vel sequi: quatenus et in hoc tantae vos humilitatis magistrum teneamus, cum videlicet non despexeritis magister sequi discipulos.

Letter 106

17   *Jerusalem Found*

BERNARD TO ALEXANDER, BISHOP OF LINCOLN

Philippus vester volens proficisci Ierosolymam, compendium viae invenit, et cito pervenit quo volebat. Transfretavit in brevi hoc mare magnum et spatiosum, et prospere navigans attigit iam littus optatum, atque ad portum tandem salutis applicuit. Stantes sunt iam pedes eius in atriis Ierusalem; et quem audierat in Ephrata, inventum in campis silvae libenter adorat in loco ubi steterunt pedes eius. Ingressus est sanctam civitatem, sortitus est cum illis hereditatem, quibus merito dicitur: *Iam non estis hospites et advenae, sed estis cives sanctorum et domestici Dei.* Cum quibus intrans et exiens, tamquam unus e sanctis, gloriatur et ipse cum caeteris dicens: *Conversatio nostra in coelis est.* Factus est ergo non curiosus tantum spectator, sed et devotus habitator, et civis conscriptus Ierusalem, non autem terrenae huius, cui Arabiae mons Sina coniunctus est, quae servit cum filiis suis; sed liberae illius, quae est sursum mater nostra.

Et, si vultis scire, Clara-vallis est. Ipsa est Ierusalem, ei quae in coelis est, tota mentis devotione, et conversationis imitatione, et cognatione quadam spiritus sociata. Haec requies eius, sicut ipse promittit, in saeculum saeculi: elegit eam in habitationem sibi; quod apud eam sit, etsi nondum visio, certe exspectatio verae pacis, illius utique de qua dicitur: *Pax Dei, quae exsuperat omnem sensum.* Verum hoc suum bonum, etsi desuper accepit, in vestro tamen beneplacito hoc facere cupit, immo se fecisse confidit, sciens vos Sapientis non ignorare sententiam: quod *filius* utique *sapiens sit gloria patris.* Rogat autem paternitatem vestram, rogamus et nos cum illo et pro illo, quatenus de praebenda sua quod ipse suis creditoribus constituit, immobiliter stare faciatis: ne in aliquo fraudator (quod absit) debiti, et praevaricator pacti inveniatur; et ita munus contriti cordis quod offert quotidie, non recipiatur, dum frater quispiam habet aliquid adversus eum. Precatur deinde, ut domus quam ipse matri suae in terra ecclesiae construxit, cum terra quam ibi delegavit, eidem matri, quamdiu vixerit, concedatur. Haec pro Philippo.

Reliqua haec pauca pro vobis, ipso quidem intimante, immo vero inspirante Deo, adiicienda putavimus, hortari vos in caritate praesumentes, ne casuri gloriam mundi quasi stantem aspiciatis, et vere stantem amittatis; ne plus vobis aut pro vobis vestra diligatis, et sic vos et vestra perdatis: ne blandiens praesens prosperitas sui vobis finem abscondat, et adversitas sine fine succedat; ne laetitia temporalis luctum vobis aeternum et operiat quem parit, et pariat quem operit: ne mors longe esse putetur, et praeoccupet improvidum; et vita dum longa exspectatur, cito deserat male conscium, sicut scriptum est: *Cum dixerint, Pax et securitas; tunc subitaneus superveniet eis interitus, tamquam in utero habenti, et non effugient.* Valete.

Letter 64

THE PAPACY

What is the role of the papacy; and how ought a pope to conduct himself in the most exalted and dangerous position in the world, so as to fulfil his responsibilities and save his own soul? To the first question there are many simple answers, such as that given by Bede in his account of the Synod of Whitby (664). This is richly elaborated by St. Bernard; while in answer to the second question he lays down one central principle: *Vaca considerationi*, 'keep time for consideration'. This 'consideration' he defines as 'thought concentrated on the search for truth'—*intensa ad vestigandum cogitatio, vel intensio animi vestigantis verum*—and ranging over four fields: 'yourself, things below you, things around you, and things above you.' He is to start then from self-knowledge, and work outwards. Two passages illustrate this self-examination, and a third shows something of the perils around him—the endless litigation, and the scramble for wealth and power at the fountain-head of preferment.

But it is not a one-sided picture that he presents. He answers the demand that Pascal was to formulate five hundred years later: 'True religion ought to teach man's greatness and his wretchedness; it should lead to esteem and to contempt for ourselves'—and the treatise ends with a picture of 'the things above' and the glories of Heaven.

ST. BERNARD (1090–1153)

18 *Your Greatness*

Age, indagemus adhuc diligentius qui sis, quam geras videlicet pro tempore personam in Ecclesia Dei. Quis es? Sacerdos magnus, summus Pontifex. Tu princeps episcoporum, tu heres Apostolorum, tu primatu Abel, gubernatu Noe, patriarchatu Abraham, ordine Melchisedech, dignitate Aaron, auctoritate Moyses, iudicatu Samuel, potestate Petrus, unctione Christus. Tu es cui claves traditae, cui oves creditae sunt. Sunt quidem et alii coeli ianitores, et gregum pastores: sed tu tanto gloriosius, quanto et differentius utrumque prae caeteris nomen haereditasti. Habent illi sibi assignatos greges, singuli singulos: tibi universi crediti, uni unus. Nec modo ovium, sed et pastorum tu unus omnium pastor. Unde id probem quaeris? Ex verbo Domini. Cui enim, non dico episcoporum, sed etiam Apostolorum sic absolute et indiscrete totae commissae sunt oves? *Si me amas, Petre, pasce oves meas.* Quas? illius vel illius populos civitatis, aut regionis, aut certi regni? *Oves meas,* inquit. Cui non planum, non designasse aliquas, sed assignasse omnes? Nihil excipitur, ubi distinguitur nihil.

Ergo, iuxta canones tuos, alii in partem sollicitudinis, tu in plenitudinem potestatis vocatus es. Aliorum potestas certis arctatur limitibus: tua extenditur et in ipsos, qui potestatem super alios acceperunt. Nonne, si causa exstiterit, tu episcopo coelum claudere, tu ipsum ab episcopatu deponere etiam et tradere satanae potes? Stat ergo inconcussum privilegium tuum tibi tam in datis clavibus, quam in ovibus commendatis. Accipe aliud, quod nihilominus praerogativam confirmat tibi. Discipuli navigabant, et Dominus apparebat in littore; quodque iucundius erat, in corpore redivivo. Sciens Petrus quia Dominus est, in mare se misit, et sic venit ad ipsum, aliis navigio pervenientibus. Quid istud? Nempe signum singularis pontificii Petri, per quod non navem unam, ut caeteri quique suam, sed saeculum ipsum susceperit gubernandum. Mare enim saeculum est; naves, Ecclesiae. . . . Ita cum quisque caeterorum habeat suam, tibi una commissa est grandissima navis; facta ex omnibus ipsa universalis Ecclesia, toto orbe diffusa.

De Consideratione, II. 8 (15, 16)

19 *Your Wretchedness*

Nec modo quid natus, sed et qualis natus, oportet attendas, si non vis tuae considerationis fructu et utilitate fraudari. Tolle proinde nunc haereditaria haec perizomata ab initio maledicta. Dirumpe velamen foliorum celantium ignominiam, non plagam curantium. Dele fucum fugacis honoris huius, et male coloratae nitorem gloriae, ut nude nudum consideres, quia nudus egressus es de utero matris tuae. Numquid infulatus? numquid micans gemmis, aut floridus sericis, aut coronatus pennis, aut suffarcinatus metallis? Si cuncta haec, veluti nubes quasdam matutinas, velociter transeuntes et cito pertransituras, dissipes et exsuffles a facie considerationis tuae, occurret tibi homo nudus, et pauper, et miser, et miserabilis; homo dolens quod homo sit, erubescens quod nudus sit, plorans quod natus sit, murmurans quod sit; homo natus ad laborem, non ad honorem; homo natus de muliere . . . ; brevi vivens tempore, ideoque cum metu; repletus multis miseriis, et propterea cum fletu. Et vere multis, quia corporis et animae simul. Quid enim calamitate vacat nascenti in peccato, fragili corpore, et mente sterili? Vere ergo repletus, cui infirmitas corporis, et fatuitas cordis cumulatur traduce sordis, mortis addictione. Salubris copula, ut cogitans te summum Pontificem, attendas pariter vilissimum cinerem non fuisse, sed esse. Imitetur cogitatio naturam; imitetur et, quod dignius est, Auctorem naturae, summa imaque consocians. Nonne natura in persona hominis vili limo vitae spiraculum colligavit? Nonne Auctor naturae in sui persona Verbum limumque contemperavit? Ita tibi sume formam tam de nostrae concretione originis, quam de sacramento redemptionis: ut altus sedens, non alta sapiens sis, sed humilia de te sentiens, humilibusque consentiens.

De Consideratione, II. 9 (18)

20 *Your Perils*

Quaeso te, quale est istud, de mane usque ad vesperam litigare aut litigantes audire? Et utinam sufficeret diei malitia sua! Non sunt liberae noctes. Vix relinquitur necessitati naturae, quod corpusculi pausationi sufficiat,
5 et rursum ad iurgia surgitur. Dies diei eructat lites, et nox nocti indicat malitiam: usque adeo non est respirare in bonis, non est alternam capessere requiem, non vel rara interseri otia. Non ambigo te quoque ista deplorare: at frustra istud, si non et emendare studueris. Interim tamen
10 sic semper facias hortor, nec te umquam ad ista duraveris quolibet usu vel assiduitate.

'But', you say, 'everywhere the strong oppress the poor; we dare not fail to succour the oppressed, we cannot refuse justice to the suffering. Unless causes are pleaded, and both sides heard, how can judgement be given between the parties?' I reply:

Agitentur causae, sed sicut oportet. Nam is modus qui frequentatur exsecrabilis plane, et qui, non dico Ecclesiam, sed nec forum deceret. Miror namque quemadmodum
15 religiosae aures tuae sustinent huiusmodi disputationes advocatorum et pugnas verborum, quae magis ad subversionem quam ad inventionem proficiunt veritatis. . . . Hi sunt qui docuerunt linguas suas loqui mendacium, diserti adversus iustitiam, eruditi pro falsitate. Sapientes
20 sunt ut faciant malum, eloquentes ut impugnent verum. Hi sunt qui instruunt a quibus fuerant instruendi, adstruunt non comperta, sed sua; struunt de proprio calumnias innocentiae, destruunt simplicitatem veritatis, obstruunt iudicii vias. . . . Plena est ambitiosis Ecclesia;
25 non est iam quod exhorreat in studiis et molitionibus ambitionis, non plus quam spelunca latronis in spoliis viatorum.

De Consideratione, I. 3 (4); 10 (13)

THE CHRISTIAN LIFE 39

VIRTUE AND VICE

Much theological thought (and medieval thought in general) was schematized into patterns, where like was balanced by unlike, and key numbers such as three, seven, twelve, played an important part. So there were seven Virtues, made up of the four 'cardinal' virtues of Greek philosophy—justice, prudence, temperance, and fortitude—together with the three 'theological' virtues of faith, hope, and charity. These in turn were balanced against the Seven Deadly Sins of pride (*superbia*), covetousness (*avaritia*), lust (*luxuria*), anger (*ira*), gluttony (*gula*), envy (*invidia*), and sloth or gloom (*accidia, tristitia*). The two sets do not precisely correspond with one another, but they are the sources from which the characteristic features or temptations of the Christian life derive, while at the same time they provide a groundwork for instruction. In monasteries this fell to the Novice-Master, and Cistercians in particular, who only accepted novices from the age of fifteen upwards, set great store by their moral formation.

A picture of this is given by a Cistercian novice-master from the Rhineland, Caesarius of Heisterbach (*c.* 1180–*c.* 1240), in a long work entitled *Dialogus Miraculorum*. He illustrates every abstract discussion (under such large headings as *De tentatione*, *De daemonibus*, *De praemio mortuorum*) by some vivid instance whose truth he vouches for. Some are very tall stories, but none the less interesting for that: in fact they were so popular that about a hundred manuscripts of this and his other works survive, and the *Dialogus* ran through five or six printed editions between 1475 and 1605.

(An English version of the Seven Deadly Sins is given by Chaucer in his *Parson's Tale*. He was drawing on a thirteenth-century *Summa Vitiorum*; and there was a vast intermediate literature of religious manuals in Latin and the vernaculars, all of them looking back to Gregory the Great. But the supreme picture of vice and virtue, where the whole of medieval thought is minutely articulated and exemplified in saint and sinner, in their three worlds of horror, of purgatorial suffering, and of bliss, is to be found in Dante's *Divine Comedy*.)

21   *Virtue and Vice*

NOVICIUS: Quibus armis resistendum est his septem vitiis, de quibus iam sermo in longum protractus est?

MONACHUS: Virtutibus eis oppositis. NOVICIUS: Quid sunt virtutes vel unde dicuntur? MONACHUS: Virtutes sunt qualitates mentis, quibus recte vivitur. Dicuntur autem virtutes, quasi contra vitia stantes. Stare debet contra superbiam humilitas, contra iram lenitas, contra invidiam caritas, contra tristitiam spiritalis iocunditas, contra avaritiam largitas, contra gulam potus cibique parcitas, contra luxuriam castitas. Quod si in pugna tentationum virtutes vitiis effectae fuerint superiores, victoriam meritum, et meritum praemium sequitur aeternum. Quod perseveranti se daturum pollicitus est Dominus noster Iesus Christus, qui est via in exemplo, veritas in promisso, vita in praemio. Ipsi cum Patre et Spiritu sancto honor et imperium in saecula saeculorum. Amen.

Dialogus Miraculorum; Conclusion of Book IV, De Tentatione

22 *Avarice*

Abbas quidam, ut puto de ordine nigro, sicut ex relatione cuiusdam Abbatis ordinis nostri didici, hospitalis erat valde, et circa pauperes multum misericors. Et quia in operibus misericordiae fervens fuit, tales dispensatores domui suae ordinare studuit, qui non eius fervorem impedirent, sed magis incenderent. Quanto plures hospites suscepit, quanto plus caritatis pauperibus exhibuit, tanto illi et domui eius Dominus amplius benedixit. Post cuius mortem, successor eius stimulatus avaritia, pietatis officialibus amotis, et eis quos tenaciores noverat institutis, ait: Praedecessor meus nimis erat dapsilis et indiscretus, officiales eius nimis prodigi. Sic ordinare debemus expensas monasterii atque temperare, ut si forte seges nostra grandinata fuerit, et tempora cara emerserint, habeamus unde pauperibus subveniamus. Huiusmodi verbis avaritiam suam pallians, hospitalitatem prorsus exclusit, et consueta beneficia pauperibus subtraxit. Caritate subtracta, proficere non potuit monasterii substantia, imo in brevi ad tantam devenit paupertatem, ut vix haberent fratres quod manducarent. Die quadam vir quidam venerandae canitiei venit ad portarium, quaesivit hospitium. Quem ille quidem clanculo et cum timore collegit, atque hospitalitatis officia pro posse et tempore illi exhibens, adiecit: Non te scandalizare debet, bone vir, quod tam negligenter te procuro, quia necessitas in causa est. Aliquando vidi talem statum huius monasterii, ut si venisset Episcopus, cum magna caritate et abundantia fuisset susceptus. Respondit ille: Duo fratres expulsi sunt de monasterio isto; nisi illi duo fuerint reversi, nunquam bonus erit status eius. Unus eorum vocatur Date, alter vero Dabitur. Sicque ab oculis eius recessit. Puto aliquam fuisse personam angelicam, per quam Dominus primam fratrum illorum revocare voluit caritatem. Portarius, cum esset laicus, nomina eadem retinuit, Abbati et fratribus audita recitavit. Resumta est hospitalitas, et coepit eis mox Dominus benedicere ut prius.

Dialogus Miraculorum, Book IV, ch. 68

23 *Simplicity*

Inter omnia virtutum antidota contra tentationum incommoda ipsosque tentatores daemones, maioris efficaciae esse videtur usus simplicitatis. Haec virtus felle caret totius amaritudinis, irae, invidiae atque rancoris, caret et oculo venenato suspicionis, denteque canino detractionis. . . . Haec opus per se malum facit bonum, et econverso, sicut in sequenti capitulo satis aperto tibi ostendam exemplo.

Novicius: Bene hoc concedo, quia Salvatorem dixisse recolo: *Si oculus tuus fuerit simplex, totum corpus tuum lucidum erit.*

Monachus: Revera, ubi simplex fuerit intentio, ibi necesse est ut lucida sequatur actio; sicut econtrario oculus nequam, id est, intentio mala atque perversa, totum corpus, id est opus, efficit tenebrosum. . . . Virtus simplicitatis a Christo discipulis praedicatur: *Estote, inquit, prudentes sicut serpentes, et simplices sicut columbae.* Simplicitati coniungit prudentiam, propter vecordiam. Item dicit: *Nisi conversi fueritis, et efficiamini sicut pueri,* id est, humiles et simplices, *non intrabitis in regnum caelorum.* Simplicitas via est ad Deum, grata angelis, hominibus delectabilis. Unde ceteris virtutibus omissis, quantae sit efficaciae sancta simplicitas paucis explicabo exemplis.

Simplicity Rewarded

Dominus Wido Abbas Cisterciensis, postea Cardinalis, cum missus fuisset Coloniam ad electionem confirmandam . . . retulit ibidem quandam sanctae simplicitatis historiam, satis iocundam satisque mirabilem. Dicebat domum quandam ordinis nostri in terra cuiusdam nobilis viri atque potentis fuisse sitam. Quam idem tyrannus, eo quod Deum non timeret, neque hominem revereretur, multis modis saepe molestavit. De annona, vino et pecoribus, quotiens et quantum voluit, tulit, quantum voluit fratribus dimisit. Cumque hoc ex consuetudine et quasi pro lege habens actitaret, et conventus, querimoniis multis inutiliter delatis, gemens taceret, die quadam maximam partem rapuit armenti, praecipiens illam ad castrum suum minari. Quo cognito, Abbas et fratres satis turbabantur, in quorum consilio quid facto opus esset, satis tractabatur. Visum est eis aliquem ire debere ad castrum, per quem saltem

merces ei innotesceret, maxime Abbatem. Qui respondit: 40
Ego non ibo, quia monendo illum nihil proficimus, sed
aërem tantummodo verberamus. Simili modo excusante
se Priore et cellerario, subiunxit Abbas: Estne hic aliquis,
qui adhuc semel ire velit? Tacentibus cunctis, unus
divinitus inspiratus, promte respondit: Monachus ille 45
vadat, hominem senem ac simplicissimum nominans.
Vocatus est monachus; si ire vellet ad castrum inquiritur,
obedit, mittitur. Qui cum ab Abbate recederet, ex multa
cordis sui simplicitate verbum hoc protulit: Pater, inquit,
si aliqua portio mihi fuerit restituta, recipiam, an non? 50
Respondit: Quicquid rehabere poteris, accipias in nomine
Domini. Melius est aliquid, quam nihil. Abiit ille, venit
ad castrum, nuncium Abbatis et fratrum cum orationibus
deferens tyranno. Et quia simplicitas iusti, secundum Iob,
lampas est contemta in oculis malorum, tyrannus sermones 55
eius parvipendens et irridens ait: Domine, exspectate,
donec pransus fueritis, tunc enim respondebitur vobis.
Hora prandii ad mensam communem positus est, et
cibaria communia, carnes scilicet in bona quantitate, ei
sicut ceteris sunt appositae. Vir sanctus verbi Abbatis sui 60
reminiscens, et carnes, quae tam laute ministrabantur, de
pecoribus monasterii sui esse non dubitans, quantum ex
carnibus sumere potuit, cum ceteris, ne inobediens esset,
manducavit. Dominus castri ex opposito cum uxore
residens, et quia monachus manducaret carnes, satis 65
considerans, finito prandio hominem vocavit seorsum et
ait: Dicite mihi, bone domine, solet conventus vester
manducare carnes? Respondente illo: Nequaquam;
adiecit: Quid cum exeunt? Nec intus, inquit, nec extra
carnes comedunt. Tunc tyrannus: Et quare vos comedistis 70
hodie illas? Respondit monachus: Cum Abbas meus huc
me mitteret, praecepit mihi, ut quicquid ex pecoribus
rehabere possem, accipere non recusarem. Et quia mihi

constabat carnes appositas fuisse monasterii mei, item
quia timui nil amplius mihi fore restituendum, nisi
quantum dentibus capere possem, comedi propter obedi-
entiam, ne omnino vacuus redirem. Et quia Deus sim-
plicem non proiicit, nec porrigit manum impiis, scilicet
contra illum, audito eius verbo, et in simplicitate eius
motus, imo a Spiritu sancto, qui per os senis loquebatur,
admonitus, respondit vir nobilis: Exspectate me hic, ego
consilium habebo cum uxore mea, quid vobis faciam. Ad
quam cum venisset, et senis ei verba per ordinem reci-
tasset, adiecit: Timeo celerem Dei super me vindictam, si
vir iste tam simplex et tam rectus aliquam nunc a me passus fuerit repulsam. Similiter et illa respondit, quia eodem
spiritu accensa fuit. Reversus ad senem, ait: Bone pater,
propter sanctam simplicitatem vestram, quae me ad
misericordiam inflexit, monasterio vestro quicquid adhuc
de pecoribus superest restituam, de illatis a me iniuriis in
quantum potero satisfaciam, et nunquam ab hac die illud
turbabo. Ad quod verbum senex gratias illi referens, cum
rapina ad monasterium laetus rediit, et Abbate et fratribus
stupentibus, verba potentis retulit. Pacem ab illo tempore
habentes, quanta esset virtus simplicitatis exemplo
didicerunt.

Dialogus Miraculorum, II. 1, 2

THE FOUR LAST THINGS

Death, Judgement, Hell, and Heaven—these are the 'Four Last
Things' which haunted many of the writers in this book: 'religious'
for the most part, who had forsaken father and mother, wife and
children and lands, for the sake of the hundredfold promised to them,
and everlasting life. Each idea is present in the New Testament, but
every sentence there seems to have grown to a volume, as thought
and imagination and fear played upon it over the centuries; so that

together the effect seems more overpowering than in the early Church —and certainly more so than in our own day. Not that these conceptions remained static: there was a certain shift of emphasis in the central Middle Ages, as God, the stern judge, came to be counterbalanced by a new sense of the humanity of Christ, and the compassion of his Mother. But the tenderness of the second half of the *Dies Irae* is still balanced by the dread of the first; and the promises of the New Testament appear in the liturgy alongside the shadowy hopes and fears and the terrifying metaphors—the pit and the lion's mouth—of the Psalms.

But hope triumphed over fear in the vision of the Holy City, the New Jerusalem, and the everlasting sabbath, or day of rest, which recalls and renews the seventh day of Creation: the consummation with which Augustine concludes his account of the *City of God*. 'Tunc vacabimus et videbimus, videbimus et amabimus, amabimus et laudabimus. Ecce quod erit in fine sine fine. Nam quis alius noster est finis nisi pervenire ad regnum cuius nullus est finis?'[1]

Meanwhile there is the journey, and the familiar contrast between *in via* and *in patria*; the metaphor of a 'Pilgrim's Progress' already announced in the New Testament.[2] Sometimes the *patria* lies across the sea, *mare huius saeculi*, where men are uncertain and tempest-tossed; to be crossed on the bark of Peter, or clinging to the *lignum crucis*. It follows too that this life is an exile, from the day when man was first expelled from Paradise till the day of his return. One can add the New Testament metaphors of battle and victory (one that was adopted by monks as peculiarly their own from the fourth century onwards), of work and reward, of marriage song and feast. But another one is perhaps still more inclusive: that of Dante's *Divine Comedy*, where life and death, this world and the next, justice and mercy are combined in a single vision at once terrifying and exultant: that of a drama of which God is the author, in which all men must play a part whether they will or no (for to refuse to act is still a choice, and a damning one). But each choice has eternal significance; and no one knows the day or hour at which he will quit the stage, whether by battle, murder, or slow decay, or heroic choice, or sullen refusal. 'Watch therefore . . . .'

[1] *De Civitate Dei*, XXII. 30.
[2] Heb. 11. 10–16; 13. 14.

ST. BERNARD (1090–1153)

24 *The Death of Gerard (1138)*

St. Bernard's gifts had been demanded as abbot of a great community and founder of daughter-houses, and in effect head of the Cistercian Order, and as writer, preacher, correspondent, and statesman with commitments all over Europe. Meanwhile his brother Gerard, apart from accompanying him on one journey to Italy, had remained behind as cellarer of Clairvaux, largely responsible for the material welfare of some 300 monks.

This lament fills most of Sermon 26, one of 86 devoted to a running commentary on the Song of Songs. The present selection represents about a quarter of the original: each theme is stated and rephrased and balanced against its opposing themes as in a musical composition, his emotion expressing itself now in bare simplicity, now in an elaboration of antitheses and word-play which explore and at the same time relieve his anguish.

Quousque enim dissimulo, et ignis, quem intra meipsum abscondo, triste pectus adurit, interiora depascitur? Clausus latius serpit, saevit acrius. Quid mihi et cantico huic, qui in amaritudine sum? Vis doloris abducit in-
5 tentionem, et indignatio Domini ebibit spiritum meum. Subtracto siquidem illo, per quem mea in Domino studia utcumque libera esse solebant, simul et cor meum dereliquit me. Sed feci vim animo meo ac dissimulavi usque huc, ne affectus fidem vincere videretur. Denique
10 plorantibus aliis, ego, ut advertere potuistis, siccis oculis secutus sum invisum funus, siccis oculis steti ad tumulum, quousque cuncta peracta sunt exsequiarum solemnia. Indutus sacerdotalibus, solitas in eum orationes proprio ore complevi, terram propriis manibus ex more ieci super
15 dilecti corpus, terram mox futurum. Qui me intuebantur flebant, et mirabantur quod non flerem ipse, cum non illum quidem, sed me potius, qui illum amisissem, omnes

THE CHRISTIAN LIFE

miserarentur. Cuius enim vel ferreum pectus super me ibi non moveretur, quem videret Girardo superstitem? Commune damnum; sed prae meo non reputabatur infortunio. At ego, quibus poteram viribus fidei, reluctabar affectui, nitens vel invitus non moveri frustra addictione naturae, universitatis debito, conditionis usu, potentis iussu, iudicio iusti, flagello terribilis, Domini voluntate. . . . Fateor, victus sum. Exeat, necesse est, foras quod intus patior. Exeat sane ad oculos filiorum, qui scientes incommodum, planctum humanius aestiment, dulcius consolentur.

Scitis, o filii, quam intus sit dolor meus, quam dolenda plaga mea. Cernitis nempe quam fidus comes deseruit me in via hac qua ambulabam, quam vigil ad curam, quam non segnis ad opus, quam suavis ad mores. Quis ita mihi pernecessarius? Cui ego aeque dilectus? Frater erat genere, sed religione germanior. Dolete, quaeso, vicem meam vos, quibus haec nota sunt. Infirmus corpore eram, et ille portabat me; pusillus corde eram, et confortabat me; piger et negligens, et excitabat me; improvidus et obliviosus, et commonebat me. Quo mihi avulsus est? Quo mihi raptus e manibus, homo unanimis, homo secundum cor meum? Amavimus nos in vita: quomodo in morte sumus separati? Amarissima separatio, et quam non posset omnino efficere, nisi mors! Quando enim me vivus vivum desereres? Omnino opus mortis, horrendum divortium. . . .

Gratias tibi, frater, de omni fructu meorum, si quis est, in Domino studiorum! Tibi debeo si profeci, si profui. Tu intricabaris, et ego tuo beneficio feriatus sedebam mihi, aut certe divinis sanctius obsequiis occupabar, aut doctrinae filiorum utilius intendebam. Cur enim securus intus non essem, cum te scirem agentem foris, manum dexteram meam, lumen oculorum meorum, pectus meum

et linguam meam? Et quidem indefessa manus, oculus simplex, pectus consilii, lingua loquens iudicium, sicut scriptum est: *Os iusti meditabitur sapientiam, et lingua eius*
55 *loquetur iudicium.*

Sed quid dixi foris agentem illum, quasi interna Girardus nesciret ac spiritualium expers esset donorum? Norunt, qui illum norunt spirituales, quam verba eius spiritum redolerent. Norunt contubernales, quam mores
60 eius et studia non carnem saperent, sed ferverent spiritu. Quis illo rigidior in custodia disciplinae? Quis in castigando corpus suum districtior, suspensior in contemplando, subtilior in disserendo? Quotiens cum eo disserens ea didici quae nesciebam, et qui docturus adveneram,
65 doctus magis abscessi! Nec mirum de me, cum magni ac sapientes viri idipsum nihilominus ex illo sibi accidisse testentur. Non cognovit litteraturam, sed habuit litterarum inventorem sensum, habuit et illuminantem Spiritum. Nec in maximis tantum, sed et in minimis maximus erat.
70 Quid, verbi gratia, in aedificiis, in agris, in hortis, aquis, cunctis denique artibus seu operibus rusticorum, quid, inquam, vel in hoc rerum genere Girardi subterfugit peritiam? Caementariis, fabris, agricolis, hortulanis, sutoribus atque textoribus facile magister erat. Cumque
75 omnium iudicio omnibus esset sapientior, solius in sui oculis non erat sapiens. ... Affectum meum confessus sum, et non negavi. Carnalem quis dixerit? Ego humanum non nego, sicut nec me hominem. Si nec hoc sufficit, nec carnalem negaverim. Nam et *ego carnalis sum, venumdatus*
80 *sub peccato*, addictus morti, poenis et aerumnis obnoxius. Non sum, fateor, insensibilis ad poenas: mortem horreo meam et meorum. Meus Girardus erat, meus plane. An non meus erat, qui frater sanguine fuit, professione filius, sollicitudine pater, consors spiritu, intimus affectu? Is
85 recessit a me: sentio, laesus sum, et graviter. ...

God grant that I may follow you—you for whom the night was as the day, as you died with a song of praise on your lips.

Accitus sum ad id miraculi: videre hominem in morte exultantem et insultantem morti. *Ubi est, mors, victoria tua? Ubi est, mors, stimulus tuus?* Iam non stimulus, sed iubilus. Iam cantando moritur homo, et moriendo cantat. Usurparis ad laetitiam, mater maeroris; usurparis ad gloriam, gloriae inimica; usurparis ad introitum regni, porta inferi, et fovea perditionis ad inventionem salutis, idque ab homine peccatore. . . . Girardus te non formidat, larvalis effigies. Girardus per medias fauces tuas transit ad patriam, non modo securus, sed et laetabundus et laudans.

THOMAS OF CELANO (*c.* 1190–1260)

25 *The Day of Judgement*

Dies irae, dies illa,
solvet saeclum in favilla,
teste David cum Sibylla.

Quantus tremor est futurus,
quando iudex est venturus,
cuncta stricte discussurus!

Tuba mirum sparget sonum
per sepulchra regionum,
coget omnes ante thronum.

Mors stupebit et natura,
cum resurget creatura
iudicanti responsura.

Liber scriptus proferetur,
in quo totum continetur,
unde mundus iudicetur.

Iudex ergo cum censebit,
quidquid latet apparebit:
nil inultum remanebit.

Quid sum miser tunc dicturus,
20 quem patronum rogaturus,
dum vix iustus sit securus?

Rex tremendae maiestatis,
qui salvandos salvas gratis,
salva me, fons pietatis!

25 Recordare, Iesu pie,
quod sum causa tuae viae;
ne me perdas illa die.

Quaerens me sedisti lassus;
redemisti, crucem passus;
30 tantus labor non sit cassus.

Iuste iudex ultionis,
donum fac remissionis
ante diem rationis.

Ingemisco tanquam reus,
35 culpa rubet vultus meus:
supplicanti parce, Deus.

Qui Mariam absolvisti
et latronem exaudisti,
mihi quoque spem dedisti.

40 Preces meae non sunt dignae,
sed tu, bonus, fac benigne,
ne perenni cremer igne.

Inter oves locum praesta
et ab haedis me sequestra
statuens in parte dextra.

Confutatis maledictis,
flammis acribus addictis,
voca me cum benedictis.

Oro supplex et acclinis,
cor contritum quasi cinis:
gere curam mei finis.

HILDEBERT OF LAVARDIN (1056–1133)

26 *The World to Come*

Reus mortis non despero,
Sed in morte vitam quaero.
Quo te placem nil praetendo
Nisi fidem, quam defendo.
Fidem vides; hac imploro,
Leva fascem, qua laboro,
Per hoc sacrum cataplasma
Convalescat aegrum plasma.
   Extra portum iam delatum,
Iam foetentem, tumulatum
Vitta ligat, lapis urget,
Sed, si iubes, hic resurget.
Iube, lapis revolvetur,
Iube, vitta disrumpetur,
Exiturus nescit moras,
Postquam clamas: Exi foras!
   In hoc salo mea ratis
Infestatur a piratis,

Hinc assultus, inde fluctus,
20 Hinc et inde mors et luctus.
Sed tu, bone nauta, veni,
Pro me ventos, mare leni,
Fac abscedant hi piratae,
Duc ad portum salva rate.
25 Infecunda mea ficus,
Cuius ramus ramus siccus,
Incidetur, incendetur,
Si promulgas, quae meretur.
Sed hoc anno dimittatur,
30 Stercoretur, fodiatur,
Quodsi necdum respondebit,
Flens hoc loquor, tunc ardebit.
Tu intrare me non sinas
Infernales officinas,
35 Ubi maeror, ubi metus,
Ubi foetor, ubi fletus,
Ubi probra deteguntur,
Ubi rei confunduntur,
Ubi tortor semper caedens,
40 Ubi vermis semper edens,
Ubi totum hoc perenne,
Quia perpes mors gehennae.
Me receptet Sion illa,
Sion, David urbs tranquilla,
45 Cuius faber auctor lucis,
Cuius portae lignum crucis,
Cuius claves lingua Petri,
Cuius cives semper laeti,
Cuius muri lapis vivus,
50 Cuius custos rex festivus.
In hac urbe lux sollennis,
Ver aeternum, pax perennis,

In hac odor implens caelos,
In hac festum semper melos.
Non est ibi corruptela, 55
Non defectus nec querela,
Non minuti, non deformes,
Omnes Christo sunt conformes.
Urbs caelestis, urbs beata,
Super petram collocata, 60
Urbs in portu satis tuto,
De longinquo te saluto.
Te saluto, te suspiro,
Te affecto, te requiro.
Quantum tui gratulentur, 65
Quam festive conviventur,
Quis affectus eos stringat
Aut quae gemma muros pingat,
Quis chalcedon, quis iacinthus,
Norunt illi, qui sunt intus. 70
In plateis huius urbis
Sociatus piis turbis
Cum Moyse et Elia
Pium cantem Alleluia.

De Trinitate, ll. 96–127, 162–203

PART THREE

HISTORY AND BIOGRAPHY

Sive enim historia de bonis bona referat, ad imitandum bonum auditor sollicitus instigatur; seu mala commemoret de pravis, nihilominus religiosus ac pius auditor sive lector, devitando quod noxium est ac perversum, ipse sollertius ad exsequenda ea, quae bona ac Deo digna esse cognoverit, accenditur.

Bede, *Ecclesiastical History* (Preface)

SEVEN historians or biographers are represented here; in chronological order:

BEDE (*c.* 671–735), the Northumbrian monk, who is discussed more fully later;

EADMER (*c.* 1055–*c.* 1124), a monk of Canterbury, and biographer of his archbishop, Anselm (three passages from this life are included in other sections of this book);

THE UNKNOWN AUTHOR—knight and layman—of the *Gesta Francorum et aliorum Hierosolomitanorum*, an account of the First Crusade (1095–9), in which he served;

ROBERT THE MONK, of Rheims, who wrote a more popular account of the same Crusade, the *Historia Hierosolymitana, c.* 1120;

WILLIAM OF MALMESBURY (*c.* 1090–*c.* 1142), who aspired to continue the work of Bede, and wrote the *Gesta Regum Anglorum* and *Gesta Pontificum Anglorum*—both among the most important sources for his times—besides smaller monastic biographies, etc.;

JOCELIN OF BRAKELOND (*fl.* 1200), a monk of Bury St. Edmunds, who wrote a domestic chronicle of his monastery under Abbot Samson; and

MATTHEW PARIS (*c.* 1200–*c.* 1259), a monk of St. Albans, whose *Chronica Majora* was a rewriting of an earlier chronicle of the house, with an extensive continuation on a national and European scale, making him the most important English historian of his time. (A passage from this work is included in a later section.)

HISTORY AND BIOGRAPHY

It is worth looking at the general proportions first: six monks to one layman—and, broadly speaking, these are representative of Europe as a whole. For about six hundred years, from the eighth to the fourteenth century, history was written almost entirely by clerks or 'religious'; and in England at least these were nearly all Benedictine monks. (Italy was an exception, with its town chronicles going back to the tenth century.) But many of the laity at least made good listeners, and Charlemagne, who could barely write his name, listened eagerly to history, including, we are told, that stiff work, Augustine's *City of God*.

The author of the *Gesta* was a knight serving under Bohemond, one of the many Normans who had carved out lordships for themselves in the tenth–eleventh centuries in southern Italy and Sicily. Of those from this island two are Anglo-Saxons, Eadmer bridging the Norman Conquest, and experiencing its new and often harsh régime while remaining rooted in his native tradition. William of Malmesbury was an Anglo-Norman of mixed parentage, and in that way well fitted to see both sides of the new order; while Jocelin and Matthew Paris can both be called 'Englishmen' in the growing sense of a united nation.

The knight tells a vivid and straightforward tale, with little learning but the Vulgate to fall back on. Eadmer's treatment of his subject is fairly simple, and all the better for that; but William of Malmesbury was steeped in the Latin poets as well as prose writers, and spreads his wings in flowery passages, writing dramatic speeches for his characters and inserting quotations to hit off a situation or to display his own wide reading. Matthew Paris was ideally placed to continue this tradition whereby national history grew up within the framework of the monastic chronicle. St. Albans was only a day's ride from London, on the road to the North; and an observant monk did not need to go out into the world, since the world came to him. Henry III visited the abbey nine times between 1220 and 1259, sometimes staying a week: he knew that Matthew was writing a history of his times, and treated him with much friendliness. Foreign visitors as well as important Englishmen would pass through—there was stabling for 300 horses in the Guest House; the Master of the Temple in Scotland probably told him about King Loui sIX's Crusade (1248–52), and there was a steady stream of bishops, clerics, and monks from other monasteries.

At the same time, owing to the temper of the times and to the writers themselves in their particular setting, history tended to be closely bound up with the Church. Bede set out to write the 'ecclesiastical' history of the English nation, and it is only indirectly the chief source for the politics of the period. William of Malmesbury's *Historia Regum* is balanced by his *Historia Pontificum*; and monastic historians in general tend to see the hand of God in trivial incidents, and are never far from hagiography and miracle stories, or on the other hand from those which give warning to the wicked. So the ghost story is at home here, with tales of witchcraft and devilry; and the historian is conscious of his double mission: to record, instruct, and entertain; and to point a moral. Yet, apart from the emphasis and colouring given by Christianity, with its rewards and punishments in another world, there is nothing specifically medieval here: Livy and Tacitus felt much the same. This moral purpose of history, with its Christian overtones, is perhaps englished best by Caxton in his Preface to Malory's *Morte Darthur* in 1485: 'Herein may be seen noble chivalry, courtesy, humanity, friendliness, hardiness, love, friendship, cowardice, murder, hate, virtue and sin. Do after the good and leave the evil, and it shall bring you to good fame and renown. And for to pass the time this book shall be pleasant to read in, but for to give faith and belief that all is true that is contained herein, ye be at your liberty: but all is written for our doctrine, and for to beware that we fall not to vice nor sin, but to exercise and follow virtue, by which we may come and attain to good fame and renown in this life, and after this short and transitory life to come into everlasting bliss in heaven.'

THE VENERABLE BEDE (*c.* 671–735)

Bede, 'the only teacher of the first rank between Gregory the Great and the eleventh century,'[1] is one of the glories of Anglo-Saxon, and indeed European, culture, and in his company the 'Dark Ages' seem much less dark—though the light of Northumbrian Christianity was within a century all but extinguished by Viking raids, followed by massive invasions. The cathedral-monastery of Durham, where his bones were finally buried, was later to dominate the north, but Lindisfarne and Jarrow were never rebuilt.

He was fortunate in the time both of his birth and of his death, escaping the destruction that was to come, but born late enough to reap the fruits of *Benedict Biscop*'s work. This Anglo-Saxon monk (*c.* 628–90),

[1] D. Knowles, op. cit., p. 24.

after a period in Gaul with Wilfrid of Ripon, and three journeys to Rome, returned to England with *Theodore of Tarsus*, archbishop of Canterbury (669–93), himself a turning-point in the history of the English Church. After a spell as abbot in Canterbury, Benedict founded the monasteries of Monkwearmouth and Jarrow in his native Northumbria (674, 681), bringing in stonemasons and glaziers from Gaul, and in three more journeys to Rome brought back the arch-chanter of St. Peter's, relics, paintings—above all, books. (We are swamped by them, and take them for granted, forgetting that one can almost plot the curve of a civilization by the books it produces or circulates. Boniface, another Benedictine, writing home from Germany, begs for two things: more missionaries, and more books— and his murderers, expecting rich plunder, found only a few books. From the library at Jarrow sprang that of York, the finest, it is said, north of the Alps, built up by Bede's pupil, Archbishop Egbert (734–66); from York came Alcuin, the chief executor of Charlemagne's educational reforms; and so it went on.)

In this setting then he lived out a life of prayer and scholarship, of learning and teaching from the age of seven to the day of his death. His *Ecclesiastical History of the English Nation* is only a part of his lifework, tracing the story of Christianity in Britain, with some background geography and history, down to his own day. The legendary and the miraculous may bulk too large for the modern mind, but the latter he has in common with all the Middle Ages, and for that matter with much of New Testament Christianity. His chronology is scrupulous (he wrote three books on the subject)—in fact it was he who established in history our modern system of dating *Anno Domini*. He consulted written sources whenever possible, and made special efforts to obtain them from the archives of Canterbury and Rome; e.g., he incorporates a series of letters from Gregory the Great to Augustine and others; he was close enough in time to have spoken with those who had seen Paulinus in his northern mission in 625, and with the latest events he was himself contemporary. His Latin is fluent and clear, where some of his contemporaries were tortuous, his spirit serene, gentle, and generous, except where at moments his anti-Celtic bias gets the better of him. He can be seen as a type of the scholar-monks who set their mark on the religion and culture of the 'Benedictine centuries', and wrote its history for the next five hundred years or so—Bede did much here to create a pattern and a precedent; but, more than that, one has only to read him to find him lovable and individual.

THE CONVERSION OF NORTHUMBRIA
625–64

The Roman Empire had left Christianity as one of its last legacies to Britain; but the British Church of the fifth and sixth centuries, scattered and weakened by the invaders, did not even attempt to convert them. Two more forces were needed: the Roman mission of Augustine and his companions to Kent in 597, and the Celtic mission radiating out from Iona, where Irish monks had settled under Columba in 563. Each had its unique contribution to make; and the two currents finally converged, and clashed, at the Synod of Whitby in 664. Here Roman unity was argued out, and imposed by King Oswy of Northumbria—and was ultimately accepted by the Welsh and Irish too.

27 *Edwin, 616–32*

When King Edwin of Northumbria married the daughter of King Ethelbert of Kent in 625, she was accompanied north by Paulinus, a Roman monk, as her bishop-chaplain; and Edwin, reminded by Paulinus of his deliverance from his enemies, and of an earlier promise to accept the faith, summons his Council to debate the matter.

Quibus auditis, rex suscipere quidem se fidem, quam docebat, et velle et debere respondebat. Verum adhuc cum amicis principibus et consiliariis suis sese de hoc conlaturum esse dicebat, ut, si et illi eadem cum illo
5 sentire vellent, omnes pariter in fonte vitae Christo consecrarentur. Et adnuente Paulino, fecit, ut dixerat. Habito enim cum sapientibus consilio, sciscitabatur singillatim ab omnibus, qualis sibi doctrina haec eatenus inaudita et novus divinitatis, qui praedicabatur, cultus
10 videretur.

Cui primus pontificum ipsius Coifi continuo respondit: 'Tu vide, rex, quale sit hoc, quod nobis modo praedicatur; ego autem tibi verissime, quod certum didici, profiteor, quia nihil omnino virtutis habet, nihil utilitatis religio illa, quam hucusque tenuimus. Nullus enim tuorum studiosius quam ego culturae deorum nostrorum se subdidit; et nihilominus multi sunt, qui ampliora a te beneficia quam ego et maiores accipiunt dignitates, magisque prosperantur in omnibus, quae agenda vel adquirenda disponunt. Si autem dii aliquid valerent, me potius iuvare vellent, qui illis inpensius servire curavi. Unde restat, ut si ea, quae nunc nobis nova praedicantur, meliora esse et fortiora, habita examinatione perspexeris, absque ullo cunctamine suscipere illa festinemus.'

Cuius suasioni verbisque prudentibus alius optimatum regis tribuens assensum, continuo subdidit, 'Talis', inquiens, 'mihi videtur, rex, vita hominum praesens in terris, ad conparationem eius, quod nobis incertum est, temporis, quale cum te residente ad caenam cum ducibus ac ministris tuis tempore brumali, accenso quidem foco in medio, et calido effecto caenaculo, furentibus autem foris per omnia turbinibus hiemalium pluviarum vel nivium, adveniens unus passerum domum citissime pervolaverit; qui cum per unum ostium ingrediens, mox per aliud exierit. Ipso quidem tempore, quo intus est, hiemis tempestate non tangitur, sed tamen parvissimo spatio serenitatis ad momentum excurso, mox de hieme in hiemem regrediens, tuis oculis elabitur. Ita haec vita hominum ad modicum apparet; quid autem sequatur, quidve praecesserit, prorsus ignoramus. Unde si haec nova doctrina certius aliquid attulit, merito esse sequenda videtur.' His similia et ceteri maiores natu ac regis consiliarii divinitus admoniti prosequebantur.

Adiecit autem Coifi quia vellet ipsum Paulinum diligentius audire de Deo, quem praedicabat, verbum facientem. Quod cum iubente rege faceret, exclamavit auditis eius sermonibus dicens: 'Iam olim intellexeram

nihil esse, quod colebamus; quia videlicet, quanto studiosius in eo cultu veritatem quaerebam tanto minus
50 inveniebam. Nunc autem aperte profiteor, quia in hac praedicatione veritas claret illa, quae nobis vitae, salutis, et beatitudinis aeternae dona valet tribuere. Unde suggero, rex, ut templa et altaria, quae sine fructu utilitatis sacravimus, ocius anathemati et igni contrada-
55 mus.' Quid plura? praebuit palam adsensum evangelizanti beato Paulino rex, et, abrenuntiata idolatria, fidem se Christi suscipere confessus est. Cumque a praefato pontifice sacrorum suorum quaereret, quis aras et fana idolorum cum septis, quibus erant circumdata, primus
60 profanare deberet; ille respondit: 'Ego. Quis enim ea, quae per stultitiam colui, nunc ad exemplum omnium aptius quam ipse per sapientiam mihi a Deo vero donatam destruam?' Statimque, abiecta superstitione vanitatis, rogavit sibi regem arma dare et equum emissarium, quem
65 ascendens ad idola destruenda veniret. Non enim licuerat pontificem sacrorum vel arma ferre, vel praeter in equa equitare. Accinctus ergo gladio accepit lanceam in manu, et ascendens emissarium regis, pergebat ad idola. Quod aspiciens vulgus, aestimabat eum insanire. Nec distulit
70 ille, mox ut adpropiabat ad fanum, profanare illud, iniecta in eo lancea, quam tenebat; multumque gavisus de agnitione veri Dei cultus, iussit sociis destruere ac succendere fanum cum omnibus septis suis. Ostenditur autem locus ille quondam idolorum non longe ab Eburaco ad
75 orientem, ultra amnem Doruventionem, et vocatur hodie Godmunddingaham, ubi pontifex ipse, inspirante Deo vero, polluit ac destruxit eas, quas ipse sacraverat, aras.

Historia Ecclesiastica Gentis Anglorum, II. 13

The king, his nobles, and commons were baptized in York on Easter Day 627, in the first York Minster, which the King built of timber. Before its successor in stone was completed, he was defeated and killed by a coalition of Welsh Christians and Mercian heathen in 632. Paulinus fled by sea to Kent, taking with him the queen and her children. One Roman priest remained at his post, and survived to take part in the Synod of Whitby (664); but the mass-conversion collapsed, till Oswald (633–41), prince of a rival line who had been converted in exile at Iona, defeated the British and summoned Irish monks from Iona to re-convert his kingdom—and Aidan was sent to him as bishop.

Each had an essential part to play; and Oswald was for Bede a model of the Christian king, as Aidan was of bishops: a king Dei gratia, *who fought for the faith and worked for it, co-operating humbly and generously with his bishop,*[1] *and finally died for it.*

After Oswald's death in battle at the hands of Penda, the heathen king of Mercia, the southern half of Northumbria fell to Oswin. Ten years later he was driven out and murdered by his northern rival, Oswy, but this was a dynastic quarrel, and the Christianization of Northumbria went steadily forward.

28 *Oswin and Aidan, 641–51*

Donaverat equum optimum antistiti Aidano, in quo ille, quamvis ambulare solitus, vel amnium fluenta transire, vel si alia quaelibet necessitas insisteret, viam peragere posset. Cui cum parvo interiecto tempore pauper quidam occurreret elimosynam petens, desiliens ille praecepit equum, ita ut erat stratus regaliter, pauperi dari; erat enim multum misericors, et cultor pauperum, ac velut pater miserorum. Hoc cum regi esset relatum, dicebat episcopo, cum forte ingressuri essent ad prandium:

---

[1] 'Kings are most kingly when helping bishops': so a seventh-century Visigoth king in Spain. Conversely, 'From Bede all English readers became familiar with the idea . . . that monks should co-operate most closely with bishops and temporal rulers for the good of the Church and the country' (D. Knowles, op. cit., p. 24).

'Quid voluisti, domine antistes, equum regium, quem te conveniebat proprium habere, pauperi dare? Numquid non habuimus equos viliores plurimos, vel alias species, quae ad pauperum dona sufficerent, quamvis illum eis equum non dares, quem tibi specialiter possidendum elegi?' Cui statim episcopus: 'Quid loqueris,' inquit, 'rex? Numquid tibi carior est ille filius equae, quam ille filius Dei?' Quibus dictis intrabant ad prandendum. Et episcopus quidem residebat in suo loco. Porro rex, venerat enim de venatu, coepit consistens ad focum calefieri cum ministris; et repente inter calefaciendum recordans verbum, quod dixerat illi antistes, discinxit se gladio suo, et dedit illum ministro, festinusque accedens ante pedes episcopi conruit, postulans, ut sibi placatus esset, 'quia numquam', inquit, 'deinceps aliquid loquar de hoc aut iudicabo, quid vel quantum de pecunia nostra filiis Dei tribuas.' Quod videns episcopus, multum pertimuit, ac statim exsurgens levavit eum, promittens se multum illi esse placatum, dum modo ille residens ad epulas tristitiam deponeret. Dumque rex, iubente ac postulante episcopo, laetitiam reciperet, coepit e contra episcopus tristis usque ad lacrimarum profusionem effici. Quem dum presbyter suus lingua patria, quam rex et domestici eius non noverant, quare lacrimaretur, interrogasset: 'Scio', inquit, 'quia non multo tempore victurus est rex; numquam enim ante haec vidi humilem regem. Unde animadverto illum citius ex hac vita rapiendum; non enim digna est haec gens talem habere rectorem.' Nec multo post dira antistitis praesagia tristi regis funere, de quo supra diximus, impleta sunt.

Sed et ipse antistes Aidan non plus quam XII° post occisionem regis, quem amabat, die, id est pridie Kalendas Septembres, de saeculo ablatus, perpetua laborum suorum a Domino praemia recepit.

Historia Ecclesiastica, III. 14

HISTORY AND BIOGRAPHY 63

29 *The Synod of Whitby, 664*

The synod of Whitby was precipitated by a clash between the Celtic and Roman methods of calculating the date of Easter. This led more than once to King Oswy of Northumbria's celebrating Easter while his Kentish-born queen was still fasting on Palm Sunday. About this time Agilbert, the bishop of Wessex, arrived at the Northumbrian court, representing the Gallic and Roman tradition, and bringing with him a young Northumbrian, Wilfrid (634–709), who had spent three years in Lyons and had visited Rome: a formidable character already, and with forty-five stormy years as bishop still to come. Accordingly the king summoned a synod to settle the matter. On the Celtic side were Colman, bishop of Lindisfarne, representing the tradition of Iona, and Hilda, abbess of Whitby; on the Roman were James the Deacon and Romanus, the queen's chaplain, besides Agilbert and Wilfrid.

Primusque rex Oswiu praemissa praefatione, quod oporteret eos, qui uni Deo servirent, unam vivendi regulam tenere, nec discrepare in celebratione sacramentorum caelestium, qui unum omnes in caelis regnum expectarent; inquirendum potius, quae esset verior traditio, et hanc ab omnibus 5 communiter esse sequendam; iussit primo dicere episcopum suum Colmanum, qui esset ritus et unde originem ducens ille, quem ipse sequeretur. Tum Colmanus: 'Pascha,' inquit, 'hoc, quod agere soleo, a maioribus meis accepi, qui me huc episcopum miserunt, quod omnes 10 patres nostri, viri Deo dilecti, eodem modo celebrasse noscuntur. Quod ne cui contemnendum et reprobandum esse videatur, ipsum est, quod beatus evangelista Iohannes, discipulus specialiter Domino dilectus, cum omnibus, quibus praeerat, ecclesiis celebrasse legitur.' Quo haec et 15 his similia dicente, iussit rex et Agilberctum proferre in medium morem suae observationis, unde initium haberet, vel qua hunc auctoritate sequeretur. Respondit Agilberctus: 'Loquatur, obsecro, vice mea discipulus meus

Wilfrid presbyter, quia unum ambo sapimus cum ceteris, qui hic adsident, ecclesiasticae traditionis cultoribus; et ille melius ac manifestius ipsa lingua Anglorum, quam ego per interpretem, potest explanare, quae sentimus.' Tum Wilfrid, iubente rege ut diceret, ita exorsus est: 'Pasca, quod facimus,' inquit, 'vidimus Romae, ubi beati apostoli Petrus et Paulus vixere, docuere, passi sunt, et sepulti, ab omnibus celebrari; hoc in Italia, hoc in Gallia, quas discendi vel orandi studio pertransivimus, ab omnibus agi conspeximus; hoc Africam, Asiam, Aegyptum, Greciam, et omnem orbem, quacumque Christi ecclesia diffusa est, per diversas nationes et linguas, uno ac non diverso temporis ordine geri conperimus; praeter hos tantum et obstinationis eorum conplices, Pictos dico et Brettones, cum quibus de duabus ultimis oceani insulis, et his non totis, contra totum orbem stulto labore pugnant.' Cui haec dicenti respondit Colmanus: 'Mirum quare stultum appellare velitis laborem nostrum, in quo tanti apostoli, qui super pectus Domini recumbere dignus fuit, exempla sectamur; cum ipsum sapientissime vixisse omnis mundus noverit.' At Wilfridus: . . .

There follow three pages of detailed argument, in which Wilfrid is given the lion's share. He ends with the assertion: 'I do not deny that your fathers were holy men who served God according to their lights. But had some expert (catholicus calculator) *reached them with more perfect knowledge of catholic observance, no doubt they would have obeyed him, since you yourself have shown their obedience to God's commands.'*

'Tu autem et socii tui, si audita decreta sedis apostolicae, immo universalis ecclesiae, et haec litteris sacris confirmata sequi contemnitis, absque ulla dubietate peccatis. Etsi enim patres tui sancti fuerunt, numquid universali, quae per orbem est, ecclesiae Christi eorum est paucitas uno de angulo extremae insulae praeferenda? Et si sanctus erat, ac potens virtutibus ille Columba vester, immo et noster, si Christi erat, num praeferri potuit beatissimo apostolorum principi, cui Dominus ait: *"Tu es Petrus, et super hanc petram aedificabo ecclesiam meam, et portae inferi non praevalebunt adversus eam, et tibi dabo claves regni caelorum"?'*

Haec perorante Wilfrido, dixit rex: 'Verene, Colmane, haec illi Petro dicta sunt a Domino?' Qui ait: 'Vere, rex.' At ille: 'Habetis', inquit, 'vos proferre aliquid tantae potestatis vestro Columbae datum?' At ille ait: 'Nihil.' Rursum rex: 'Si utrique vestrum', inquit, 'in hoc sine ulla controversia consentiunt, quod haec principaliter Petro dicta, et ei claves regni caelorum sint datae a Domino?' Responderunt: 'Etiam', utrique. At ille ita conclusit: 'Et ego vobis dico quia hic est ostiarius ille, cui ego contradicere nolo; sed, in quantum novi vel valeo, huius cupio in omnibus oboedire statutis; ne forte, me adveniente ad fores regni caelorum, non sit qui reseret, averso illo, qui claves tenere probatur.'

Haec dicente rege, faverunt adsidentes quique sive adstantes maiores una cum mediocribus, et abdicata minus perfecta institutione, ad ea, quae meliora cognoverant, sese transferre festinabant.

Historia Ecclesiastica, III. 25

WILLIAM RUFUS (1087–1100)

WILLIAM OF MALMESBURY (*c.* 1080–*c.* 1143)

30 *The Siege of Mont-Saint-Michel, 1091*

William the Conqueror had three surviving sons. To the eldest, Robert, he left Normandy, to William England, and to the youngest, Henry, no lands, but 5,000 lb. of silver. Henry bought the peninsula of Cotentin, including Mont-Saint-Michel, from Robert, while

William tried to wrest Normandy from him. The two elder brothers patched up their quarrel in 1091, Robert ceded to William lands he had already sold to Henry, and both turned on Henry and besieged him in the almost impregnable fortress of Mont-Saint-Michel.

In ea obsidione praeclarum specimen morum in rege et comite apparuit; in altero mansuetudinis, in altero magnanimitatis. Utriusque exempli notas pro legentium notitia affigam.

5 Egressus rex tabernaculo, vidensque eminus hostes superbum inequitantes, solus in multos irruit, alacritate virtutis impatiens, simulque confidens nullum sibi ausurum obsistere: moxque occiso sub feminibus deturbatus equo, quem eo die quindecim marcis argenti emerat, etiam per
10 pedem diu tractus est; sed fides loricae obstitit ne laederetur. Iamque miles qui deiecerat manum ad capulum aptabat ut feriret, cum ille, periculo extremo territus, exclamat, 'Tolle, nebulo! Rex Angliae sum!' Tremuit, nota voce iacentis, vulgus militum; statimque reverenter
15 de terra levato equum alterum adducunt. Ille, non expectato ascensorio, sonipedem insiliens, omnesque circumstantes vivido perstringens oculo, 'Quis', inquit, 'me deiecit?' Mussitantibus cunctis, miles audacis facti conscius non defuit patrocinio suo, dicens: 'Ego, qui te
20 non putarem esse regem, sed militem.' Tum vero rex placidus, vultuque serenus, 'Per vultum', ait, 'de Luca', sic enim iurabat, 'meus a modo eris, et meo albo insertus laudabilis militiae praemia reportabis.' Macte animi amplissime rex, quod tibi praeconium super hoc dicto
25 rependam? A magni quondam Alexandri non degener gloria, qui Persam militem se a tergo ferire conatum, sed pro perfidia ensis spe sua frustratum, incolumem pro admiratione fortitudinis conservavit.

Iam vero ut de mansuetudine comitis dicam. Cum
30 obsidio eo usque processisset ut aqua deesset obsessis,

misit Henricus nuntios comiti, qui eum de siti sua conveniant; impium esse ut eum aqua arceant, quae esset communis mortalibus: aliter, si velit, virtutem experiatur; nec pugnet violentia elementorum, sed virtute militum. Tum ille, genuina mentis mollitie flexus, suos qua praetendebant laxius habere se iussit, ne frater siticulosus potu careret: quod cum relatum regi esset, ut semper calori pronus erat, comiti dixit, 'Belle scis actitare guerram, qui hostibus praebes aquae copiam; et quomodo eos domabimus si eis in pastu et in potu indulserimus?' At ille renidens illud come et merito famosum verbum emisit: 'Papae, dimitterem fratrem nostrum mori siti? Et quem alium habebimus si eum amiserimus?' Ita rex, deridens mansueti hominis ingenium, resolvit praelium; infectaque re quam intenderat, quod eum Scottorum et Walensium tumultus vocabant, in regnum se cum ambobus fratribus recepit.

De Gestis Regum Anglorum, IV, §§ 309-10

31 *Back to Normandy, 1099*

William coveted not only Normandy, but Maine to the south of it. He seized its capital, Le Mans (*Cenomannis*), in 1097, and desultory fighting went on for two years. In June 1099 news reached him that Le Mans was being besieged by its feudal lord, Count Helias.

Veruntamen sunt quaedam de rege praeclarae magnanimitatis exempla, quae posteris non invidebo. Venationi in quadam silva intentum nuntius detinuit ex transmarinis partibus, obsessam esse civitatem Cenomannis, quam nuper fratre profecto suae potestati adiecerat. Statim ergo ut expeditus erat retorsit equum, iter ad mare convertens. Admonentibus ducibus exercitum advocandum, paratos componendos, 'Videbo', ait, 'quis me sequetur; putatis me non habiturum homines? si cognovi iuventutem meam, etiam naufragio ad me venisse volet.' Hoc igitur modo pene solus ad mare pervenit. Erat tunc nubilus aer et ventus contrarius; flatus violentia terga maris verrebat. Illum statim transfretare volentem nautae exorant ut pacem pelagi et ventorum clementiam operiatur. 'Atqui', inquit rex, 'nunquam audivi regem naufragio interiisse. Quin potius solvite retinacula navium, videbitis elementa iam conspirata in meum obsequium.' Ponto transito obsessores, eius audita fama, dissiliunt. Auctor turbarum, Helias quidam, capitur; cui ante se adducto rex ludibundus, 'Habeo te, magister!' dixit. At vero illius alta nobilitas, quae nesciret in tanto etiam periculo humilia sapere, humilia loqui: 'Fortuitu', inquit, 'me cepisti; sed si possem evadere, novi quid facerem.' Tum Willelmus, prae furore fere extra se positus, et obuncans Heliam, 'Tu,' inquit, 'nebulo! tu, quid faceres? Discede, abi, fuge! Concedo tibi ut facias quicquid poteris: et, per vultum de Luca! nihil, si me viceris, pro hac venia tecum paciscar.' Nec inferius factum verbo fuit, sed continuo dimisit evadere, miratus potius quam insectatus fugientem. Quis talia de illitterato homine crederet? Et fortassis erit aliquis qui, Lucanum legens, falso opinetur Willelmum haec exempla de Iulio Caesare mutuatum esse: sed non erat ei tantum studii vel otii ut litteras unquam audiret; immo calor mentis ingenitus, et conscia virtus, eum talia exprimere cogebant. Et profecto, si Christianitas nostra pateretur, sicut olim anima Euforbii transisse dicta est in Pythagoram Samium, ita possit dici quod anima Iulii Caesaris transierit in regem Willelmum.

IV, §§ 320-1

32   *His End, 1100*

Tertiodecimo anno, qui et extremus fuit vitae, multa adversa: hoc quoque maxime horrendum, quod visibiliter diabolus apparuit hominibus in saltibus et deviis, transeuntes allocutus. Praeterea in pago Berrucscire, in villa Hamstede, continuis quindecim diebus fons sanguinem tam ubertim manavit ut vicinum vadum inficeret. Audiebat ille haec, et ridebat; nec sua sompnia de se, nec aliorum visa, curans.

Multa de ipsius nece et praevisa et praedicta homines ferunt....

Pridie quam excederet vita, vidit per quietem se phlebotomi ictu sanguinem emittere: radium cruoris in caelum usque protentum lucem obnubilare, diem interpolare. Ita, inclamata sancta Maria, sompno excussus, lumen inferri praecepit, et cubicularios a se discedere vetuit. Tunc aliquot horis antelucanis nonnihil vigilatum. Paulo post, cum iam Aurora diem invehere meditaretur, monachus quidam transmarinus retulit Roberto filio Hamonis, viro magnatum principi, sompnium quod eadem nocte de rege viderat, mirum et horrendum: quod in quandam ecclesiam venerat, superbo gestu et insolenti, ut solebat, circumstantes despiciens; tunc, crucifixum mordicus apprehendens, brachia illi corroserit, crura pene truncaverit; crucifixum diu tolerasse, sed tandem pede ita regem depulisse ut supinus caderet: ex ore iacentis tam effusam flammam exisse, ut fumeorum voluminum orbes etiam sidera lamberent. Hoc sompnium Robertus non negligendum arbitratus, regi confestim, quod ei a secretis erat, intulit: at ille cachinnos ingeminans, 'Monachus', inquit, 'est, et causa nummorum monachiliter sompniat; date ei centum solidos.' Multum tamen motus, diu cunctatus est an in silvam sicut intenderat iret, suadentibus amicis ne suo dispendio veritatem sompniorum experiretur. Itaque ante cibum venatu abstinuit, seriis negotiis cruditatem indomitae mentis eructuans; ferunt, ea die largiter epulatum, crebrioribus quam consueverat poculis frontem serenasse. Mox igitur post cibum in saltum contendit, paucis comitatus; quorum familiarissimus erat Walterius cognomento Tirel, qui de Francia, liberalitate regis adductus, venerat. Is, ceteris per moram venationis, quo quemque casus tulerat, dispersis, solus cum eo remanserat. Iamque Phoebo in oceanum proclivi, rex cervo ante se transeunti, extento nervo et emissa sagitta, non adeo saevum vulnus inflixit; diutile adhuc fugitantem vivacitate oculorum prosecutus, opposita contra violentiam solarium radiorum manu. Tunc Walterius pulchrum facinus animo parturiens, ut, rege alias interim intento, ipse alterum cervum qui forte propter transibat prosterneret, inscius et impotens regium pectus, Deus bone! lethali arundine traiecit. Saucius ille nullum verbum emisit; sed ligno sagittae quantum extra corpus exstabat effracto, moxque supra vulnus cadens, mortem acceleravit. Accurrit Walterius: sed, quia nec sensum nec vocem hausit, perniciter cornipedem insiliens, beneficio calcarium probe evasit. Nec vero fuit qui persequeretur, illis coniventibus, istis miserantibus, omnibus postremo alia molientibus; pars receptacula sua munire, pars furtivas praedas agere, pars regem novum iamiamque circumspicere. Pauci rusticanorum cadaver, in rheda caballaria compositum, Wintoniam in episcopatum devexere, cruore undatim per totam viam stillante. Ibi infra ambitum turris, multorum procerum conventu, paucorum planctu, terrae traditum. Secuta est posteriori anno ruina turris: de qua re quae opiniones fuerint parco dicere, ne videar nugis credere; praesertim cum, pro instabilitate operis, machina ruinam fecisse potuisset etiamsi nunquam ipse ibi sepultus fuisset. Obiit anno Dominicae incarnationis millesimo centesimo, regni tertio decimo, nonas Augusti quarto, maior quadragenario, ingentia praesumens, et ingentia, si pensa Parcarum evolvere vel violentiam fortunae abrumpere et eluctari potuisset, facturus. Tanta vis erat animi, ut quodlibet sibi regnum promittere auderet. Denique ante proximam diem mortis interrogatus ubi festum suum in Natali teneret, respondit Pictavis, quod comes Pictavensis, Ierosolimam ire gestiens, ei terram suam pro pecunia invadaturus dicebatur. Ita paternis possessionibus non contentus, maiorisque gloriae spe raptatus, indebitis incubabat honoribus. Vir sacrati ordinis hominibus pro dampno animae, cuius salutem revocare laborent, maxime miserandus; stipendiariis militibus pro copia donativorum mirandus; provincialibus, quod eorum substantias abradi sinebat, non desiderandus.

IV, §§ 331-3

THE FIRST CRUSADE (1095-9)

The motives were complex and can only briefly be summarized. There was the fascination exercised by the Holy Places, which had drawn pilgrims from every nation in the Christian East and West from the fourth century onwards. The Moslem conquests of the seventh century had obliterated Christianity in most of north Africa, but tolerated it in Spain and Palestine, and complicated the traffic without stopping it; but in the 1050s Turkish hordes came flooding in from the East with their droves of horses and formidable bowmen, crushed a great Greek army in 1071, and began to overrun the whole of Asia Minor. By 1085 they had captured Antioch, and completely altered the situation.

The Greek emperor, Alexius, was now driven to rely on money and mercenaries. He already depended on a Scandinavian and English bodyguard; and in 1095 he appealed to the Pope, Urban II, for Latin help—not to recover the Holy Places, but his former possessions in Asia Minor. This misunderstanding, and mutual distrust, was to prejudice the Crusade from the start.

Urban II at the Council of Clermont in November 1095 made an impassioned appeal to the nobles and knights of the West, above all those of France—he too with mixed motives: the Turks could be a threat to Europe as well as to the East: and how good to get rid of some of the troublemakers of Christendom by means of a Holy War! The idea was spread through Europe by the bishops and by popular preachers, working on the feelings of an ignorant peasantry, to whom 'Jerusalem' was as familiar a name as that of their own villages, unqualified by the perspectives of time and distance, and the hazards of an unknown foe.

Beyond these religious motives, the feudal nobles and knights of the eleventh century were a fighting society, attracted by prospects of adventure and gain. Where Normans had already carved out fiefs in Italy by the mid century, at the expense of the Greeks, what might not be won further east? And behind the knights and soldiers, the peasants and women and camp-followers, there were possibilities of direct commercial advantage for sea-powers such as Genoa, or for freebooting vessels, who in fact helped the army more than once at critical moments, and could at the same time work for their own advantage.

The question of command presented acute problems. The Pope appointed his own Legate, Adhémar, bishop of Le Puy, who exercised some sort of general supervision, and was very capable of taking a hand in strategy. Beyond him the chief leaders were Raymond, count of Toulouse and Provence, an able man who hoped to run the whole expedition—neither he nor anyone succeeded in this aim—Robert, duke of Normandy, eldest son of William the Conqueror, and his brother-in-law Stephen of Blois, and three brothers—two of them outstanding: Godfrey of Bouillon, who brought Netherlanders and Lorrainers, and his youngest brother Baldwin. Both of these intended to carve out lordships for themselves, and both succeeded. Baldwin made sure of his before the Crusades ever reached the Holy Land, while Godfrey became king (in all but name) of Jerusalem in 1099.

Lastly there was a group of Norman knights from south Italy (one of them the writer of the *Gesta*) serving under Bohemond, prince of Taranto, perhaps the ablest soldier of them all. He was the eldest son of Robert Guiscard, recognized by the pope in 1059 as Duke of Apulia and Calabria; and the two had already tried their strength against Alexius in Macedonia. It is their fortunes that we shall chiefly follow, from Amalfi to Antioch.

HISTORY AND BIOGRAPHY

ROBERT THE MONK (*fl.* 1200)

33 *The Council of Clermont, November 1095*

There are four contemporary accounts, each with its different emphasis. Robert the Monk, of Rheims, who claims to have been present, stresses Urban's appeal to the pre-eminence and military glory of the Franks—and Urban himself was a northern Frenchman.

'Gens Francorum, gens transmontana, gens, sicuti in pluribus vestris elucet operibus, a Deo electa et dilecta, tam situ terrarum quam fide catholica, quam honore sanctae Ecclesiae, ab universis nationibus segregata, ad vos sermo noster dirigitur vobisque nostra exhortatio protenditur. Scire vos volumus quae lugubris causa ad vestros fines nos adduxerit; quae necessitas vestra cunctorumque fidelium attraxerit. Ab Iherosolimorum finibus et urbe Constantinopolitana relatio gravis emersit et saepissime iam ad aures nostras pervenit, quod videlicet gens regni Persarum, gens extranea, gens prorsus a Deo aliena, *generatio* scilicet *quae non direxit cor suum, et non est creditus cum Deo spiritus eius,* terras illorum Christianorum invaserit, ferro, rapinis, incendio depopulaverit, ipsosque captivos partim in terram suam abduxerit, partimque nece miserabili prostraverit, ecclesiasque Dei aut funditus everterit aut suorum ritui sacrorum mancipaverit. . . .

'Quibus igitur ad hoc ulciscendum, ad hoc eripiendum labor incumbit, nisi vobis, quibus prae ceteris gentibus contulit Deus insigne decus armorum, magnitudinem animorum, agilitatem corporum, virtutem humiliandi *verticem capilli* vobis resistentium?

'Moveant vos et incitent animos vestros ad virilitatem gesta praedecessorum vestrorum, probitas et magnitudo Karoli Magni regis, et Ludovici filii eius aliorumque regum vestrorum, qui regna paganorum destruxerunt et in eis fines sanctae Ecclesiae dilataverunt. Praesertim moveat vos sanctum Domini Salvatoris nostri Sepulcrum, quod ab immundis gentibus possidetur, et loca sancta, quae nunc inhoneste tractantur et irreverenter eorum immundiciis sordidantur. O fortissimi milites et invictorum propago parentum, nolite degenerari, sed virtutis priorum vestrorum reminiscimini. Quod si vos carus liberorum et parentum et coniugum detinet affectus, recolite quid in Evangelio dicat Dominus: *Qui amat patrem aut matrem super me, non est me dignus. Omnis qui reliquerit domum, aut patrem, aut matrem, aut uxorem, aut filios, aut agros, propter nomen meum, centuplum accipiet et vitam aeternam possidebit.* Non vos protrahat ulla possessio, nulla rei familiaris sollicitudo, quoniam terra haec quam inhabitatis, clausura maris undique et iugis montium circumdata, numerositate vestra coangustatur, nec copia divitiarum exuberat et vix sola alimenta suis cultoribus administrat. Inde est quod vos in invicem mordetis et contenditis, bella movetis et plerumque mutuis vulneribus occiditis. Cessent igitur inter vos odia, conticescant iurgia, bella quiescant et totius controversiae dissensiones sopiantur. Viam sancti Sepulcri incipite, terram illam nefariae genti auferte, eamque vobis subiicite, terra illa filiis Israel a Deo in possessionem data fuit, sicut Scriptura dicit, *quae lacte et melle fluit.*

'Iherusalem umbilicus est terrarum, terra prae ceteris fructifera, quasi alter Paradisus deliciarum. Hanc redemptor humani generis suo illustravit adventu, decoravit conversatione, sacravit passione, morte redemit, sepultura insignivit. Haec igitur civitas regalis, in orbis medio posita, nunc a suis hostibus captiva tenetur, et ab ignorantibus Deum ritui gentium ancillatur. Quaerit igitur et optat liberari, et ut ei subveniatis non cessat imprecari. A vobis quidem praecipue exigit subsidium,

quoniam a Deo vobis collatum est prae cunctis nationibus, ut iam diximus, insigne decus armorum. Arripite
igitur viam hanc in remissionem peccatorum vestrorum,
securi de immarcescibili gloria regni coelorum.'

Haec et id genus plurima ubi papa Urbanus urbano
sermone peroravit, ita omnium qui aderant affectus in
unum conciliavit ut adclamarent: 'Deus vult! Deus vult!'
Quod ut venerandus pontifex Romanus audivit, erectis
in coelum luminibus, Deo gratias egit et manu silentium
indicens, ait: 'Fratres carissimi, hodie est in nobis osten-
sum quod Dominus dicit per Evangelium: *Ubi duo vel tres
congregati* fuerint *in nomine meo, ibi sum in medio eorum.* . . .
Sit ergo vobis vox ista in rebus bellicis militare signum,
quia verbum hoc a Deo est prolatum. Quum in hostem
fiet bellicosi impetus congressio, erit universis haec ex
parte Dei una vociferatio: 'Deus vult! Deus vult!'

Historia Hierosolomitana, I. 1, 2

The following three passages (Nos. 34–36) are from the *Gesta Francorum*.

34 *Bohemond takes the Cross, Summer 1096*

At bellipotens Boamundus qui erat in obsidione Malfi,
Scafardi Pontis, audiens venisse innumerabilem gentem
Christianorum de Francis, ituram ad Domini Sepulchrum,
et paratam ad prelium contra gentem paganorum, coepit
diligenter inquirere quae arma pugnandi haec gens
deferat, et quam ostensionem Christi in via portet, vel
quod signum in certamine sonet. Cui per ordinem haec
dicta sunt: 'Deferunt arma ad bellum congrua, in dextra
vel inter utrasque scapulas crucem Christi baiulant;
sonum vero "Deus vult, Deus vult, Deus vult!" una voce
conclamant.' Mox Sancto commotus Spiritu, iussit

preciosissimum pallium quod apud se habebat incidi, totumque statim in cruces expendit. Coepit tunc ad eum vehementer concurrere maxima pars militum qui erant in obsidione illa, adeo ut Rogerius comes pene solus remanserit, reversusque Siciliam dolebat et merebat quandoque gentem amittere suam. Denique reversus iterum in terram suam dominus Boamundus diligenter honestavit sese ad incipiendum Sancti Sepulchri iter. Tandem transfretavit mare cum suo exercitu, et cum eo Tancredus Marchisi filius, et Richardus princeps, ac Rainulfus frater eius, et Rotbertus de Ansa, et Hermannus de Canni, et Rotbertus de Surda Valle, et Robertus filius Tostani, et Hunfredus filius Radulfi, et Ricardus filius comitis Rainulfi, et comes de Russignolo cum fratribus suis, et Boello Carnotensis, et Alberedus de Cagnano, et Hunfredus de Monte Scabioso. Hi omnes transfretaverunt ad Boamundi famulatum, et applicuerunt Bulgariae partibus; ubi invenerunt nimiam abundantiam frumenti et vini et alimentorum corporis. Deinde descendentes in vallem de Andronopoli, expectaverunt gentem suam, donec omnes pariter transfretassent. Tunc Boamundus ordinavit concilium cum gente sua, confortans et monens omnes ut boni et humiles essent; et ne depredarentur terram istam quia Christianorum erat, et nemo acciperet nisi quod ei sufficeret ad edendum.

Tunc exeuntes inde, venerunt per nimiam plenitudinem de villa in villam, de civitate in civitatem, de castello in castellum, quousque pervenimus Castoriam; ibique Nativitatem Domini solemniter celebravimus.

Gesta Francorum (*I. iv*)

The main contingents reached Constantinople between December 1096 and April 1097. They were rationed by a wary emperor, who at last extorted from most of them an unwilling oath of fealty, that in return for pay and aid they would restore to him the territories they recovered. So they crossed into Asia Minor.

For seven weeks during May and June they battered at the strong city-fortress of Nicaea, till it surrendered—not to the Crusaders, but to Alexius; then, cheated of plunder but paid with gold and fine words, they pushed southwards till they found the main Turkish army, under the sultan, waiting for them on the plains of Dorylaeum.

35   *The Battle of Dorylaeum, 1 July 1097*

... prima die qua recessimus a civitate, venimus ad quemdam pontem, ibique mansimus per duos dies. Tertia autem die, priusquam lux coepisset oriri, surrexerunt nostri; et quia nox erat non viderunt tenere unam viam, sed sunt divisi per duo agmina, et venerunt divisi per duos dies. In uno agmine fuit vir Boamundus, et Rotbertus Normannus, et prudens Tancredus, et alii plures. In alio fuit comes Sancti Egidii, et dux Godefridus, et Podiensis episcopus, et Hugo Magnus, comesque Flandrensis, et alii plures.

Tertia vero die irruerunt Turci vehementer super Boamundum, et eos qui cum ipso erant. Continuo Turci coeperunt stridere et garrire ac clamare, excelsa voce dicentes diabolicum sonum nescio quomodo in sua lingua. Sapiens vir Boamundus videns innumerabiles Turcos procul, stridentes et clamantes demoniaca voce, protinus iussit omnes milites descendere, et tentoria celeriter extendere. Priusquam tentoria fuissent extensa, rursus dixit omnibus militibus: 'Seniores et fortissimi milites Christi, ecce modo bellum angustum est undique circa nos. Igitur omnes milites eant viriliter obviam illis, et pedites prudenter et citius extendant tentoria.'

Postquam vero hoc totum factum est, Turci undique iam erant circumcingentes nos, dimicando et iaculando, ac spiculando, et mirabiliter longe lateque sagittando. Nos itaque quamquam nequivimus resistere illis, neque sufferre pondus tantorum hostium, tamen pertulimus illuc unanimiter gradum. Feminae quoque nostrae in illa die fuerunt nobis in maximo refugio, quae afferebant ad bibendum aquam nostris preliatoribus, et fortiter semper confortabant illos, pugnantes et defendentes. Vir itaque sapiens Boamundus protinus mandavit aliis, scilicet comiti de Sancto Egidio, et duci Godefrido, et Hugoni Magno, atque Podiensi episcopo, aliisque omnibus Christi militibus, quo festinent, et ad bellum citius approximent, dicens: 'Et si hodie luctari volunt, viriliter veniant.' Dux itaque Godefridus audax et fortis, ac Hugo Magnus simul venerunt prius cum suis exercitibus; episcopus quoque Podiensis prosequutus est illos, una cum suo exercitu, et comes de Sancto Egidio iuxta illos cum magna gente.

Mirabantur ergo nostri valde unde esset exorta tanta multitudo Turcorum et Arabum et Saracenorum, et aliorum quos enumerare ignoro; quia pene omnes montes et colles et valles et omnia plana loca intus et extra undique erant cooperta de illa excommunicata generatione. Factus est itaque sermo secretus inter nos laudantes et consulentes atque dicentes: 'Estote omnimodo unanimes in fide Christi et Sanctae Crucis victoria, quia hodie omnes divites si Deo placet effecti eritis.'

Continuo fuerunt ordinatae nostrorum acies. In sinistra parte fuit vir sapiens Boamundus, et Rotbertus Nortmannus, et prudens Tancredus, ac Robertus de Ansa et Richardus de Principatu. Episcopus vero Podiensis venit per alteram montanam, undique circumcingens incredulos Turcos. In sinistra quoque parte equitavit fortissimus miles Raimundus comes de Sancto Egidio. In dextera vero parte fuit dux Godefridus, et acerrimus miles Flandrensis comes, et Hugo Magnus, et alii plures, quorum nomina ignoro.

Statim autem venientibus militibus nostris, Turci et Arabes et Saraceni et Agulani omnesque barbarae nationes dederunt velociter fugam, per compendia montium et per plana loca. Erat autem numerus Turcorum, Persarum, Publicanorum, Saracenorum, Agulanorum, aliorumque paganorum trecenta sexaginta milia extra Arabes, quorum numerum nemo scit nisi solus Deus. Fugerunt vero nimis velociter ad sua tentoria, ibique eos diu morari non licuit. Iterum vero arripuerunt fugam, nosque illos persecuti sumus occidentes tota una die. Et accepimus spolia multa, aurum, argentum, equos et asinos, camelos, oves, et boves et plurima alia quae ignoramus. Et nisi Dominus fuisset nobiscum in bello, et aliam cito nobis misisset aciem, nullus nostrorum evasisset, quia ab hora tertia usque in horam nonam perduravit haec pugna. Sed omnipotens Deus pius et misericors qui non permisit suos milites perire, nec in manibus inimicorum incidere, festine nobis adiutorium misit. Sed fuerunt illic mortui duo ex nostris milites honorabiles, scilicet Gosfredus de Monte Scabioso, et Willelmus Marchisi filius frater Tancredi, aliique milites et pedites quorum nomina ignoro.

Gesta Francorum (III. ix)

The victory of Dorylaeum ensured their safe passage across Asia Minor; but to reach Syria they still had to cross the Anti-Taurus range: 'a damnable mountain which was so high and steep that none of our men dared to overtake another on the narrow path. Horses fell over the precipice, and one beast of burden dragged another down. As for the knights, they stood in a great state of gloom, wringing their hands because they were so frightened and miserable, not knowing what to do with themselves and their armour, and offering to sell their shields, valuable breastplates, and helmets for threepence or fivepence or any price they could get. Those who could not find a buyer threw their arms away and went on.'

They reached Antioch on 20 October 1097, and settled down to besiege it, harassed by sorties, hunger, and cold, and attacked in February 1098 by a formidable relief-force. They beat it off; and were heartened by the arrival of Genoese and English vessels with reinforcements, siege-engines from the emperor, and food from Cyprus. But by the summer a massive Turkish force was approaching, and the situation looked hopeless—when in the nick of time, on 3 June 1098, one of the city towers was betrayed to Bohemond, Antioch was overrun, and the Turkish garrison and population slaughtered. But the citadel still held out, the besieging army closed in, and the Christians found themselves shut up in Antioch, starving, and between two fires.

36 *Antioch, June 1098*

Pars vero quae erat in castello agebat bellum cum nostris die noctuque, sagittando, vulnerando, occidendo. Alia autem pars undique obsedit civitatem, ita ut nullus nostrorum civitatem auderet exire aut intrare, nisi nocte
5 et occulte. Ita vero eramus obsessi et oppressi ab illis, quorum numerus fuit innumerabilis. Isti autem prophani et inimici Dei ita tenebant nos inclusos in urbe Antiochiae, ut multi mortui fuerint fame, quoniam parvus panis vendebatur uno bisantio. De vino non loquar. Equinas
10 namque carnes aut asininas manducabant, et vendebant. Vendebant quoque gallinam quindecim solidis, ovum duobus solidis, unam nucem uno denario; omnia enim valde erant cara. Folia fici et vitis et cardui, omniumque

arborum coquebant et manducabant, tantam famem immensam habebant. Alii coria caballorum et camelorum et asinorum atque boum seu bufalorum sicca decoquebant, et manducabant. Istas et multas anxietates ac angustias quas nominare nequeo passi sumus pro Christi nomine et Sancti Sepulchri via deliberanda. Tales quoque tribulationes et fames ac timores passi sumus per viginti sex dies.

Stephen of Blois, who was in charge of the commissariat, had lost heart before the capture of Antioch and had withdrawn his troops to Alexandretta; and now, thinking it as good as lost, he retreated to the emperor with the news that it had fallen. The emperor, who was on his way across Asia Minor with reinforcements, summoned his senior officers (among them Guy, Bohemond's half-brother) and told them he proposed to retreat.

Cum Wido miles honestissimus talia audisset, cum omnibus statim coepit plorare, atque vehementissimo ululatu plangere; unaque voce omnes dicebant: 'O Deus verus, trinus et unus, quamobrem haec fieri permisisti? Cur populum sequentem te in manibus inimicorum incidere permisisti et viam tui itineris tuique Sepulchri liberare volentes tam cito dimisisti? Certe si verum est hoc verbum quod ab istis nequissimis audivimus, nos et alii Christiani derelinquemus te; nec te amplius rememorabimur, et unus ex nobis non audebit ulterius invocare nomen tuum.' Et fuit hic sermo valde mestissimus in tota militia, ita ut nullus illorum sive episcopus sive abbas, seu clericus seu laicus, auderet invocare Christi nomen per plures dies. Nemo namque poterat consolari Widonem plorantem et ferientem se manibus suosque frangentem digitos et dicentem: 'Heu mihi domine mi Boamunde honor et decus totius mundi, quem omnis mundus timebat et amabat! Heu mihi tristis! Non merui dolens tuam videre honestissimam speciem, qui nullam rem magis videre desiderabam. Quis mihi det ut ego moriar pro te, dulcissime amice et domine? Cur ego ex utero matris meae exiens, non statim mortuus fui? Cur ad hanc lugubrem diem perveni? Cur non demersus fui in mare? Cur non ex equo cecidi fracto collo, ut recepissem repentinum interitum? Utinam tecum recepissem felix martyrium, ut cernerem te gloriosissimum suscepisse finem!' Cumque omnes cucurrissent ad eum quatinus consolarentur eum, ut iam finem daret planctui, in se reversus ait: 'Forsitan creditis huic semicano imprudenti militi. Unquam vere non audivi loqui de militia aliqua, quam idem fecisset. Sed turpiter et inhoneste recedit, sicut nequissimus et infelix, et quicquid miser nuntiat, sciatis falsum esse.'

Interea iussit imperator suis hominibus dicens: 'Ite et conducite omnes homines istius terrae in Bulgariam, et explorate et devastate universa loca, ut cum venerint Turci, nichil possint hic reperire.' Voluissent noluissent nostri reversi sunt retrorsum, dolentes amarissime usque ad mortem; fueruntque mortui multi ex peregrinis languentes nec valentes fortiter militiam sequi; remanebantque morientes in via. Omnes vero alii reversi sunt Constantinopolim.

Gesta Francorum (IX. xxvi, xxvii)

POSTSCRIPT

On 28 June 1098, after more than three weeks of this double blockade of Antioch, Bohemond led a massive sortie and routed the besieging army; and the citadel surrendered—not to Raymond of Provence, who had been left behind in the city, but to the victorious Bohemond. 'And we rested in Antioch with joy and gladness, for five months and eight days.' There Adhémar of Le Puy died—'one of the greatest tragedies of the Crusade', for 'after his death no one possessed any overriding authority'.[1] The army finally moved southwards along the coast, capturing strongholds on the way, but the leaders were at loggerheads, and Bohemond turned back to make sure of his lordship of Antioch. The main body, greatly diminished by death, sickness, and desertion, reached Jerusalem and began the month-long siege on 7 June 1099. On 15 July the city fell, and the Crusaders, slaughtering and plundering, 'all came rejoicing and weeping from excess of gladness to worship at the Sepulchre of our Saviour Jesus'.

What happened to them all?

GODFREY OF BOUILLON, who refused the title of King of Jerusalem —there could only be one king there—but accepted that of Advocate of the Holy Sepulchre, died within a year, but passed into legend as one of the 'three noble Christian men, stalled and admitted through the universal world into the number of the nine best and worthy' (the other two, for Caxton, were King Arthur and Charlemagne).

BALDWIN, his more earthy brother, 'the ablest, the most patient, and the most far-sighted of them all',[1] had seized Edessa before ever they reached Antioch, and carved out for himself there a county, astride the Euphrates; but on Godfrey's death he was chosen to succeed him, and was crowned King of Jerusalem; and after upholding the Kingdom for eighteen years died there in 1118. 'Of all the great leaders it was Baldwin, the penniless younger son, that had triumphed.'[1]

RAYMOND OF PROVENCE had a strangely mixed career. His friendship with the emperor brought little good to either, and he never gained the place his rank and expectations claimed. Leading a fresh army across Asia Minor in 1101, he was one of the few to escape from a disastrous defeat. Arrested by Tancred as a traitor to the cause, and warned off North Syria, he spent the next three years in trying to carve out a principality further south, round Tripoli, and died in 1105 in the castle he had built there, aptly named Mount Pilgrim.

STEPHEN OF BLOIS was sent back to the East by his indignant wife in 1101, and survived (with Raymond) the first defeat he was involved in, but fell in 1102 in a battle with the Egyptians from which few escaped.

[1] S. Runciman: *History of the Crusades*, vol. i, Cambridge, 1951.

HUGH OF VERMANDOIS, who had also deserted before Antioch, returned in 1101, and died of wounds at Tarsus, never having reached Jerusalem.

ROBERT OF NORMANDY was outwitted and defeated in 1106 by his younger brother, Henry, determined to add Normandy to the crown of England, and spent the next twenty-eight years in captivity, dying in Cardiff Castle at the age of 80, and gaining a fine tomb in St. Peter's Abbey, Gloucester.

BOHEMOND, prince of Antioch, and the ablest soldier of them all, was captured in an ambush in 1100, and carried off in chains to a remote Turkish castle. He was ransomed three years later by his fellow Crusaders (his nephew, Tancred, installed in Antioch contributed nothing); then, realizing that the master-prize of the East was the Empire itself, he enlisted the support of the pope, and challenged Alexius on his western frontier of Dalmatia; was captured for a second time in 1107, acknowledged himself the emperor's vassal in Antioch—and retired to Apulia, where he lived with his French princess till his death in 1111.

TANCRED, after the fall of Jerusalem, established himself as prince of Galilee and, when Baldwin was promoted to Jerusalem in 1100, he succeeded him at Antioch as regent for his captured uncle, Bohemond; and died there in 1112, still only 36.

The writer of this chronicle simply disappears; but his 'little book' was taken to Italy by Bohemond, and was drawn on by writers of the next generation for their longer and more elaborate histories.

ABBOT SAMSON (1135–1211)

JOCELIN OF BRAKELOND (*fl.* 1200)

Abbot Samson of Bury was a striking figure in his own right, who was still more fortunate in his biographer. A Norfolk man, he began his education in the little market-town of Diss, and continued it in the schools of Paris: one of a steady stream of Englishmen who crossed the Channel, giving as well as receiving, till Henry II's edict in 1167 temporarily halted the traffic.

After a few years as a schoolmaster he entered the monastery at the age of 30, was elected abbot in 1182, and for thirty years ruled over one of the greater English houses, and played his part in the Church and in national affairs with shrewdness and vigour. But all this must be followed in the *Cronica de rebus gestis Samsonis Abbatis Monasterii Sancti Edmundi*, written shortly after 1200 by his chaplain, Jocelin.

Jocelin had an observant eye for detail, and for the foibles of his fellow monks, a ready pen, and a venturesome tongue, so that two portraits emerge from his Chronicle: Abbot Samson's and his biographer's. But beyond that is a picture in depth and breadth of an important Benedictine monastery at the end of the twelfth century, with its deep roots in tradition, in the soil and landed property, and in the feudal society of the time, where the abbot had the responsibility of a great noble in furnishing men and money for the wars, and the king was directly concerned both with the holder of the office and with the abbot's revenues. Further afield the abbey had direct relations with the papacy and, at home, with the town that had grown up outside its walls (and in fact belonged to them)—with its markets, the merchants and their dues, the pilgrims to the shrine and their offerings (King John offered nothing but a silken cloth which he borrowed from the Sacrist and never paid for), and with the poor at their gates. In fact the one thing we hear least about is the specifically religious life of the community—it is so basic and familiar that it is taken for granted—though there is plenty about monastic concerns proper: for example, the building and establishment of the church and shrine, and the problems of office and administration.

The whole account shows a community belonging to a robust tradition already 600 years old—a part of the landscape, untouched by the Cistercian Reform which was recalling men to the primitive Rule, and peopling the remote valleys of Europe with monks.

The writer outlived his abbot, after his six years' chaplaincy holding office as guestmaster and, later, almoner. His chronicle covers the years 1173–1202, sketching the disorderly state of the monastery during the last years of Abbot Hugh, before his vivid account of Samson's election and *res gestae*. It survives complete in a single manuscript (British Museum, Harley 1005), and was first printed in 1840. Carlyle was fascinated by it, and used it extensively in *Past and Present* (1843), the past being a stick with which to beat the present. To Carlyle's admirers the credit is all his: 'How vividly do the figures stand out on the faded tapestry of the monkish chronicler' (H. D. Traill). Faded tapestry? Or rather 'the most vivacious and spontaneous of all monastic writers of this, or indeed of any period of the Middle Ages' (D. Knowles, op. cit., pp. 507–8)?

37   *Who would be an Abbot!*

Alia tamen vice dixi: 'Domine, audivi te in hac nocte post matutinas vigilantem et valde suspirantem contra morem solitum.' Qui respondit: 'Non est mirum; particeps es bonorum meorum in cibo et potu, et equitaturis, et
5 similibus, set parum cogitas de procuracione domus et familie, de variis et arduis negociis cure pastoralis, que me sollicitant, que animum meum gementem et anxium faciunt.' Quibus respondi, elevatis manibus ad celum: 'Talem anxietatem mihi omnipotens et misericors Domi-
10 nus.' Audivi abbatem dicentem, quod si fuisset in eo statu quo fuit antequam monacharetur, et habuisset v. vel sex marcas redditus cum quibus sustentari possit in scolis, nunquam fieret monachus nec abbas. Alia vice dixit cum iuramento, quod, si prescivisset que et quanta esset
15 sollicitudo abbatie custodiende, libentius voluisset fieri magister almarii et custos librorum, quam abbas et dominus. Illam utique obedienciam dixit pre omnibus aliis se semper desiderasse. Et quis talia crederet? Vix ego; nec etiam ego, nisi quia, cum eo vi. annis existens die ac
20 nocte, vite scilicet meritum et sapientie doctrinam plenius agnoscerem.

    Cronica Jocelini de Brakelonda, ed. H. E. Butler, p. 36

38   *Portrait of Abbot Samson*

Abbas Samson mediocris erat stature, fere omnino calvus, vultum habens nec rotundum nec oblongum, naso eminente, labiis grossis, oculis cristallinis et penetrantis intuitus, auribus clarissimi auditus, superciliis in altum crescentibus
5 et sepe tonsis; ex parvo frigore cito raucus; die eleccionis

sue quadraginta et septem annos etatis habens, et in
monachatu decem et septem annos; paucos canos habens
in rufa barba, et paucissimos inter capillos nigros, et
aliquantulum crispos; set infra xiiii annos post eleccionem
suam totus albus efficitur sicut nix; homo supersobrius,
nunquam desidiosus, multum valens, et volens equitare
vel pedes ire, donec senectus prevaluit, que talem volun-
tatem temperavit; qui, audito rumore de capta cruce et
perdicione Jerusalem, femoralibus cilicinis cepit uti, et
cilicio loco staminis, et carnibus et carneis abstinere; carnes tamen voluit sibi anteferri sedens ad mensam, ad augmentum scilicet elemosine. Lac dulce et mel et consimilia
dulcia libencius quam ceteros cibos comedebat. Mendaces
et ebriosos et verbosos odio habuit; quia virtus sese diligit,
et aspernatur contrarium. Murmuratores cibi et potus, et
precipue monachos murmuratores condempnans, teno-
rem antiquum conservans quem olim habuit dum claustralis fuit: hoc autem virtutis in se habuit quod nunquam
ferculum coram eo positum voluit mutare. Quod cum
ego novicius vellem probare si hoc esset verum, forte
servivi in refectorio, et cogitavi penes me ut ponerem
coram eo ferculum quod omnibus aliis displiceret in
disco nigerimo et fracto. Quod cum ipse vidisset, tanquam
non videns erat; facta autem mora, penituit me hoc
fecisse, et statim, arepto disco, ferculum et discum
mutuavi in melius et asportavi: ille vero emendacionem
talem moleste tulit iratus et turbatus. Homo erat elo-
quens, Gallice et Latine, magis rationi dicendorum quam
ornatui verborum innitens. Scripturam Anglice scriptam
legere novit elegantissime, et Anglice sermocinare solebat
populo, set secundum linguam Norfolchie, ubi natus et
nutritus erat, unde et pulpitum iussit fieri in ecclesia et
ad utilitatem audiencium et ad decorem ecclesie. Videbatur quoque abbas activam vitam magis diligere quam

contemplativam, quia bonos obedienciales magis commendavit quam bonos claustrales; et raro aliquem propter solam scientiam literarum approbavit, nisi haberet scientiam rerum secularium; et cum audiret forte aliquem prelatum cedere oneri pastorali et fieri anachoritam, in hoc eum non laudavit. Homines nimis benignos laudare noluit, dicens: 'Qui omnibus placere nititur, nulli placere debet.'

Cronica, ed. H. E. Butler, pp. 39–40

PART FOUR

THE WORLD OF LEARNING

Nulla calamo agilior est sarcina, nulla iucundior. Voluptates alie fugiunt et mulcendo ledunt; calamus et in manus sumptus mulcet, et depositus delectat, et prodest non domino suo tantum sed aliis multis sepe etiam absentibus, nonnumquam et posteris post annorum milia.
Petrarch, aged 70, writing to Boccaccio, who had urged him to live less strenuously (*Senilium Rerum*, XVII. 2).

'WHERE shall wisdom be found?'[1] 'All men by nature desire to know.'[2] The search for knowledge and wisdom (the complexity of their meanings and their Christian and pagan overtones cannot be examined here) dominates the speculative thinking of Jews and Greeks, and, through the Greeks, the Romans; and all three traditions, Jewish, Christian, and Graeco-Roman, converge to challenge and enrich the Middle Ages. But 'traditions' is too impersonal a term for such vivid individuals as the unknown authors of the Wisdom books;[3] St. Paul, at once Jew and Christian, and Hellenist enough to quote their poets even if he turns his back on Greek 'wisdom';[4] Plato (even if known indirectly, through Cicero and Augustine) and, by the end of the twelfth century, Aristotle in full measure; Cicero, the high-minded eclectic, an invaluable link in the transmission, and Seneca, the near-Christian Stoic; and lastly the Fathers, who drew on pagan philosophy in order to articulate their Christian theology. These were masters to be venerated and friends to be enjoyed and lived with—and all were accessible (if one could but lay hands on them) in the world of books.

Books, then, and leisure; and the latter was mainly provided for a disordered medieval world for some five centuries (*c.* 600–1100) by the exacting yet semi-sheltered life of the cloister, with its corporate continuity, and meditation based on reading. So scholars found

[1] Job 28. 12.   [2] Aristotle, *Metaphysics*, I. 1.
[3] Job, Proverbs, Ecclesiastes, Ecclesiasticus, Wisdom.
[4] 'Videte ne quis vos decipiat per philosophiam . . . .' Col. 2. 8.

themselves committed to a triple task. The first was the study of available sources, and the building up of a growing body of commentary on them. The second task was the search for fresh material hidden away in other libraries—perhaps in other countries (for the bulk of Aristotle this meant going to Arab and Jewish scholars in Spain and Sicily, and recovering his works by means of Latin translations). Here the book-collector played a vital part. Benedict Biscop's six journeys to Rome in the seventh century and the books he brought back for his two monasteries in Northumbria were the foundation on which Bede built his scholarship, while for some of the superstructure he himself sent to Rome and Canterbury. This in its turn led to a two-way traffic, for manuscripts copied in England were to be prized on the Continent, and Bede's own works were soon to be found in every monastery in Europe. Lanfranc (1005–89) was to do the same for Bec and Canterbury, so providing a springboard for Anselm; and William of Malmesbury (*c.* 1080–1143) was librarian as well as historian, hoarding what had survived from the days of Aldhelm (d. 709), searching everywhere for more, and copying with his own hand or arranging to be copied.[1] This—the labour and delight of the copyist, sometimes an enthusiastic individual such as Petrarch, often highly organized in a monastic scriptorium, and still later on a commercial basis in the growing university cities—was the third task of scholars, ensuring the continuance of the tradition; but all three should be seen in a larger context where, in the monasteries at any rate down to the thirteenth century, scholarship was largely biblical and patristic, the by-product and background of a pattern of living to be assimilated into the blood-stream of a worshipping community.

But scholarship implied a mastery of the Latin language, both to unlock the past and to communicate with their fellow scholars. So schools were a necessity. From about the seventh to the eleventh century it fell to the monasteries and the cathedrals to supply them, each taking in a certain number of boys of good family who would return to the world of war and administration, as well as those needed to recruit their own numbers. The first great step forward was taken by Charlemagne (742–814), who was convinced of the immense importance of education, and not only recruited Alcuin (735–804) from the school of York, to supervise a palace school for bright young

---

[1] See M. R. James, *Two Ancient English Scholars*, 1931; and No. 42. (About twelve manuscripts have been identified in his hand.)

men, but by imperial rescript commanded that schools should be established throughout his empire. The text of the Vulgate was revised; manuscripts were copied and multiplied in fine minuscules which have never been bettered; and Alcuin and his pupils practised their skill in classical verse forms. It can be argued that they were too academic in their outlook, and too little creative; and when the unwieldy empire broke up, much of Charlemagne's grandiose schemes remained a pious dream. Northmen invaded France and Danes England, sacking monasteries and burning what they could not understand—among them, Bede's Jarrow never recovered. Yet Europe as a whole never completely looked back; and within a century King Alfred (849–901) was reviving education while still at war, and translating Boethius and Gregory the Great for those who could not read them in Latin. As some sort of order returned to society, schools—i.e. 'grammar' schools for the study of Latin language and literature—sprang up in towns or even villages in Europe, where a gifted priest or benefactor or a guild of craftsmen gave their support; and in the eleventh century more than one brilliant teacher emerged in French cathedral schools such as Chartres and Tours, attracting a widespread following for a generation or more, and pointing the way for the transformation that was to come.

For by the middle of the twelfth century the whole educational perspective was opening up, with the development of the universities—a kind of spontaneous combustion all over northern Europe. (The movement had begun rather earlier in Italy, where Greek and Arab influence were active in the medical school of Salerno, and the study of Roman law had never died out.) They emerged in some places, notably Paris, as an outgrowth of the cathedral schools (Oxford and Cambridge were exceptions here), and developed as a corporation or guild—*universitas*—of Masters, usually under the control of a Chancellor, who represented the bishop, though in Italy the corporation was one of students, who chose their own masters and called the tune. (A university in the modern sense of the term was known as a *studium generale*.) Their growth was phenomenal, helped by the rise of the two new Orders of Franciscans and Dominicans, each established early in the thirteenth century, and fighting each other as well as the secular clergy for the privilege of studying and teaching there. Even the old-established Benedictine houses, whose educational supremacy was by now passing away, began to set up hostels and send students there (Canterbury, Gloucester, Malmesbury, and Durham had a footing in Oxford). But apart from one or two scenes of student life, and student poems, this whole field will hardly be represented here; partly because it is too large, and still more because the universities of northern Europe were far more concerned with philosophy (its perspectives enlarged by the recovery of Aristotle), and with a highly technical theology, the *scientia scientiarum*. For these the arts were only a preliminary, and they neither concerned themselves much with literature nor produced it (outside their own technical fields), apart from the literature of revolt, concerned with the themes of satire, wine, woman, and song.

One important question remains. Behind the acquisition of a language, of books, and of education, lay the larger problem: what books? How far could the two traditions be reconciled—the Christian and the pagan? Every form of opposition or compromise can be found, depending partly on the times, and still more on temperament; for the clashes are as real as are the possibilities of reconciliation, commonly summed up in the term 'Christian humanism', but more vividly expressed in Jean Leclercq's phrase: 'l'amour des lettres et le désir de Dieu'. Petrarch, at the far end of this period, has the same problem, though not the same solution, as Jerome. The latter, fascinated by Plautus and Cicero, professed to reject them—but did he? His mastery of style shows no change. Augustine, as he looked back, was ashamed of so many tears shed for Dido, so few for his own soul; yet as he approached his conversion he was painfully conscious how rough-hewn were the Hebrew scriptures compared with the polished Latin classics. He never lost, in fact, the rhetorical skills he had practised, and it was his artistry as well as his intellect and psychological insight which fascinated succeeding generations, and set its mark on such different writers as Anselm, Bernard, and Petrarch. One whole field, too, of ancient thought—Platonic philosophy—he claimed for the Christian under the Hebrew metaphor of 'spoiling the Egyptians'.

Yet—one more of the paradoxes of Christianity—side by side with this there is a clear tradition stemming from the Wisdom books themselves, and equally visible in the New Testament. 'Knowledge breeds conceit', writes St. Paul to the Corinthians, and 'I determined not to know anything while I was among you but Jesus Christ...'. It recurs in St. Ambrose, with his 'Non in dialectica complacuit Deo salvari populum suum', and is repeated by St. Bernard the scholar, steeped in books, and with a mastery of the pen that could have come from no other source, when he maintains that only two kinds of knowledge really matter; self-knowledge, leading to humility, and knowledge of

God, leading to love of Him. After that he can add, 'Non tamen dico contemnendam scientiam litterarum, quae ornat animam et erudit eam, et facit ut possit alios erudire. Sed duo illa oportet et expedit ut praecedant.'[1]

For outside the 'life of the spirit' in the narrower sense of the term—the search of the soul for God and for union with him—lay a wide world of human endeavour, of speculative thought and creative imagination, as explored by historians, philosophers, and poets; a lesser world too of scientific observation, however inadequate, in such works as Pliny's *Natural History*.

If then one can summarize the case for the classics, it rested on the desire of all men by nature to know; and the usefulness in the broadest sense of a knowledge of the world and of human nature—and of the art of composition. It is this last point which William of Malmesbury stresses in the spirited defence which he inserts between two works of Cicero in a collection which he had been at pains to compile and copy. But in the last resort they were read as much for pleasure as for profit; and without this liberal spirit half the texts would have perished. If some of them were scandalous, well, to use St. Augustine's phrase, 'Two loves made two cities'; and the earthly city persisted alongside the heavenly inside the cloister as well as outside.

ST. AUGUSTINE (354–430)

39 *Spoiling the Egyptians*

St. Augustine's ultimate aim in his treatise on Christian education, the *De Doctrina Christiana*, is first, to interpret the Scriptures, and then to preach them. But in order to further this he is prepared to claim for his *studiosis et ingeniosis adulescentibus et timentibus deum beatamque vitam quaerentibus* whatever of value the pagan world can offer, in its knowledge of history and chronology (for God is the author of time), its arithmetic and natural sciences (within certain limits), its art of reasoning and rules of eloquence, its institutions and (within limits again) its philosophy. In short, a charter for medieval learning; though he quickly adds two cautions: the classical one of *Ne quid nimis* for all that is strictly bounded by time and space, and the Pauline *scientia inflat, caritas aedificat*. Without this, *doctus videri potest, esse autem sapiens nullo modo*.

[1] *On the Song of Songs*, Sermon 37.

Philosophi autem qui vocantur si qua forte vera et fidei nostrae accommodata dixerunt, maxime Platonici, non solum formidanda non sunt, sed ab eis etiam tamquam ab iniustis possessoribus in usum nostrum vindicanda. Sicut enim Aegyptii non tantum idola habebant et onera gravia, quae populus Israhel detestaretur et fugeret, sed etiam vasa atque ornamenta de auro et argento et vestem, quae ille populus exiens de Aegypto sibi potius tamquam ad usum meliorem clanculo vindicavit, non auctoritate propria, sed praecepto dei ipsis Aegyptiis nescienter commodantibus ea, quibus non bene utebantur, sic doctrinae omnes gentilium non solum simulata et superstitiosa figmenta gravesque sarcinas supervacanei laboris habent, quae unusquisque nostrum duce Christo de societate gentilium exiens debet abominari atque vitare, sed etiam liberales disciplinas usui veritatis aptiores et quaedam morum praecepta utilissima continent deque ipso uno deo colendo nonnulla vera inveniuntur apud eos, quod eorum tamquam aurum et argentum, quod non ipsi instituerunt, sed de quibusdam quasi metallis divinae providentiae, quae ubique infusa est, eruerunt et, quo perverse atque iniuriose ad obsequia daemonum abutuntur, cum ab eorum misera societate sese animo separat, debet ab eis auferre christianus ad usum iustum praedicandi evangelii. Vestem quoque illorum, id est, hominum quidem instituta, sed tamen accommodata humanae societati, qua in hac vita carere non possumus, accipere atque habere licuerit in usum convertenda christianum.

Nam quid aliud fecerunt multi boni fideles nostri? Nonne aspicimus quanto auro et argento et veste suffarcinatus exierit de Aegypto Cyprianus et doctor suavissimus et martyr beatissimus? quanto Lactantius? quanto Victorinus, Optatus, Hilarius, ut de vivis taceam? quanto innumerabiles Graeci? Quod prior ipse fidelissimus dei

famulus Moyses fecerat, de quo scriptum est, quod *erudi-* 35
tus fuerit *omni sapientia Aegyptiorum.*[1]
De Doctrina Christiana, II. 60–61

AELFRIC (*c.* 950–*c.* 1020)

40   *The Latin Lesson*

The *Colloquies* of Aelfric, abbot of Eynsham from 1005, represent only a small corner of the literary output of a great teacher—a leading figure in the tenth-century revival of Benedictine monasticism in Anglo-Saxon England. Brought up as a monk at Winchester, he wrote three series of sermons in the vernacular, intended for parish priests to read to their flocks, besides translating parts of the O.T. But he was at least equally concerned to raise the standard of Latin scholarship among the clergy—and the key bishops of his day were all of them monks. Hence his Latin Grammar, and Latin–English vocabularies, and these Colloquies intended to bring the language to life for the boys of the cloister. The speakers are all monks, but by a dramatic convention they assume many other roles, in order to enlarge their vocabulary and give liveliness to their lessons. Each describes his calling, then they vie with one another, till they are brought to order by the 'wise man'. He awards the primacy to the service of God and, reminding them all of their interdependence, bids each, 'sive sis sacerdos, sive monachus, seu laicus, seu miles, exerce temetipsum in hoc, et esto quod es.' The Colloquies end with a return to the schoolboys; and after a touch of light relief ('Were you beaten today?' 'No, because I behaved myself.' 'What about your companions?' 'Why do you ask me that? I daren't tell you our secrets') they too are bidden to go about the duties of their station.

PUER: Nos pueri rogamus te, magister, ut doceas nos loqui
   latialiter recte, quia idiote sumus et corrupte loquimur.
MAGISTER: Quid vultis loqui?
PUER: Quid curamus quid loquamur, nisi recta locutio sit
   et utilis, non anilis et turpis?   5

[1] Acts 7. 22.

Magister: Vultis flagellari in discendo?

Puer: Carius est nobis flagellari pro doctrina quam nescire. Sed scimus te mansuetum esse et nolle inferre plagas nobis nisi cogaris a nobis.

Magister: Interrogo te, quid mihi loqueris? Quid habes operis?

P. . . . Professus sum monachus, et psallam omni die septem synaxes cum fratribus, et occupatus sum nimis lectionibus et cantu, sed tamen, si tibi placuisset, vellem interim discere sermocinari Latina lingua.

M. Quid enim sciunt isti tui socii?

P. Alii, domine kare, sunt aratores, alii etenim opiliones, quidam quippe bubulci, quidam etiam venatores, alii autem piscatores, alii autem aucupes, quidam scilicet mercatores, quidam videlicet sutores, quidam salinatores, quidam porro pistores, quidam quoque coci.

M. Quid itaque dicis tu, arator? Quomodo exerces opus tuum?

P. O mi domine! nimium laboro. Exeo diluculo, minando boves ad campum, et iugo eos ad aratrum; non est namque tam aspera hiems, ut audeam latere domi pro timore domini mei, sed iunctis bobus et confirmato vomere et cultro aratro omni die debeo arare integrum agrum aut plus.

M. Habes aliquem socium?

P. Habeo saltem quendam puerum minantem boves cum stimulo suo, qui etiam modo raucus est pre frigore et clamatione.

M. Quid vero amplius facis in die?

P. Certe adhuc plus facio. Debeo igitur implere presepia boum foeno et adaquare eos ad laticem sive ad puteum, et fimum eorum portare foras.

M. O! O! magnus labor.

P. Etiam, magnus labor est, quia non sum liber.

THE WORLD OF LEARNING

§ 2

MAGISTER: Quid dicimus de coco, si indigemus in aliquo arte eius?

Dicit cocus: Si me expellitis a vestro collegio, manducabitis holera vestra viridia, et carnes vestras crudas, et nec saltem pingue ius potestis sine arte mea habere.

Non curamus de arte tua, nec nobis necessaria est, quia nos ipsi possumus coquere que coquenda sunt, et assare que assanda sunt.

Dicit cocus: Si ideo me expellitis, ut sic faciatis, tunc eritis omnes coci, et nullus vestrum erit dominus; et tamen sine arte mea non manducabitis.

O, monache, qui mihi locutus es, ecce, probavi te habere bonos socios et valde necessarios; qui sunt illi?

Habeo fabros, ferrarios, aurificem, argentarium, erarium, lignarium et multos alios variarum artium operatores.

. . . . .

Habes aliquem sapientem consiliarium?

Certe habeo. Quomodo potest nostra congregatio sine consiliario regi?

Quid dicis tu, sapiens? Que ars tibi videtur inter istas prior esse?

Dico tibi, mihi videtur servitium Dei inter istas artes primatum tenere, sicut legitur in evangelio: 'Primum querite regnum Dei et iustitiam eius, et hec omnia adicientur vobis.'

Et qualis tibi videtur inter artes seculares retinere primatum?

Agricultura, quia arator nos omnes pascit.

Conclusion

MAGISTER: O, probi pueri et venusti mathites, vos hortatur vester eruditor ut pareatis divinis disciplinis et observetis vosmet ubique locorum. Inceditis morigerate

cum auscultaveritis ecclesie campanas, et ingredimini in orationem, et inclinate suppliciter ad almas aras, et state disciplinabiliter, et concinite unanimiter, et intervenite pro vestris erratibus, et egredimini sine scurrilitate
35 in claustrum vel in gimnasium.

EADMER (c. 1055–c. 1124)

41   *St. Anselm: Thoughts on Education*

Quodam igitur tempore cum quidam abbas qui admodum religiosus habebatur secum de iis quae monasticae religionis erant loqueretur, ac inter alia de pueris in claustro nutritis verba consereret, adiecit, 'Quid, obsecro,
5 fiet de istis? Perversi sunt et incorrigibiles. Die et nocte non cessamus eos verberantes, et semper fiunt sibi ipsis deteriores.' Ad quae miratus Anselmus, 'Non cessatis', inquit, 'eos verberare? Et cum adulti sunt quales sunt?' 'Hebetes', inquit, 'et bestiales.' At ille, 'Quam bono omine
10 nutrimentum vestrum expendistis; de hominibus bestias nutrivistis.' 'Et nos,' ait, 'quid possumus inde? Modis omnibus constringimus eos ut proficiant, et nihil proficimus.' 'Constringitis? Dic, quaeso mihi, domine abba, si plantam arboris in horto tuo plantares, et mox illam omni
15 ex parte ita concluderes, ut ramos suos nullatenus extendere posset; cum eam post annos excluderes, qualis arbor inde prodiret?' 'Profecto inutilis, incurvis ramis et perplexis.' 'Et hoc ex cuius culpa procederet nisi tua, qui eam immoderate conclusisti? Certe hoc facitis de pueris
20 vestris. Plantati sunt per oblationem in horto ecclesiae, ut crescant et fructificent Deo. Vos autem in tantum terroribus, minis et verberibus undique illos coarctatis, ut nulla penitus sibi liceat libertate potiri. Itaque indiscrete oppressi

pravas et spinarum more perplexas infra se cogitationes
congerunt, fovent, nutriunt; tantaque eas vi nutriendo
suffulciunt, ut omnia quae illarum correctioni possent
adminiculari obstinata mente subterfugiant. Unde fit ut,
quia nihil amoris, nihil pietatis, nihil benevolentiae sive
dulcedinis circa se in vobis sentiunt, nec illi alicuius in
vobis boni postea fidem habeant, sed omnia vestra ex odio
et invidia contra se procedere credant. Contingitque modo
miserabili, ut, sicut deinceps corpore crescunt, sic in eis
odium, et suspicio omnis mali, crescat, semper proni et
incurvi ad vitia. Cumque ad nullum in vera fuerint
caritate nutriti, nullum nisi depressis superciliis oculove
obliquo valent intueri. Sed propter Deum vellem mihi
diceretis quid causae sit quod eis tantum infesti estis.
Nonne homines, nonne eiusdem sunt naturae cuius vos
estis? Velletisne vobis fieri quod illis facitis, siquidem quod
sunt vos essetis? Sed esto. Solis eos percussionibus et fla-
gellis ad bonos mores vultis informare. Vidistis unquam
aurificem ex lamina auri vel argenti solis percussionibus
imaginem speciosam formasse? Non puto. Quid tunc?
Quatinus aptam formam ex lamina formet, nunc eam suo
instrumento leniter premit et percutit, nunc discreto leva-
mine lenius levat et format. Sic et vos, si pueros vestros
cupitis ornatis moribus esse, necesse est ut cum depressioni-
bus verberum impendatis eis paternae pietatis et mansuetudinis levamen atque subsidium.' Ad haec abbas, 'Quod
levamen? quod subsidium? Ad graves et maturos mores
illos constringere laboramus.' Cui ille, 'Bene quidem. Et
panis et quisque solidus cibus utilis et bonus est eo uti
valenti. Verum, subtracto lacte, ciba inde lactantem
infantem, et videbis eum ex hoc magis strangulari quam
recreari. Cur hoc, dicere nolo, quoniam claret. Attamen
hoc tenete, quia sicut fragile et forte corpus pro sua
qualitate habet cibum suum, ita fragilis et fortis anima

habet pro sui mensura victum suum. Fortis anima delectatur et pascitur solido cibo, patientia scilicet in tribu-
60 lationibus, non concupiscere aliena, percutienti unam maxillam praebere alteram, orare pro inimicis, odientes diligere, et multa in hunc modum. Fragilis autem et adhuc in Dei servitio tenera lacte indiget, mansuetudine videlicet aliorum, benignitate, misericordia, hilari ad-
65 vocatione, caritativa supportatione, et pluribus huiusmodi. Si taliter vestris et fortibus et infirmis vos coaptatis, per Dei gratiam omnes, quantum vestra refert, Deo adquiretis.' His abbas auditis ingemuit, dicens, 'Vere erravimus a veritate, et lux discretionis non luxit nobis.' Et cadens in
70 terram ante pedes eius, se peccasse, se reum esse confessus est; veniamque de praeteritis petiit, et emendationem de futuris repromisit.

De Vita et Conversatione Anselmi, I. 22

42   *A Defence of the Classics*

The following paragraph is an aside by William of Malmesbury[1] (*c.* 1080–*c.* 1143)—a personal note inserted in a collection of Cicero's philosophical works and speeches which he had been at pains to compile and copy. It shows at a glance his labours and frustrations (it was only one of many collections he made for his monastery library and his own delight), and the rights he claimed as monk and scholar to the freedom of the pagan world.[2]

It is worth continuing his brief citation from the *Confessions*, to see how—each of them in search of 'wisdom'—Augustine was moving forward from the classical to the Christian world, while William is returning from the Christian to the classical, in the to-and-fro which makes up much of the texture of this book.

Dicit item Cicero in principio secundi libri de divinatione se composuisse librum in quo introduxit Hortensium

[1] See introduction to Part Three; and Nos. 30–32, 67–69.
[2] For a full discussion see M. R. James, *Two Ancient English Scholars*, Glasgow, 1931.

THE WORLD OF LEARNING 101

hortantem ad studium philosophie. Dicit eciam ibidem se
sex libros de republica composuisse. Qui libri quia in
Anglia non reperiuntur, ego Willelmus Malmesburgensis
more meo hic apposui quicquid de materia et intentione
eorum in beato Augustino invenire potui. Simul et hic
inventa occasione notandum puto, ne quis me repre-
hendat quot libros gentilium lego et scribo. Qui enim hac
intentione illos legit quia fastidit vel vilipendit divinas
scripturas graviter et penaliter peccat; unde et beatus
Hieronimus se castigatum et cesum profitetur in libro ad
Eustochium de virginitate servanda. Qui vero eos ideo
legit ut si quid ornate et eloquenter dicunt ipse in scriptis
suis ad Dei et sanctorum eius gloriam opportune trans-
ferat, tenens apostoli regulam ut omnia probet, quod
bonum est teneat, ab omni specie mala se abstineat,
nullo modo eum delectione gentilium librorum peccare
crediderim. . . .

Ex libro tertio Confessionum beati Augustini 'usitato
discendi ordine perveneram in librum cuiusdam Ciceronis,
cuius linguam fere omnes mirantur, pectus non ita. Sed
ille liber exhortationem ipsius continet ad philosophiam
et vocatur Hortensius. Ille vero liber mutavit affectum
meum et ad te ipsum, Domine, mutavit preces meas et
vota ac desideria fecit alia.'

Cambridge University Library, MS. Dd. 13. 2

Here—his point established—William breaks off. Augustine continues:

Viluit mihi repente omnis vana spes et immortalitatem
sapientiae concupiscebam aestu incredibili et surgere
coeperam ut ad te redirem. . . . Et ego illo tempore, scis
tu, lumen cordis mei, . . . non illam aut illam sectam,
sed ipsam quaecumque esset sapientiam ut diligerem et
quaererem et adsequerer et tenerem atque amplexarer

fortiter excitabar sermone illo et accendebar et ardebam.

Confessions, III. 4. 7

MATTHEW PARIS (*c.* 1200–59)

43   *Trouble at Oxford, 1238*

The setting of the following story is an Oxford already crowded with Masters and Scholars—all of them 'clerks' and most of them poor—living in halls or hostels centred round the 'Schools', twenty years or so before the first fully collegiate foundations of Balliol and Merton. In the foreground is the visit to England of the Papal Legate Otho (Otto), Cardinal Bishop of Palestrina, who spent nearly four years here (1237–41), investigating various grievances and abuses, and holding an important Council in London. In the background, in spite of Englishmen's recognition of the *plenitudo potestatis* of the Roman see, there is a growing resentment at its financial exactions, and at the intrusion of foreigners, especially *Italici homines*, into English benefices. Lastly there is Matthew Paris himself,[1] 'equipped at every point with healthy English prejudices; against the Welsh and Scots, against the French and foreigners in general, against Jacks-in-office, against innovators or reformers . . . a hard hitter and a good hater . . . full of life and its dramatic interests, its tragic and its comic elements, its crimes and its scandals.'[2]

Tunc vero temporis dominus legatus cum Oxoniam adventasset, et honore summo, prout decuit, reciperetur, hospitatus est in domo Canonicorum, scilicet abbatia de Oseneie. Clerici vero scholares eidem xenium honora-
5 bile in poculentis et esculentis transmiserunt ante prandii tempus. Et post prandium, ut eum salutarent et reverenter visitarent, ad hospitium suum venerunt. Quibus advenientibus, ianitor quidam transalpinus, minus quam deceret

[1] See introduction to Part Three.
[2] A. L. Smith, *Church and State in the Middle Ages*, 1913, pp. 167–71.

aut expediret facetus, et more Romanorum vocem exaltans, et ianuam aliquantulum patefactam tenens, ait, 'Quid quaeritis?' Quibus clerici, 'Dominum legatum, ut eum salutemus.' Credebant enim confidenter, ut essent honorem pro honore recepturi. Sed ianitor, convitiando loquens, in superbia et abusione introitum omnibus procaciter denegavit. Quod videntes clerici, impetuose irruentes intrarunt; quos volentes Romani reprimere, pugnis et virgis caedebant; et dum obiurgantes ictus et convitia geminarent, accidit quod quidam pauper capellanus Hyberniensis ad ostium coquinae staret, et ut quippiam boni pro Deo acciperet, instanter, more pauperis et famelici, postulaverat. Quem cum magister coquorum legati (frater legati erat ille, et ne procuraretur aliquid venenosum, quod nimis timebat legatus, ipsum ipsi officio praefecerat, quasi hominum specialissimo) audivit, nec exaudivit, iratus in pauperem, proiecit ei scilicet in faciem aquam ferventem, haustam de lebete ubi carnes pingues coquebantur. Ad hanc iniuriam exclamavit quidam clericus de confinio Walliae oriundus, 'Proh pudor! ut quid haec sustinemus?' Et arcum, quem portavit, tetendit (dum enim tumultus accreverat excitatus, clericorum aliqui arma, quae ad manus venerunt, arripuerant), et ipse missa sagitta corpus coci, quem clerici satirice Nabuzardan, id est, principem coquorum, vocabant, transverberavit. Corruente igitur mortuo, clamor excitatur. Ad quem stupefactus legatus, et nimis perterritus timore qui posset in constantissimum virum cadere, in turrim ecclesiae indutus capa canonicali se recepit, seratis post terga ostiis. Ubi cum noctis opacae conticinium tumultum pugnae diremisset, legatus, vestimentis canonicalibus exutis, equum suum optimum ascendit expeditus, et ducatu eorum qui vada secretiora noverunt, amnem, qui proximus erat, licet cum periculo, transivit, ut ad protectionem alarum regis ocius avolaret. Clerici enim furia invecti legatum etiam in abditis secretorum latebris quaerere non cessabant, clamantes et dicentes: 'Ubi est ille usurarius, simonialis, raptor reddituum, et sititor pecuniae, qui, regem pervertens et regnum subvertens, de spoliis nostris ditat alienos?' Insequentium autem adhuc clamores cum fugiens legatus audiret, dixit intra se,

'Cum furor in cursu est, currenti cede furori.'

Et patienter omnia tolerans, *factus* est *sicut homo non audiens, et non habens in ore suo redargutiones*. Cum autem, ut praedictum est, amnem vix pertransisset, paucis, pro difficultate transitus, comitantibus, caeteris in abbatia latitantibus, ad regem [apud Abendone commorantem] anhelus et turbidus usque pervenit; et lacrimabiliter, singultibus sermones suos interrumpentibus, rei gestae ordinem, gravem super hoc reponens querimoniam, tam regi quam suis collateralibus explicavit. Cuius querulis sermonibus cum rex attonitus nimis compateretur, misit properanter comitem Waranniae cum armata manu Oxoniam, eos qui latuerant Romanos eripere et scholares arripere. Inter quos captus est truculenter magister Odo legista, et ipse cum aliis triginta vinculis et carceri in castro de Waligeford, quod non multum distat ab Oxonia, ignominiose mancipatus. Legatus vero contrito laqueo liberatus, episcopis convocatis nonnullis, Oxoniam supposuit interdicto, et omnes illi enormi facto consentaneos excommunicavit. Postea in bigis, more latronum, ad arbitrium legati Londonias sunt transvecti, et ibidem carceri et vinculis arctaeque custodiae, redditibus spoliati et anathemate innodati, mancipantur.

The Legate, who had been on his way north, returned to London and summoned all the bishops to him to discuss the affair.

Finally at their intercession he consented to lift the ban on Oxford and on the guilty clerks. They were to walk on foot from St. Paul's to the Legate's lodging at Charing Cross—the last stage barefoot, and stripped of their academic dress—and there humbly beg his pardon. Quod et factum est.

Chronica Majora (R.S., vol. 3, pp. 481–4)

44 *In Praise of Books*

Richard de Bury (1287–1345), the author of *Philobiblon* (the Love of Books), was a scholar whose ruling passion fought a losing battle against the cares of state and high office. After studying at Oxford he became tutor to Prince Edward, afterwards Edward III (1327–77), and from then on was never free from responsibilities, whether in the court at home or as ambassador abroad. He visited Paris, Flanders, Germany, and the Papal Court at Avignon, where he met Petrarch, and finally became bishop of Durham from 1333 to his death: a stormy spot where Scottish invasions were at least as important as the cares of a diocese.

His passion for books inevitably suggests a comparison with Petrarch, but Richard's range of reading and style are very different: the latter highly elaborate, rhythmical, loaded with scriptural quotations and allusions—in short, though less than twenty years Petrarch's senior, he belongs far more in outlook to the Middle Ages. He planned to bequeath his library to a college in Oxford, but died in debt, and it seems certain that his books (like Petrarch's) were dispersed, and never reached their destination.

Thesaurus desiderabilis sapientie et scientie, quem omnes homines per instinctum nature desiderant, cunctas mundi transcendit divitias infinite, cuius respectu lapides pretiosi vilescunt, cuius comparatione argentum lutescit et aurum obryzum exigua fit arena, cuius splendore tenebrescunt 5
visui sol et luna, cuius dulcore mirabili amarescunt gustui mel et manna. O valor sapientie non marcescens ex tempore, virtus virens assidue, omne virus evacuans

ab habente! O munus celeste liberalitatis divine, descendens a Patre luminum, ut mentem rationalem provehas usque celum! Tu es intellectus celestis alimonia, quam qui edunt adhuc esurient, quam qui bibunt adhuc sitient, et languentis anime harmonia letificans, quam qui audit nullatenus confundetur. Tu es morum moderatrix et regula: secundum quam operans non peccabit. 'Per te reges regnant et legum conditores iusta decernunt.' Per te, deposita ruditate nativa, elimatis ingeniis atque linguis, vitiorum sentibus coëffossis radicitus, apices consequuntur honoris, fiuntque patres patrie et comites principum qui, sine te, conflassent lanceas in ligones et vomeres vel cum filio prodigo pascerent forte sues.

Quo lates potissime, preelecte thesaure, et ubi te reperient anime sitibunde?

In libris proculdubio posuisti tabernaculum tuum, ubi te fundavit Altissimus, lumen luminum, liber vite. Ibi te omnis qui petit accipit et qui querit invenit, et pulsantibus improbe citius aperitur. In his cherubim alas suas extendunt, ut intellectus studentis ascendat et a polo ad polum prospiciat, a solis ortu et occasu, ab aquilone et mari. In his incomprehensibilis ipse Deus altissimus apprehensibiliter continetur et colitur; in his patet natura celestium, terrestrium et infernorum; in his cernuntur iura, quibus omnis regitur politia, hierarchie celestis distinguuntur officia et demonum tyrannides describuntur . . . . In libris mortuos quasi vivos invenio, in libris futura prevideo, in libris res bellice disponuntur, de libris prodeunt iura pacis. Omnia corrumpuntur et tabescunt in tempore, et Saturnus quos generat devorare non cessat: omnem mundi gloriam operiret oblivio, nisi Deus mortalibus librorum remedia providisset.

Alexander, orbis domitor, Iulius et Urbis et orbis invasor, qui, et marte et arte primus, in unitate persone

assumpsit imperium, fidelis Fabricius et Cato rigidus
hodie caruissent memoria, si librorum suffragia defuissent.
Turres ad terram sunt dirute, civitates everse, putredine
perierunt fornices triumphales, nec quicquam reperiet
rex vel papa, quo perennitatis privilegium conferatur
commodius quam per libros. . . .
Postremo pensandum quanta doctrine commoditas sit
in libris, quam facilis, quam arcana, quam tuto libris
humane ignorantie paupertatem sine verecundia denudamus. Hi sunt magistri qui nos instruunt sine virgis et
ferula, sine verbis et cholera, sine pannis et pecunia. Si
accedis, non dormiunt; si inquirens interrogas, non
abscondunt; non remurmurant, si oberres; cachinnos
nesciunt, si ignores. O libri soli liberales et liberi, qui omni
petenti tribuitis et omnes manumittitis vobis sedulo servientes! Quot rerum millibus typice viris doctis recommendamini in scriptura nobis divinitus inspirata! Vos enim
estis profundissime sophie fodine, ad quas sapiens filium
suum mittit, ut inde thesauros effodiat; vos putei aquarum
viventium, quos pater Abraham primo fodit, Isaac
eruderavit quosque nituntur obstruere Palestini. Vos estis
revera spice gratissime, plene granis, solis apostolicis
manibus confricande, ut egrediatur cibus sanissimus
famelicis animabus. Vos estis urne auree, in quibus manna
reconditur, atque petre melliflue, immo potius favi mellis,
ubera uberrima lactis vite, promptuaria semper plena,
vos lignum vite et quadripartitus fluvius paradisi, quo
mens humana pascitur et aridus intellectus imbuitur et
rigatur; vos arca Noe et scala Jacob . . . pera David,
de qua limpidissimi lapides extrahuntur ut Goliath prosternatur. Vos estis aurea vasa templi, arma militie
clericorum, quibus tela nequissimi destruuntur, olive fecunde, vinee Engadi, ficus sterilescere nescientes, lucerne
ardentes, semper in manibus pretendende; et optima

queque scripture libris adaptare poterimus, si loqui libeat figurate.

Philobiblon, ch. 1, with ommissions

PETRARCH (1304–74)

(Francesco Petrarca)

Petrarch is a major figure in many ways. A Christian through and through—uncomfortably so, as we see in his *Secretum*—he was neither monk nor theologian nor scholastic philosopher, and had little use for the universities of his day. He was a cleric only in a nominal sense, but a classical scholar to his finger-tips, with the additional sympathy and imagination of a poet. A man who could say of Cicero 'Interdum non paganum philosophum sed apostolum loqui putes', and could use the fly-leaf of his Virgil as a family Bible to record the deaths of his family and friends, was seeing classical literature in a new dimension, and in the round, instead of as a comparatively flat and secondary background; and he proved to be opening a new chapter in the long story of Humanism.

He was born at Arezzo, where his father, a lawyer, was a political exile from Florence, but the family moved when he was nine to Provence, where the newly established papal court at Avignon offered good prospects to a whole host of people on the make. After studying the classics as a boy, he devoted five years to law at Bologna, the chief centre of legal studies for Europe as a whole; but his heart was already given to literature, and rejecting law and medicine, he turned to the only other major profession, the Church. He took the tonsure, and perhaps minor orders, in 1330, and from now on was assured of a living, indeed, of several livings, for as he became more widely known, one canonry after another was added (at one time he held five in Italy and France); but of corresponding duties he did virtually none. There is a touch of conscience about this in his will, where he asks that if he should die in Parma, he may be buried in the cathedral, 'ubi per multos annos archidiaconus fui inutilis et semper fere absens'. More than once he was offered a bishopric and a papal secretaryship, but these he refused, preferring the freedom of a scholar's life. For this neglect was no pretext for idleness; few men can have packed more into their lives of study, travel, and, above all, writing.

The first half of his life centred upon Avignon, where he held a minor post in Cardinal Giovanni Colonna's household, one which permitted him to travel north to Paris and Cologne, and south to Rome, sometimes on missions, sometimes simply to visit friends. But when he was 33 he acquired a small property in Vaucluse (*Vallis Clausa*), a retired valley some fifteen miles from Avignon, which more than anywhere else in his wandering life meant home. Here, with a bailiff and a servant or two, a couple of horses, and a dog, he worked at making a garden, fished in the river, or wandered through the woods alone, nursing an unrequited passion for Laura, a married woman whom he had merely glimpsed in a church in Avignon on Good Friday 1327—a distant worship in the Provençal tradition which fed his melancholy and flowered richly in his Italian verse. He worked on classical texts, collecting and comparing manuscripts, copying, and employing copyists, pondering the problems they raised and living with their characters, writing his own works, at once derivative and personal, and always letters to his friends.

Books and friends—these are the two main ingredients of his life: perhaps in that order, but both are indispensable. Besides Cicero (the philosopher, rather than the orator or statesman), Virgil, Livy, and Seneca, one calls for special mention—St. Augustine—whom he refers to some 600 times in his letters, and as often again in his other works. He steeped himself in the *Confessions*, and Augustine came to represent for him his better, or at any rate his Christian, self. There was much in common between the two. Each was a man of acute sensibilities, who laid bare his innermost feelings for posterity, though Augustine was ultimately unyielding, while Petrarch remained hesitant and divided—a 'modern man' in this as in other ways. So when he came in mid life to analyse for himself the tug of war in him between the Church and the 'world'—the fame he thirsted for, and the yoke of love he could not or would not shake off (his 'two golden chains', as he calls them), set against the renunciations of Christianity in its medieval setting, he dramatized it in his *Secretum*, or *Dialogus de contemptu mundi*. Here Franciscus stands up to Augustinus for three long rounds, and neither wins—and each is Petrarch.

What then were the master-ideas he looked for and found in his reading? They can be marshalled roughly under three heads. First he looked for guidance on how to live; and this he found almost equally in the pagan philosophers and the Christian saint. But the last word remains with Christianity: 'Non Ciceronianus certe nec Platonicus, sed Christianus sum.'

Secondly, he looked for knowledge, *scientia*: not the 'natural science' to which we tend to confine the term, but knowledge of the world of men, as recorded in history, and knowledge of himself.

Lastly, he looked for mastery of language, whether in prose or verse: *eloquentia*; both to enjoy it in the classical authors and to practise it himself.

His Latin prose works are massive, and it was to these, not to his vernacular 'trifles', that he looked for lasting fame. (History has reversed his verdict.) Only one section here calls for comment: his *Letters*. It was in 1349 that he conceived the idea of forming a collection of them for the benefit of his friends and himself; the whole to form something of a self-portrait, and a picture of his life. The collection grew till it ultimately reached a total of some 600 letters and became a full-scale literary enterprise. Some were expanded to essay length, and some, such as the letters to dead authors, were written for the purpose of the collection. But the overriding intention holds good, and most of them are genuine in every sense, reflecting his ideas and experiences over some forty years.

Books and friends, society and solitude, philosophy and religion, the troubles of his century, and his own unresting pen: these in constantly shifting order harassed or soothed his spirit and bound together his restless life in a real unity. His enthusiasms were caught by his friends and passed on to the growing number of his successors. His achievements were enlarged and more than doubled by the recovery of Greek literature, which he looked for but did not live to see. The discovery of new manuscripts and fresh authors, and finally the invention of printing, transformed the scholar's world, and put a library within the reach of almost everyone. In short his scholarship was caught up and absorbed in the rising tide of Humanism. But as a poet he remains unique; unique too in his combination of poetry and scholarship, each fertilizing the other. And as an individual, with his affections, his foibles and vanities, his anxieties and convictions, he remains a many-sided and lovable figure, mirrored, as he wished to be, in his correspondence, *Posteritati*.

Note. The range and variety of his interests are inadequately represented in this short selection from his Letters, chosen to illustrate his share in the 'World of Learning'.

45 *Student Days at Bologna, c. 1320*

To Guido Sette, archbishop of Genoa, a fellow Italian, and one of Petrarch's earliest school-friends in Provence
1367

... Inde Bononiam perreximus, qua nil puto iucundius nilque liberius toto esset orbe terrarum. Meministi plane qui studiosorum conventus, quis ordo, que vigilantia, que maiestas preceptorum: iurisconsultos veteres redivivos crederes! Quorum hodie prope nullus est ibi, sed pro tam multis et tam magnis ingeniis una urbem illam invasit ignorantia; hostis utinam et non hospes, vel si hospes at non civis seu, quod multum vereor, regina: sic michi omnes videntur abiectis armis manum tollere. Quenam ibi preterea tunc ubertas rerum omnium, queve fertilitas, ut iam prescripto cognomine per omnes terras 'pinguis Bononia' diceretur. ...

Sentis, puto, ut dulci quadam cum amaritudine inter hec mala et bonarum memoriam rerum versor; heret memorie mee, credo et tue, indelebile fixumque vestigium illius temporis, quo studiosorum unus ibi agebam. Venerat iam etas ardentior, iam adolescentiam ingressus et debito et solito plus audebam. Ibam cum equevis meis; dies festos vagabamur longius, sic ut sepe nos in campis lux desereret, et profunda nocte revertebamur, et patentes erant porte; siquo casu clause essent nullus erat urbi murus; vallum fragile iam disiectum senio urbem cingebat intrepidam. Nam quid muro seu quid vallo tanta opus erat in pace? Sic pro uno multi erant aditus, quisque commodiorem sibi carpebat ingressum: nil difficile, nil suspectum erat. Ut muro, ut turribus, ut propugnaculis, ut armatis custodibus, ut nocturnis

excubiis opus esset, interne primum venena tyrannidis, post externorum fecere hostium insidie atque insultus.
Senilium Rerum, X. 2

46 *The Ascent of Mont Ventoux*

To Dionigi da Borgo San Sepolcro   26 April 1336

Dionigi was an Augustinian canon who was lecturing on divinity and philosophy at the university of Paris from 1317. Petrarch seems to have met him there in 1333, when Dionigi gave him a copy of the *Confessions*. The book went with him everywhere for forty years, until he gave it away to a young Augustinian, as the script was now too small for him to read. (The forty years' companionship are described in a letter accompanying the gift, written in 1374, six months before Petrarch's death.)

Altissimum regionis huius montem, quem non immerito Ventosum vocant, hodierno die, sola videndi insignem loci altitudinem cupiditate ductus, ascendi. Multis iter hoc annis in animo fuerat; ab infantia enim his in locis,
5 ut nosti, fato res hominum versante, versatus sum. Mons autem hic late undique conspectus fere semper in oculis est. . . .

Dies longa, blandus aer, animorum vigor, corporum robur ac dexteritas et siqua sunt eiusmodi, euntibus
10 aderant; sola nobis obstabat natura loci. Pastorem exacte etatis inter convexa montis invenimus, qui nos ab ascensu retrahere multis verbis enisus est, dicens se ante annos quinquaginta eodem iuvenilis ardoris impetu supremum in verticem ascendisse, nichilque inde retulisse
15 preter penitentiam et laborem, corpusque et amictum lacerum saxis ac vepribus, nec unquam aut ante illud tempus aut postea auditum apud eos quenquam ausum esse similia. Hec illo vociferante, nobis, ut sunt animi

THE WORLD OF LEARNING 113

iuvenum monitoribus increduli, crescebat ex prohibitione
cupiditas. Itaque senex, ubi animadvertit se nequicquam
niti, aliquantulum progressus inter rupes, arduum callem
digito nobis ostendit, multa monens multaque iam
digressis a tergo ingeminans. Dimisso penes illum siquid
vestium aut rei cuiuspiam impedimento esset, soli duntaxat ascensui accingimur alacresque conscendimus.

*My brother took the steep path to the summit, while I self-
indulgently hoped to reach it by an easier route along the lower
slopes—and soon found myself in trouble, and no nearer my goal.
With an effort I caught him up, and we set off again together; but
once more I shirked the difficulty. . . . Then, my thoughts turning
from the material to the spiritual, 'This', I said, 'is what happens
in our striving for the blessed life. There too our goal is set on
high; and narrow, we are told, is the way that leads to it. On then
to those heights; or else lie sluggishly in the valley of your sins,
where if death overtakes you, you will be lost for ever.'*

*Spurred by these thoughts I sprang up and at last made my way
to the summit.*

Primum omnium spiritu quodam aeris insolito et specta-
culo liberiore permotus, stupenti similis steti. Respicio:
nubes erant sub pedibus; iamque michi minus incredibiles
facti sunt Athos et Olimpus, dum quod de illis audieram
et legeram, in minoris fame monte conspicio. Dirigo
dehinc oculorum radios ad partes italicas, quo magis
inclinat animus; Alpes ipse rigentes ac nivose, per quas
ferus ille quondam hostis romani nominis transivit, aceto,
si fame credimus, saxa perrumpens, iuxta michi vise sunt,
cum tamen magno distent intervallo. Suspiravi, fateor, ad
italicum aerem animo potius quam oculis apparentem,
atque inextimabilis me ardor invasit et amicum et patriam
revidendi . . . . Occupavit inde animum nova cogitatio
atque a locis traduxit ad tempora. Dicebam enim ad me

ipsum: 'Hodie decimus annus completur, ex quo, puerilibus studiis dimissis, Bononia excessisti; et, o Deus immortalis, o immutabilis Sapientia, quot et quantas morum tuorum mutationes hoc medium tempus vidit! Infinita pretereo; nondum enim in portu sum, ut securus preteritarum meminerim procellarum. Tempus forsan veniet, quando eodem quo gesta sunt ordine universa percurram, prefatus illud Augustini tui: 'Recordari volo transactas feditates meas et carnales corruptiones anime mee, non quod eas amem, sed ut amem te, Deus meus'. Michi quidem multum adhuc ambigui molestique negotii superest. Quod amare solebam, iam non amo; mentior: amo, sed parcius; iterum ecce mentitus sum: amo, sed verecundius, sed tristius; iantandem verum dixi. Sic est enim; amo, sed quod non amare amem, quod odisse cupiam; amo tamen, sed invitus, sed coactus, sed mestus et lugens. Et in me ipso versiculi illius famosissimi sententiam miser experior:

Odero, si potero; si non, invitus amabo.

Possessed by these thoughts I seemed to have forgotten where I was, and why I had come, when I came to myself—for the sun was sinking, the shadow of the mountain was lengthening, and it was time to leave. Westward lay the Pyrenees, beyond the range of human sight. On my right were the mountains of central France; to the left the Mediterranean and Aigues Mortes could be clearly seen. Below us lay the Rhône.

Que dum mirarer singula et nunc terrenum aliquid saperem, nunc exemplo corporis animum ad altiora subveherem, visum est michi *Confessionum* Augustini librum, caritatis tue munus, inspicere; quem et conditoris et donatoris in memoriam servo habeoque semper in manibus: pugillare opusculum, perexigui voluminis sed

THE WORLD OF LEARNING

infinite dulcedinis. Aperio, lecturus quicquid occurreret; 65
quid enim nisi pium et devotum posset occurrere? Forte
autem decimus illius operis liber oblatus est. Frater
expectans per os meum ab Augustino aliquid audire,
intentis auribus stabat. Deum testor ipsumque qui aderat,
quod ubi primum defixi oculos, scriptum erat: 'Et 70
eunt homines admirari alta montium et ingentes fluctus
maris et latissimos lapsus fluminum et occeani ambitum et
giros siderum, et relinquunt se ipsos.' Obstupui, fateor;
audiendique avidum fratrem rogans ne michi molestus
esset, librum clausi, iratus michimet quod nunc etiam 75
terrestria mirarer, qui iampridem ab ipsis gentium philosophis
discere debuissem nichil preter animum esse mirabile,
cui magno nichil est magnum.

Tunc vero montem satis vidisse contentus, in me ipsum
interiores oculos reflexi, et ex illa hora non fuit qui me 80
loquentem audiret donec ad ima pervenimus; satis michi
taciti negotii verbum illud attulerat. . . .

*It was not by chance, I was convinced, that these words were
directed to me, and to me alone; and I remembered how Augustine,
and Antony before him, were converted by opening a book and
reading . . . and I thought how vainly men seek in the distractions
of the world without for that which can only be found within. . . .
Possessed by such thoughts, I looked back; and the mountain
seemed barely a cubit's height, compared with the far-ranging
human spirit—if only it does not sink in the mire of this earthly
life.*

Hos inter undosi pectoris motus, sine sensu scrupulosi
tramitis, ad illud hospitiolum rusticum unde ante lucem
moveram, profunda nocte remeavi, et luna pernox gratum 85
obsequium prestabat euntibus. Interim ergo, dum
famulos apparande cene studium exercet, solus ego in
partem domus abditam perrexi, hec tibi, raptim et ex

tempore, scripturus; ne, si distulissem, pro varietate
locorum mutatis forsan affectibus, scribendi propositum
deferveret. Vide itaque, pater amantissime, quam nichil
in me oculis tuis occultum velim, qui tibi nedum univer-
sam vitam meam sed cogitatus singulos tam diligenter
aperio; pro quibus ora, queso, ut tandiu vagi et instabiles
aliquando subsistant, et inutiliter per multa iactati, ad
unum, bonum, verum, certum, stabile se convertant. Vale.
VI Kal. Maias, Malausane.

Familiarium Rerum, IV. 1, §§ 1, 7–8, 17–21,
26–29, 35–36

47   *Come to Vaucluse!* (1)

To Giovanni Colonna, an elderly Dominican living near
Rome   30 May 1342

. . . Illic tandem in terram depositus, ad dexteram me
videbis. Ubi enim procul ab Italia possim esse tran-
quillius? Videbis autem modicis sed umbrosis ortulis
angustoque contentum hospitio, sed quod tanti hospitis
adventu factum putes angustius; videbis quem desideras,
optime valentem, nullius egentem rei, nil magnopere de
fortune manibus expectantem; videbis a mane ad vesperam solivagum herbivagum montivagum fontivagum
silvicolam ruricolam; hominum vestigia fugientem, avia
sectantem, amantem umbras, gaudentem antris roscidis
pratisque virentibus, execrantem curas curie, tumultus
urbium vitantem, abstinentem liminibus superborum,
vulgi studia ridentem, a letitia mestitiaque pari spatio
distantem; totis diebus ac noctibus otiosum, gloriantem
musarum consortio, cantibus volucrum et nimpharum
murmure, paucis servis sed multis comitatum libris; et

nunc domi esse, nunc ire, nunc subsistere, nunc querula in
ripa nunc tenero in gramine lassatum caput et fessa membra
proicere; et que non ultima solatii pars est, neminem
accedere nisi perraro, qui vel millesimam vaticinari possit suarum particulam curarum; ad hec, modo obnixum
defixumque oculis tacere, modo multa secum loqui,
postremo se ipsum et mortalia cuncta contemnere. Ecce,
pater, dum te voco, veniendi laborem abstulisse videor:
si enim hec perlegis et fidem habes, abunde me vides.
Vale iantandem; dum enim colloqui videor, epystolam
me scribere sum oblitus.

Ad fontem Sorgie, III Kal. Iunias (1342).

Fam. VI. 3, §§ 69–71

48   *Come to Vaucluse!* (2)

To the Bishop of Viterbo   15 February 1353

Your recent illness will perhaps remind you of the frailty of human beings—and your recovery will endear you even more to your friends.

Tandem illud in animum inducas, nichil quod sciam,
posse nunc cum hac solitudine comparari, in qua te Socrates noster et ego cupidissime expectamus, ubi facile
divina ope suffultus et corpus recreare et serenare animum queas. Nullus hic tyrannus minax, nullus civis in-
solens; non obtrectatoris rabidi lingua mordacior, non
ira, non civilis factio, non querimonie, non insidie, non
clamor, non strepitus hominum, non tubarum clangor,
non fragor armorum; nulla preterea avaritia, nullus livor,
nulla prorsus ambitio, nullum superbi limen cum tremore
subeundum; sed gaudium et simplicitas et libertas et
inter divitias pauperiemque status optabilis; sed sobria et

humilis et mansueta rusticitas, gens innocua, plebs inermis, regio pacifica, cuius presul vir optimus et bonorum amicissimus consequens erit ut te in fratrem habeat, quoniam nos habet in filios. Quid de aliis loquar? aer hic blandus ac suaves aure, tellus aprica, fontes nitidi, piscosum flumen, umbrosum nemus, antra humida recessusque herbidi et prata ridentia; hic mugitus boum, avium cantus murmurque nimpharum penitusque abdita et ex re nomen habens clausa vallis et amena. In circuitu autem certatim Bacho grati colles ac Minerve, neve in his que ad esum potumque pertinent parasitico more, quod non soleo, curiosius immorer, breviter sic habe: quicquid seu in terris seu in aquis hic nascitur, tale esse ut in Paradiso deliciarum, sicut theologi loquuntur, sive, ut poete, in campis Elysiis natum putes. Siquid vero, ut est animus hominis sepe voluptuosior quam oportet, exiguo ruri desit, facile finitimorum locorum ubertate supplebitur. Postremo, ne singula prosequar, hic tibi quies exoptata et votiva tranquillitas et, qua nulle studioso animo divitie cariores, librorum copia ingens adest fideliumque convictus atque obsequium amicorum. Versaberis cum sanctis cum philosophis cum poetis cum oratoribus cum historicis; nos duo quantum sine satietate tua fuerit, latus tibi utrunque cingemus; nos tibi iam nunc animis occurrimus et ab occupate vite tempestatibus redeunti portum hunc quietissimum preparamus. . . . Inter tuorum vota igitur, pater amabilis, vive, oro, feliciter et vale et veni et propera supra vires animum attollens, ac sepe tibi et omnibus virtutibus tuis dicens poeticum illud famosissimum:

Durate et vosmet rebus servate secundis.

Fam. XVI. 6, §§ 20–25, 27

49 *To M. Tullius Cicero, 16 June 1345*

In June 1345 Petrarch discovered in the library of the cathedral at Verona a volume containing Cicero's letters to Atticus, and those to his brother Quintus, and to Brutus; and, greatly excited, he set out to copy them himself. It proved to be a discovery of Cicero the man, as opposed to the orator and philosopher whom he already knew and loved, and he was shocked to find that his idol had feet of clay, and that in the maelstrom of events he had been torn by ambition, hopes, and fears, and had abandoned the philosophic detachment which Petrarch admired and had tried to practise for so many years.

Cicero, it can be argued, deserves more sympathy than Petrarch was prepared to give; and within a generation of the latter's death the Florentine humanists, whose republic was facing a similar threat from the growing despotism of Milan, were lauding Cicero for the very involvement which Petrarch condemned. It was the duty, they held, of every citizen to offer all his gifts in the service and defence of free institutions; and one of them, in fact, wrote a reply to Petrarch from Cicero in the nether world in defence of his own conduct, and of the active, as opposed to the contemplative, life.

§ 1

FRANCISCUS PETRARCHA M. T. CICERONI S.

Epistolas tuas, diu multumque perquisitas atque ubi minime rebar inventas, avidissime perlegi, audivi multa te dicentem, multa deplorantem, multa variantem, M. Tulli, et qui iam pridem qualis preceptor aliis fuisses noveram, nunc tandem quis tu tibi esses agnovi. Unum hoc vicissim a vera caritate profectum non iam consilium sed lamentum audi, ubicunque es, quod unus posterorum, tui nominis amantissimus, non sine lacrimis fundit. O inquiete semper atque anxie, vel ut verba tua recognoscas, *o preceps et calamitose senex*, quid tibi tot contentionibus et prorsus nichil profuturis simultatibus voluisti? Ubi et etati et professioni et fortune tue conveniens otium reliquisti? Quis te falsus glorie splendor senem adolescentium bellis implicuit et per omnes iactatum casus ad indignam philosopho mortem rapuit? Heu et fraterni consilii immemor et tuorum tot salubrium preceptorum, ceu nocturnus viator lumen in tenebris gestans, ostendisti secuturis callem, in quo ipse satis miserabiliter lapsus es. ... Quis te furor in Antonium impegit? Amor credo reipublice, quam funditus iam corruisse fatebaris. Quodsi pura fides, si libertas te trahebat, quid tibi tam familiare cum Augusto? Quid enim Bruto tuo responsurus es? 'Siquidem', inquit, 'Octavius tibi placet, non dominum fugisse sed amiciorem dominum quesisse videberis.'... Doleo vicem tuam, amice, et errorum pudet ac miseret, iamque cum eodem Bruto 'his artibus nichil tribuo, quibus te instructissimum fuisse scio'. Nimirum quid enim iuvat alios docere, quid ornatissimis verbis semper de virtutibus loqui prodest, si te interim ipse non audias? Ah quanto satius fuerat philosopho presertim in tranquillo rure senuisse, *de perpetua illa*, ut ipse quodam scribis loco, *non de hac iam exigua vita cogitantem*, nullos habuisse fasces, nullis triumphis inhiasse, nullos inflasse tibi animum Catilinas. Sed hec quidem frustra. Eternum vale, mi Cicero.

Apud superos, ad dexteram Athesis ripam, in civitate Verona Transpadane Italie, XVI Kalendas Quintiles, anno ab ortu Dei illius quem tu non noveras, MCCCXLV.

Fam. XXIV. 3

§ 2

AD EUNDEM

Franciscus Ciceroni suo salutem. Si te superior offendit epystola—verum est enim, ut ipse soles dicere, quod ait familiaris tuus in *Andria*:

Obsequium amicos, veritas odium parit—

accipe quod offensum animum ex parte mulceat, ne semper odiosa sit veritas; quoniam veris reprehensionibus irascimur, veris laudibus delectamur. Tu quidem, Cicero, quod pace tua dixerim, ut homo vixisti, ut orator dixisti, ut philosophus scripsisti; vitam ego tuam carpsi, non ingenium non linguam, ut qui illud mirer, hanc stupeam; neque tamen in vita tua quicquam preter constantiam requiro, et philosophice professioni debitum quietis studium et a civilibus bellis fugam, extincta libertate ac sepulta iam et complorata republica. Vide ut aliter tecum ago ac tu cum Epycuro multis in locis sed expressius in libro *De finibus* agebas; cuius enim ubilibet vitam probas, rides ingenium. Ego nichil in te rideo, vite tantum compatior, ut dixi; ingenio gratulor eloquiove. O Romani eloquii summe parens, nec solus ego sed omnes tibi gratias agimus, quicunque Latine lingue floribus ornamur; tuis enim prata de fontibus irrigamus, tuo ducatu directos, tuis suffragiis adiutos, tuo nos lumine illustratos ingenue profitemur; tuis denique, ut ita dicam, auspiciis ad hanc, quantulacunque est, scribendi facultatem ac propositum pervenisse. Accessit et alter poetice vie dux; ita enim necessitas poscebat, ut esset et quem solutis et quem frenatis gressibus preeuntem sequeremur, quem loquentem, quem canentem miraremur, quoniam cum bona venia amborum, neuter ad utrunque satis erat, ille tuis equoribus, tu illius impar angustiis.

Fam. XXIV. 4, §§ 1–5

PART FIVE

WINE, WOMAN, AND SONG

Et quid erat quod me delectabat, nisi amare et amari?
                                  Augustine, *Confessions*, II. 2
*Ars est artium ars amoris, cuius magisterium ipsa sibi
retinuit natura, et Deus auctor naturae.*
   William of St. Thierry, *De Natura et Dignitate Amoris*, I. 1

At about the same time as the 'new wave' of monasticism was flooding outwards from Cîteaux to cover all Europe, reinforcing the ideals of asceticism and unworldliness, while adding new warmth, out of the heart of this asceticism, to the concept of friendship—in the same twelfth century a fresh upsurge of more earthly love and laughter and learning, of wit and satire, was spreading out, this too from the land of France, to find a ready welcome in Germany and Italy, Spain and England. It was a complex movement, rich in contrasts and new relationships, harmonies and discords. Four of these will be touched on here, though they resist any closely ordered treatment: the relationship between clerical and lay, between the learned and popular, between Latin and the vernaculars, and between the sacred and profane.

How deep into the past plunge the roots of this new flowering, and how diverse its sources and nourishment, it is impossible to determine. 'As far back as we can go, church, court, and people exist side by side, and in a thousand ways, mostly incalculable, their poetry and songs are shared. . . . The Latin lyric is omnipresent, and everywhere contemporaneous with the vernacular.'[1] The latter emerged in the first brilliance in Provence, then in the heyday of a sunlit civilization, where courtly poets began to set a new fashion in their own tongue; so much so that one of them has been called 'the first modern poet.'[2]

---

[1] Peter Dronke, *Medieval Latin and the Rise of European Love-Lyric*, Oxford, 1965, vol. i, pp. 263, 285.

[2] William, count of Poitiers (*fl.* 1100): see W. P. Ker, *Medieval English Literature*, p. 48. He adds 'he uses the kind of verse which everyone uses now'—but that was 1912.

From Provence the new movement quickly spread to France, Italy, and the rest. But the fashion of the age demanded a new elegance and refinement, and here the Latin of the clerks had much to offer, backed as it was by the experiments in rhythm and rhyme of the medieval centuries, and by the full-grown literature of the classical world—long familiar, but with potentialities still not fully explored. So Latin and the vernaculars, learned and popular, drawing on the same springs of youth and gaiety, subtlety and skill, but with less sophistication than the Roman poets, their models, lending and borrowing themes and treatment, metre and rhyme, joined forces; and from the fusion of the two modern European poetry was born.

But Latin too could be 'popular' in a different way. Being international in language, the new verse passed from hand to hand and from country to country; it was adopted[1] and adapted and copied into collections,[2] to serve as a wandering scholar's handbook, or for the delight of a monastery, or of some wealthy bishop. Most of the finest lyrics are in fact anonymous, and were enjoyed as the common possession of the scholars' world.

Popular then, but learned in the fullest sense. Here the master was Ovid, with his *Art of Love*, his gallery of heroines, and all the riches of his mythology and story-telling; so that in the field of love, so one of them claimed, it was the clerk who taught the layman.

> Quid Dione valeat, quid amoris deus,
> primus novit clericus et instruxit meus;
> miles est per clericum factus cythereus.

Many of these poems then are learned, or over-learned; but one can fall in love without benefit of Ovid, and the simpler lyrics are elemental in their origin and appeal.

The last and most complex relationship was the meeting and fusion of sacred and profane. It could hardly be otherwise in a society steeped in both Christianity and the classics, and invigorated by a new adventurousness in ideas and in the world of action (it was the

---

[1] Thomas Wright, for example, in the 1830s, on the evidence of some manuscripts, claimed as English many poems which are now believed to be French in origin.

[2] e.g. the *Carmina Burana*, which takes its name from the Bavarian monastery of Benediktbeuern; the *Arundel Collection* (in the British Museum), the *Cambridge Songs*, etc. See Raby, *Secular Poetry*, vol. 2, pp. 256 ff. and *passim*.

age of the Crusades, and of the cathedral schools which were the forerunners of the universities). A society too where the tug of war between sacred and secular was the stronger since secular learning as a whole was the province of the clergy, and the prospects offered there to bright young men ranged far beyond our notions of a clerical career.

To glance briefly at detail, the Scriptures and the liturgy, and in particular its music, were all pressed into service. The Sequence pointed the way to a whole field of lyric poetry; a hymn could provide a metre, or lend itself to genial parody—and parody was not always genial. The Mass could be rewritten in the service of Bacchus, the prayers ending with the formula *Per omnia pocula poculorum*—'Ever wine without end'. Finally the Scriptures (since the Middle Ages were not overburdened with our scrupulous time-sense) furnished a wealth of 'modern instances'. So there was constant interplay between sacred and profane, sometimes friendly, sometimes a rough-and-tumble, sometimes a savage enmity between the two worlds: in modern terms, anything from peaceful coexistence to a shooting war. And a civil war at that, for these 'two worlds' met head-on in the Church, whose most savage critics were to be found among the clergy themselves. Two factors above all provoked them: the power and wealth of the hierarchy, and the celibacy, or official celibacy, of the clergy. *Femina, dulce malum*, writes a twelfth-century monk, borrowing the phrase from Ovid. His emphasis was on the *malum*, but the writers who interest us here are wholly concerned with the *dulce*; and the *malum*, along with the mischief of power and wealth, will be discussed under Satire.

> Tuum, Venus, haurio
> venis ignem bibulis.
> tuis, Flora, sitio
> favum de labellulis.
> Flora, flore singulari
> preminens puellulis,
> solum sola me solari
> soles in periculis.

We are a long way from St. Bernard, and the passion that drew men heavenwards: in short,

> The love of God which leads to realms above
> Is contre-carréd by the God of Love.

WINE, WOMAN, AND SONG

We are carried back, then, to the pagan world, where Venus and Cupid, Bacchus, and the rest represent in their own way another form of the 'sacred'; primeval forces which had to a real extent been smothered, or at any rate fenced off in the written word of monks and clerks behind the warning signs of *Luxuria* and *Gula*: DANGER: KEEP OUT. But besides the theological abasement of sex, and its pagan exaltation, there is a third solution, this also rooted in the classics, and reappearing in the twelfth century alongside the pagan one—that of a philosophic humanism. When the two lovers, Phyllis and Flora, decide to refer their dispute to the Court of Love, after all the poetic pageantry Cupid calls in as his judges *Usus et Natura*, Experience and Human Nature. These are to find a permanent home in European thought; while the gods and goddesses too will be inseparable for many centuries from art and literature.

A fourth answer claims in justice a mention, even though it was not directly aimed at lay society and the normal love of men and women: William of St. Thierry's *Tractatus de arte et dignitate amoris*; a theological exaltation of love, written *c.* 1120, and so contemporary with this new movement, and in fact intended as an answer to it. It is an analysis of love, as implanted in Nature, and taught by her. But Nature herself is the work of God and, unless corrupted, looks to God as her goal; and the *magisterium* of lesser masters, still more of such as Ovid, is explicitly rejected. The writer was a Benedictine abbot who later became a Cistercian monk out of love for St. Bernard; and his treatise, which became known as the *Anti-Nasonem*, was intended for his own novices, already well schooled in the poets, who had chosen the harder school of St. Benedict. Here, within the larger setting of a love of God, they were to find their fulfilment in a love of the brethren. *Amicitia*, a central theme of monastic thought and experience, is first cousin to *amor*, and a Christian *caritas* was the basis of the Cistercian Rule, the *Carta Caritatis*. The theme was elaborated by Ailred of Rievaulx (1109–67), most lovable of English Cistercians, in his *De spiritali amicitia*; and this answer too, though monastic in origin and in primary intention, has larger implications which have been woven into European thought and experience, finding an echo in the sixteenth-century Flemish weaver who, writing to his wife, signs himself 'your married friend'.

50 *Begone, dull Care!*

Omittamus studia:
dulce est desipere,
et carpamus dulcia
iuventutis tenere.
5 Res est apta senectuti
seriis intendere
insudandoque virtuti
vitia rependere.
　　Velox etas preterit
10 studio detenta,
lascivire suggerit
tenera iuventa.

Ver etatis labitur,
hiems nostra properat;
15 vita damnum patitur,
cura carnem macerat.
Sanguis aret, hebet pectus,
minuuntur gaudia,
nos deterret iam senectus
20 morborum familia.
　　Velox etas preterit, etc.

Imitemur superos!
digna est sententia,
et amores teneros
25 iam venentur otia.
Voto nostro serviamus:
mos est iste iuvenum,
ad plateas descendamus
et choreas virginum.
30 　　Velox etas preterit, etc.
Anon., twelfth century, from the Carmina Burana

51 *The Archpoet's Confession*

Aestuans intrinsecus ira vehementi
in amaritudine loquor meae menti:
factus de materia levis elementi
folio sum similis de quo ludunt venti.

Cum sit enim proprium viro sapienti
supra petram ponere sedem fundamenti,
stultus ego comparor fluvio labenti
sub eodem aëre nunquam permanenti.

Feror ego veluti sine nauta navis,
ut per vias aeris vaga fertur avis.
Non me tenent vincula, non me tenet clavis,
quaero mei similes et adiungor pravis.

Mihi cordis gravitas res videtur gravis,
iocus est amabilis dulciorque favis.
Quidquid Venus imperat, labor est suavis,
quae nunquam in cordibus habitat ignavis.

Via lata gradior more iuventutis,
implico me vitiis, immemor virtutis,
voluptatis avidus magis quam salutis,
mortuus in anima curam gero cutis.

. . . . .

Secundo redarguor etiam de ludo,
sed cum ludus corpore me dimittat nudo,
frigidus exterius, mentis aestu sudo,
tunc versus et carmina meliora cudo.

Tertio capitulo memoro tabernam,
illam nullo tempore sprevi neque spernam

donec sanctos angelos venientes cernam,
cantantes pro mortuis 'requiem aeternam'.

Meum est propositum in taberna mori,
30 ut sint vina proxima morientis ori.
Tunc cantabunt laetius angelorum chori:
'sit Deus propitius huïc potatori!'

Poculis accenditur animi lucerna,
cor imbutum nectare volat ad superna.
35 Mihi sapit dulcius vinum de taberna,
quam quod aqua miscuit praesulis pincerna.

Ecce meae proditor pravitatis fui,
de qua me redarguunt servientes tui.
Sed eorum nullus est accusator sui,
40 quamvis velint ludere saeculoque frui.

Iam nunc in praesentia praesulis beati
secundum dominici regulam mandati
mittat in me lapidem, neque parcat vati,
cuius non est animus conscius peccati.

52 *A Drinking Song*

Iam lucis orto sidere
statim oportet bibere:
bibamus nunc egregie
et rebibamus hodie.

5 Quicumque vult esse frater,
bibat semel, bis, ter, quater:
bibat semel et secundo,
donec nihil sit in fundo.

Bibat ille, bibat illa,
bibat servus et ancilla,
bibat hera, bibat herus:
ad bibendum nemo serus.

Potatoribus pro cunctis,
pro captivis et defunctis,
pro imperatore et papa,
bibo vinum sine aqua.

Haec est fides potatica,
sociorum spes unica:
qui bene non potaverit,
salvus esse non poterit.

Longissima potatio
sit nobis salutatio:
et duret ista ratio
per infinita secula.
                    Amen.

53 *The Debate between Wine and Water*

Cum tenerent omnia medium tumultum,
post diversas epulas et post vinum multum,
postquam voluptatibus ventris est indultum,
me liquerunt socii vino iam sepultum.

Ast ego vel spiritu, vel in carne gravi,
raptus sum et tertium celum penetravi,
ubi secretissima quedam auscultavi,
que post in concilio fratrum revelavi.

Cum sederet siquidem in excelsis Deus
et cepisset spiritus trepidare meus,
statim in iudicio Thetis et Lyeus
intrant et alteruter actor fit et reus.

AQUA

Meum decus admodum Deus ampliavit,
quando me de puteo potum postulavit:
de torrente, siquidem, attestante Davit,
bibit et propterea caput exaltavit.

VINUM

Te quamvis aquaticus bibat Nazareus,
quantum salutiferus sit effectus meus
patet, dum Apostolus mandat, immo Deus,
ut me propter stomachum bibat Timotheus.

AQUA

Medicine Naaman liquerant humane,
nec prodesse poterant cuti male sane,
cui voces prophetice non fuerunt vane,
postquam fuit septies lotus in Jordane.

VINUM

Cesus a latronibus Hierosolymita,
visus a presbitero, visus a levita,
incuratus forsitan excessisset vita,
ni fuissent vulnera vino delenita.

AQUA

Fructum temporaneum reddit excolenti
lignum, quod est proximum aque decurrenti:
potus aque frigide viro sitienti
prodest, bono nuntio longe venienti.

VINUM

Si quis causa qualibet cessit a Lyeo,
non resultat canticum neque laus in eo;

si refectus fuerit tandem potu meo, 35
tunc cantabit: *Gloria in excelsis Deo.*

Ad hanc vocem civibus celi concitatis,
quasi rationibus vini comprobatis,
inclamarunt fortibus vocibus elatis:
terre pax hominibus bone voluntatis! 40

Quibus ego vocibus, tale post examen,
excitatus expuli somnii velamen;
et laudavi, concinens, patrem, natum, flamen
usque ad: *in gloria Dei patris, amen.*

54 *Phyllis and Flora*

'*The sweete and civill Contention of two amorous Ladyes*'[1]

Anni parte florida, celo puriore,
picto terre gremio vario colore,
dum fugaret sidera nuntius Aurore,
liquit somnus oculos Phyllidis et Flore.

Placuit virginibus ire spatiatum, 5
nam soporem reicit pectus sauciatum;
equis ergo passibus exeunt in pratum,
ut et locus faciat ludum esse gratum.

Eunt ambe virgines et ambe regine:
Phyllis coma libera, Flora torto crine. 10
Non sunt forme virginum, sed forme divine,
et respondent facies luci matutine.

[1] The subtitle of an Elizabethan translation by 'R. S., Esquire', 1598.

Nec stirpe nec facie nec ornatu viles
et annos et animos habent iuveniles;
15 sed sunt parum impares et parum hostiles,
nam huic placet clericus, et huic placet miles.

Non eis distantia corporis aut oris,
omnia communia sunt intus et foris;
sunt unius habitus et unius moris:
20 sola differentia modus est amoris.

Susurrabat modicum ventus tempestivus,
locus erat viridi gramine festivus,
et in ipso gramine defluebat rivus
vivus atque garrulo murmure lascivus.

25 Consedere virgines; herba sedem dedit.
Phyllis iuxta rivulum, Flora longe sedit;
et dum sedit utraque et in sese redit,
amor corda vulnerat et utramque ledit.

Amor est interius latens et occultus
30 et corde certissimos elicit singultus;
pallor genas inficit, alternantur vultus,
sed in verecundia pudor est sepultus.

Phyllis in suspirio Floram deprehendit,
et hanc de consimili Flora reprehendit;
35 altera sic alteri mutuo rependit,
tandem morbum detegit et vulnus ostendit.

Ille sermo mutuus multum habet more,
et est quidem series tota de amore;
amor est in animis, amor est in ore.
40 Tandem Phyllis incipit et arridet Flore.

'Miles', inquit, 'inclite, mea cura, Paris,
ubi modo militas et ubi moraris?
o vita militie, vita singularis,
sola digna gaudiis Dionei laris!'

Dum puella militem recolit amicum, 45
Flora ridens oculos iacit in obliquum
et in risu loquitur verbum inimicum:
'amas', inquit, 'poteras dicere, mendicum.

Sed quid Alcibiades agit, mea cura,
res creata dignior omni creatura, 50
quem beavit omnibus gratiis natura?
o sola felicia clericorum iura!'

Floram Phyllis arguit de sermone duro
et sermone loquitur Floram commoturo;
nam 'ecce virgunculam', inquit, 'corde puro 55
cuius pectus nobile servit Epicuro!

Surge, surge, misera de furore fedo!
solum esse clericum Epicurum credo;
nichil elegantie clerico concedo,
cuius implet latera moles et pinguedo. 60

A castris Cupidinis cor habet remotum,
qui somnum desiderat et cibum et potum.
O puella nobilis, omnibus est notum,
quod est longe militis ab hoc voto votum.

Solis necessariis miles est contentus, 65
somno, cibo, potui non vivit intentus.
Amor illi prohibet ne sit somnolentus;
cibus, potus militis amor et iuventus.'

Flora repels the attack, and praises the clerk

'Dixisti de clerico quod indulget sibi,
70 servum somni nominas et potus et cibi!
Sic solet ab invido probitas describi.
Ecce parum, patere, respondebo tibi.

Tot et tanta, fateor, sunt amici mei,
quod nunquam incogitat aliene rei;
75 celle mellis, olei, Cereris, Lyei,
aurum, gemme, pocula famulantur ei.

In tam dulci copia vite clericalis,
quod non potest aliqua pingi voce talis,
volat et duplicibus semper plaudit alis
80 Amor indeficiens, Amor immortalis.

Sentit tela Veneris et Amoris ictus,
non tamen est clericus macer et afflictus:
quippe nulla copie parte derelictus,
cui respondet animus domine non fictus.'

Phyllis retorts with praises of her knight

85 'Non est ullus adeo fatuus et caecus,
cuï non appareat militare decus.
Tuus est in otio quasi brutum pecus,
meum tegit galea, meum portat equus.

Meus armis dissipat inimicas sedes:
90 et si forte prelium solus intrat pedes,
dum tenet Bucephalum suus Ganymedes,
ille me commemorat inter ipsas cedes.

Redit fusis hostibus et pugna confecta,
et me sepe respicit galea reiecta.
Ex his et ex aliis ratione recta 95
est vita militie mihi preelecta.'

55 *In Praise of his Mistress*

Sidus clarum
puellarum,
flos et decus omnium,
rosa veris,
quae videris 5
clarior quam lilium;

Tui forma
me de norma
regulari proiicit.
Tuus visus 10
atque risus
Veneri me subicit.

Pro te deae
Cythereae
libens porto vincula, 15
et alati
sui nati
corde fero spicula.

Ut in lignis
ardet ignis 20
siccis cum subducitur,
sic mens mea
pro te, dea,
fervet et comburitur.

25 Dic, quis durus,
    quis tam purus,
    carens omni crimine,
    esse potest,
    quem non dotes
30 tuae possint flectere?

    Vivat Cato,
    Dei dato
    qui sic fuit rigidus,
    in amore
35 tuo flore
    captus erit fervidus.

    Fore suum
    crinem tuum
    Venus ipsa cuperet,
40 si videret;
    et doleret
    suum quod exuperet.

    Frons et gula
    sine ruga
45 et visus angelicus
    te coelestem,
    non terrestrem,
    denotant hominibus.

    Tibi dentes
50 sunt candentes,
    pulchre sedent labia,
    quae siquando
    ore tango
    mellea dant suavia.

Quare precor, 55
mundi decor,
te satis summopere,
ut amoris,
non doloris,
causa sis hoc pectore. 60
Anon., twelfth century, from the Ripoll Collection

56 *Love's Companion*

O comes amoris, dolor,
cuius mala male solor,
 an habes remedium?
Dolor urget me, nec mirum,
quem a predilecta dirum, 5
 en, vocat exilium,
cuius laus est singularis,
pro qua non curasset Paris
 Helene consortium.

Sed quid queror me remotum 10
illi fore, que devotum
 me fastidit hominem,
cuius nomen tam verendum,
quod nec michi presumendum
 est, ut eam nominem? 15
Ob quam causam mei mali
me frequenter vultu tali
 respicit, quo neminem.

Ergo solus solam amo,
cuius captus sum ab hamo, 20
 nec vicem reciprocat.

Quam enutrit vallis quedam,
quam ut paradisum credam,
   in qua pius collocat
hanc creator creaturam
vultu claram mente puram,
   quam cor meum invocat.

Gaude, vallis insignita,
vallis rosis redimita,
   vallis flos convallium.
Inter valles vallis una,
quam collaudat sol et luna,
   dulcis cantus avium.
Te collaudat philomena,
vallis dulcis et amena,
   mestis dans solacium.
Anon., twelfth century, from the Carmina Burana

57   *Love and Reason*

Vacillantis trutine
      libramine
   mens suspensa fluctuat
      et estuat
   in tumultus anxios,
dum se vertit et bipertit
motus in contrarios.
      O langueo;
causam languoris video
      nec caveo,
videns et prudens pereo.

Me vacare studio
      vult ratio;

sed dum amor alteram
    vult operam,
in diversa rapior.
Ratione cum Dione
    dimicante crucior.
        O langueo, etc.

    Sicut in arbore
frons tremula, navicula
    levis in equore,
    dum caret anchore
subsidio, contrario
flatu concussa fluitat:
    sic agitat,
sic turbine sollicitat
    me dubio
hinc amor, inde ratio.
        O langueo, etc.

    Sub libra pondero
quid melius, et dubius
    mecum delibero.
    Nunc menti refero
delicias venerias;
que mea michi Florula
    det oscula;
qui risus, que labellula,
    que facies,
frons, naris aut cesaries.
        O langueo, etc.

His invitat et irritat
    amor me blandiciis;
    sed aliis

45   ratio sollicitat
    et excitat me studiis.
        O langueo, etc.

Nam solari me scolari
    cogitat exilio.
50   Sed, ratio,
    procul abi! Vinceris
sub Veneris imperio.
    O langueo, etc.

Anon., twelfth century, from the Arundel Collection

58 *Reluctant Celibates*

Non est Innocentius, immo nocens vere,
qui quod Deus docuit, studet abolere;
iussit enim Dominus feminas habere,
sed hoc noster pontifex iussit prohibere.

5 Gignere nos precipit Vetus Testamentum;
ubi Novum prohibet, nusquam est inventum;
a modernis latum est istud documentum,
ad quod nullum ratio prebet argumentum.

Nonne de militibus milites procedunt?
10 et reges a regibus qui sibi succedunt?
per locum a simili omnes iura ledunt,
clericos qui gignere crimen esse credunt.

Zacharias habuit prolem et uxorem,
nec prole quem genuit memini maiorem;
15 baptizavit etenim nostrum Salvatorem;
pereat, qui teneat novum hunc errorem!

Si fortasse memor es illius diei,
in quo fabricaverant vitulum Iudei,

Levi dedit infulam et progeniei;
ergo qui non gignerant omnes erunt rei.   20

Paulus coelos rapitur ad superiores,
ubi multas didicit res secretiores,
ad nos tandem rediens, instruensque mores,
  uas, inquit, habeant quilibet uxores.

Propter hoc et alia dogmata doctorum,   25
reor esse melius, et magis decorum,
quisque suam habeat, et non proximorum,
ne incurrat odium vel iram eorum.

Ecce iam pro clericis multum allegavi,
necnon pro presbyteris multa comprobavi,   30
Pater noster nunc pro me, quoniam peccavi,
dicat quisque presbyter cum sua suavi.

Anon., twelfth century

59 *A Cursing Song*

Raptor mei pilei morte moriatur:
mors sit subitanea nec prevideatur;
et pena continua post mortem sequatur,
nec campis Elysiis post Lethen fruatur.

Raptor mei pilei seva morte cadat: 5
illum febris, scabies et tabes invadat,
hunc de libro Dominus vite sue radat,
hunc tormentis Aeacus cruciandum tradat.

Eius vita brevis sit pessimusque finis,
nec vivat feliciter hic diebus binis,   10
laceret hunc Cerberus dentibus caninis,
laceratum gravius torqueat Erinys.

Excommunicatus sit agro vel in tecto,
nullus eum videat lumine directo,
solus semper sedeat similis deiecto;
hinc penis Tartareis crucietur lecto.

Hoc si quis audierit excommunicamen,
et non observaverit presulis examen;
nisi resipuerit corrigens peccamen,
anathema fuerit. Fiat, fiat! amen.
> *Anon., twelfth century, from the Carmina Burana*

Note. The *Carmina Burana*, here cited as the source of many of these poems, is 'the most famous and extensive collection of medieval Latin songs and poems'; 'the work of many poets and from more than one country'.[1] Many of these pieces are to be found in other manuscripts, published and unpublished, all over Europe. The ascription, then, is not necessarily exclusive, but points the reader to a familiar and accessible collection.

[1] Raby, *Secular Latin Poetry*, ii. 256, 266.

PART SIX

SATIRE AND COMPLAINT[1]

Pecunia $\begin{cases} \text{maket wrong rith} \\ \text{maket day nith} \\ \text{maket frend fo} \\ \text{maket wele wo}^2 \end{cases}$

THE title of this section represents more clearly than that of any other its double origin, classical and Christian. Satire proper is a large enough term, and difficult to pin down, ranging from a humorous and ironical to a scathing commentary on the crimes or follies of mankind. It is winged by wit and indignation, and commonly aimed at specific targets; and since verse gives the keenest cutting edge, *facit indignatio versum*.[3] But Complaint is yet larger in its condemnation, when it is rooted in the conviction that all mankind has gone astray, since all are involved in Adam's Fall. The material in that case will be endless, with the widest generalizations alongside attacks on particular depravities; and (a second consequence) the weapon will be wielded as of right by the clergy, the appointed shepherds of the flock, charged to 'preach the word, be urgent in season and out of season, convince, rebuke, and exhort'.[4] It will be related, in fact, to the background of preaching, year in and year out, to redeemed yet almost irredeemable humanity; and the vices to be scourged will be found not only in contemporary society, but set out in Scripture and the Fathers, and reinforced by the Roman satirists from Horace to Juvenal.

---

[1] The double title was first used by J. E. Wells in his *Manual of the Writings in Middle English, 1050–1400*, 1916. It was adopted by G. R. Owst in *Literature and Pulpit in Medieval England*, 1933, and is critically examined by J. Peter, *Complaint and Satire in early English Literature*, 1956.

[2] 'A fragment of verse inscribed in friar John of Grimston's sermon notebook': see G. R. Owst, *Literature and Pulpit in Medieval England*, Cambridge, 1933, p. 317.

[3] Juvenal, I. 79.   [4] 2 Tim. 4. 2.

For the two conceptions inevitably overlap. Both look to some ideal, whether of reason or revelation, or to some established order of society (for Christians it might be the monastic life); or again to some golden age in the past when men actually practised (or so they believe) what is now merely preached. The targets too are much the same in all ages: the corruptions of wealth, and power, and privilege; greed and stupidity in every form; and (since men usually do the writing) the mischief of woman, man's undoing. How convenient to have a permanent scapegoat in the other half of the human race!

But the higher the ideals, the deeper the shadows they cast; and the monk or clerk looking out on the world after a thousand years of Christianity saw men still choosing the primrose path, Lazarus lying at the rich man's gate, and the poor going naked, while the *servus servorum Dei* was clad in silk, Money sat in the seat of power, bought office in Church as well as State, perverted justice, and trampled on innocence, while woman still tempted man to his ruin. There was another side to Christianity: the forgiveness till seventy times seven, the silence in the face of persecution. But the satirist is not given to silence:

Semper ego auditor tantum? numquamne reponam?[1]

and his medieval successor drew the same conclusion: *Propter Sion non tacebo*.

How far are we to believe them? Where rage and wit combine, they can produce an unforgettable picture; but it is not necessarily the portrait of an individual or an age. Nor is that the satirist's aim. His business is to bring to light all that privilege gets away with, and convention tolerates or conceals. Thanks to the cast of his mind his own age is the worst of all possible ages—and thanks to human nature he is never short of material. Two targets are worth a closer look. The attacks on woman are sometimes satire, sometimes the sober conviction of a celibate society (to be set against the very different convictions of more reluctant clerks). So John of Salisbury has a long chapter in his *Policraticus* 'De molestiis et oneribus coniugiorum, secundum Hieronymum et alios philosophos'. His philosophers range from Socrates and Aristotle to Stoics and Epicureans; 'ut si qui Christianae religionis abhorrent rigorem, discant vel ab ethnicis castitatem.' It is true that he pays lip-service to marriage; but after citing the pagan maxim 'Non est uxor ducenda sapienti' (the restriction is admittedly selective), he throws into the scale all the weight

[1] Juvenal, I. 1

of Jerome, the worst misogynist of them all. Some of the writers show neither philosophy nor wit, but exploit the ingenuity of the Schools and the techniques of Ovid, while inverting his subject; parading the same list of anti-heroines, Delilah, Bathsheba (who has to take the blame for David), and the author of all our troubles, Eve.

The Roman *Curia* is a more complex problem. On the one hand is the need of a vast bureaucracy for money, and the advantages, in some directions, of a centralized government. On the other hand is the view that 'the twelfth-century renaissance was finally betrayed by many agents, and chief among them the greed, the tyranny, and the fatal secular success of the Roman *Curia*'. The tragedy, according to this view, was that the Davids, for all their courage and skill, could neither slay Goliath, nor reform him.

60 *Money Talks*

Munera conturbant reges rursusque serenant,
   munera dant pacem, munera bella parant.
Munera pontifices subvertunt, munera reges,
   munera ius statuunt destituuntque simul.
Munera stultorum linguas dant esse disertas,   5
   munera cum clamant cetera quaeque tacent.
Munera pervertunt leges, decreta refellunt,
   evacuantque patrum iura rigore suo.

. . . . .

Munera iudicii libram moderantur et ipsam
   protinus inflectunt, quo data pensa trahunt.   10
Munera mortifero dant pocula plena veneno,
   excaecant oculos, praecipitantque gradus.
Omnia vincit amor, sed amorem munera vincunt,
   quod si quis dubitet, ponderet haec et eum.
Munera virtutum suffocant germina, sanctos   15
   irritant, reprobos mortis ad ima trahunt.

Munera corrumpunt mores pariuntque recepta
    damna pudicitiae, dona cupita procis.
Munera pontifices extollunt, munera reges,
20   munera dant apices exhilarantque duces.

        .   .   .   .   .

Munera praecedunt, quoties mala multa sequuntur,
    munera cum veniunt proxima causa subest.
Munera si cessent, cessabunt iurgia, lites,
    Mars cadet, et Veneris nullus amicus erit.
25 Munera si cessent, sine sanguine tempore pacis,
    quod nunquam potuit, Roma subacta ruet.
Munera si cessent, primatum pallia multo
    constabunt levius et meliore foro.
Munera si cessent, abbatum cornua longa
30   ponderis et precii iure minoris erunt.
Munera si cessent, regis revocatus ab aula
    monachus in claustrum limina sacra teret.
Munera si cessent, grex cum pastore quiescet,
    iunctus et amborum spiritus unus erit.
35 Munera si cessent, Deus in cellas Cluniaci
    forte revertetur et remanebit ibi.
Munera si cessent, Iudam cum Simone clerus
    tollet, et e medio coget abire sui.
In quorum manibus crebro tractantur iniqua,
40   dextera muneribus esse referta solent.
Munera si cessent, miseris mortalibus ultra
    clamor, nec luctus, nec dolor ullus erit.
Munera si cessent, pariter cum Simone Iudas
    decidet, et loculos perdet uterque suos.

Nigel de Longchamps, Speculum Stultorum, 2593–2648, with omisions

61 *Money is King*

In terris summus rex est hoc tempore Nummus.
Nummum mirantur reges et ei famulantur;
Nummo venalis favet ordo pontificalis;
Nummus in abbatum cameris retinet dominatum;
Nummum nigrorum veneratur turba priorum.   5
Nummus magnorum iudex est consiliorum.
Nummus bella gerit, nec si vult pax sibi deerit;
Nummus agit lites, quia vult deponere dites;
erigit ad plenum de stercore Nummus egenum.   9
Omnia Nummus emit venditque, dat et data demit.
Nummus adulatur, Nummus post blanda minatur;
Nummus mentitur, raro verax reperitur.
Nummus avarorum deus est et spes cupidorum;
Nummus in errorem mulierum ducit amorem;
Nummus venales dominas facit imperiales;   15
Nummus raptores facit ipsos nobiliores.

. . . . .

Si Nummus loquitur, pauper tacet, hoc bene scitur.
Nummus maerores reprimit relevatque labores;
Nummus, ut est certum, stultum facit esse disertum.
In Nummi mensa sunt splendida fercula densa;   20
Nummus laudatos comedit pisces piperatos;
Francorum vinum Nummus bibit atque marinum.
Nummus formosas vestes gerit et preciosas;
Nummo splendorem dant vestes exteriorem;
Nummus eos gestat lapides quos India prestat;   25
Nummus dulce putat quod eum gens tota salutat.
Nummus adoratur, quia virtutes operatur:
vile facit carum, quod dulce est reddit amarum,
et facit audire surdum claudumque salire.
De Nummo quaedam maiora prioribus edam: 30

vidi cantantem Nummum, missam celebrantem;
Nummus cantabat, Nummus responsa parabat.
Vidi quod flebat dum sermonem faciebat,
et subridebat, populum quia decipiebat.
Carmina Burana

62 *O Most Pernicious Woman!* (1)

Femina, dulce malum, mentem roburque virile
    frangit blanditiis insidiosa suis.
Femina, fax Sathanae, gemmis radiantibus, auro,
    vestibus, ut possit perdere, compta venit.
5 Quod natura sibi sapiens dedit, illa reformat;
    quicquid et accepit dedecuisse putat.
Pingit acu, et fuco liventes reddit ocellos;
    Sic oculorum, inquit, gratia maior erit.
Est etiam teneras aures quae perforat, ut sic
10   aut aurum aut charus pendeat inde lapis.
Altera ieiunat mense, minuitque cruorem,
    ut prorsus quare palleat ipsa facit.
Nam quae non pallet sibi rustica quaeque videtur;
    Hic decet, hic color est verus amantis, ait.
15 Haec quoque diversis sua sordibus inficit ora;
    sed quare melior quaeritur arte color?
Arte supercilium rarescit, rursus et arte
    in minimum mammas colligit ipsa suas.
Arte quidem videas nigros flavescere crines;
20   nititur ipsa suo membra movere loco.
Sic fragili pingit totas in corpore partes,
    ut quicquid nata est displicuisse putes.
O quos in gestus se mollis femina frangit!
    Et placet in blaesis subdola lingua sonis.
25 Dulcia saepe canit, componit sedula gressum,
    ut quadam credas arte movere pedem.

Saepe auditores eius facundia torquet,
  et modo ridendo, et modo flendo placet.
Mille modis nostras impugnat femina mentes,
  et multos illi perdere grande lucrum est.   30
Nil est in rebus muliere nocentius, et nil
  quo capiat plures letifer hostis habet.
Nec nos in totum iactamus crimina sexum,
  tempore sed nostro rara pudica manet.
Sed carnem foenum clamat sacer ille propheta,   35
  fac procul a foeno flamma sit ista tuo.
          Anon., twelfth centuṭy, De Vita Monachorum

63   *O Most Pernicious Woman!* (2)

Ve nunc, cras et heri, qui credulus est mulieri:
vos adulescentes, sensu, ratione carentes,
vos insensati, vos divitiis mutilati,
que loquar audite; si sunt facienda videte.
Artibus illarum mendosis blandiloquarum   5
ne sit deceptus, videat sapiens et ineptus,
nec quidquam veri temere credat mulieri.
Si tuba Maronis, facundia vel Ciceronis,
vel vox Nasonis, sapientia vel Salomonis
ore meo flueret, vix dicere lingua valeret   10
tot scelerum partes, quot femina noverit artes.
Femina Samsonem decepit et Salomonem,
expulit Heliam, vita privavit Uriam.

          . . . . .

Femina cum plorat lacrimis ad iniqua laborat;
Femina damnavit quicquid Deus ipse creavit.   15
          Anon., twelfth century, De Vita Monochorum

64 *The Gospel according to the Mark of Silver*[1]

There are many versions of this 'Gospel', ranging from the twelfth to the fifteenth century, this being the earliest and shortest.[2] All are constructed on the same pattern, consisting of a cento of verses from Scripture; and most are attacking the same objects: the Roman Curia, with its simony, bribery, and corruption from doorkeeper to pope and cardinal. Some are merely outrageous; but in this instance at least parody is the weapon chosen by Satire to uphold the very purposes of the Gospel, and reassert in contemporary terms its condemnation of 'lawyers and Pharisees, hypocrites . . . blind guides . . . who pay tithes of mint and cummin; but have overlooked the weightier demands of the Law, justice, mercy, and good faith'.[3]

Initium sancti evangelii secundum Marcas argenti. In illo tempore: Dixit Papa Romanis: 'Cum venerit filius hominis ad sedem maiestatis nostre, primum dicite: "Amice, ad quid venisti?" At ille si perseveraverit pulsans nil
5 dans vobis, eiicite eum in tenebras exteriores.' Factum est autem, ut quidam pauper clericus veniret ad curiam domini Pape, et clamavit dicens: 'Miseremini mei saltem vos, hostiarii Pape, quia manus paupertatis tetigit me. Ego vero egenus et pauper sum, ideo peto ut subveniatis
10 calamitati et miserie mee.' Illi autem audientes indignati sunt valde et dixerunt: 'Amice, paupertas tua tecum sit in perditione. Vade retro, Sathanas, quia non sapis ea que sapiunt nummi. Amen, amen, dico tibi: Non intrabis in gaudium domini tui, donec dederis novissimum qua-
15 drantem.'

Pauper vero abiit et vendidit pallium et tunicam et universa que habuit, et dedit cardinalibus et hostiariis et

---

[1] The pun is a favourite one in both prose and verse: e.g.

> Nummus est pro numine, et pro Marco marca,
> Et est minus celebris ara quam sit arca.

[2] Other versions are given in P. Lehmann, *Die Parodie im Mittelalter*.
[3] Matt. 23. 23.

camerariis. At illi dixerunt: 'Et hoc quid est inter tantos?'
Et eiecerunt eum ante fores, et egressus foras flevit amare
et non habens consolationem. Postea venit ad curiam
quidam clericus dives incrassatus, inpinguatus, dilatatus,
qui propter seditionem fecerat homicidium. Hic primo
dedit hostiario, secundo camerario, tertio cardinalibus. At
illi arbitrati sunt inter eos quod essent plus accepturi.
Audiens autem dominus Papa cardinales et ministros
plurima dona a clerico accepisse infirmatus est usque ad
mortem. Dives vero misit sibi electuarium aureum et argenteum, et statim sanatus est. Tunc dominus Papa ad se
vocavit cardinales et ministros et dixiteis: 'Fratres, videte
ne aliquis vos seducat inanibus verbis. Exemplum enim
do vobis, ut quemadmodum ego capio, ita et vos capiatis.'

Carmina Burana

65   *The Roman Curia*

'Radix Omnium Malorum Avaritia'[1]

Propter Sion non tacebo,
set ruinas Rome flebo,
quousque iustitia
rursus nobis oriatur
et ut lampas accendatur
iustus in ecclesia.

Sedet vilis et in luto
princeps, facta sub tributo;
quod solebam dicere,
Romam esse derelictam,
desolatam et afflictam,
expertus sum opere.

---

[1] An ingenious adaptation of 'Radix enim omnium malorum est cupiditas' (1 Tim. 6. 10). (The acrostic is attributed to the twelfth-century English satirist, Walter Map.)

Vidi, vidi caput mundi,
instar maris et profundi
15 vorax guttur Siculi;
ibi mundi bitalassus,
ibi sorbet aurum Crassus
et argentum seculi.

Ibi latrat Scilla rapax
20 et Caribdis auri capax
potius quam navium;
fit concursus galearum
et conflictus piratarum,
id est cardinalium.

25 Sirtes insunt huic profundo
et Sirenes toti mundo
minantes naufragium;
os humanum foris patet,
in occulto cordis latet
30 informe demonium.

Canes Scille possunt dici
veritatis inimici,
advocati curie,
qui latrando falsa fingunt,
35 mergunt simul et confringunt
carinam pecunie.

Qui sunt Sirtes vel Sirenes?
qui sermone blando lenes
attrahunt bizantium;
40 spem pretendunt lenitatis,
set procella parcitatis
supinant marsupium.

Cardinales, ut predixi,
novo iure crucifixi
vendunt patrimonium; 45
Petrus foris, intus Nero,
intus lupi, foris vero
sicut agni ovium.

Tales regunt Petri navem,
tales habent eius clavem, 50
ligandi potentiam;
hi nos docent, set indocti,
hi nos docent et nox nocti
indicat scientiam.

Tunc occurrunt cautes rati, 55
donec omnes sunt privati
tam nummis quam vestibus;
tunc securus it viator,
quia nudus et cantator
fit coram latronibus. 60

Qui sunt cautes? Ianitores,
per quos, licet seviores
tigribus et beluis,
intrat dives ere plenus,
pauper autem et egenus 65
pellitur a ianuis.

Set ne rursus in hoc mari
me contingat naufragari,
dictis finem faciam,
quia, dum securus eo, 70
ne submergar, ori meo
posui custodiam.

Walter of Châtillon (fl. 1170)

66 *The Poor Scholar*

Qui virtutes appetit, labitur in imum,
querens sapientiam irruit in limum;
imitemur igitur hec dicentem mimum:
o cives, cives, querenda pecunia primum.

5 Hec est, que in sinodis confidendo tonat,
in electionibus prima grande sonat;
intronizat presules, dites impersonat:
et genus et formam regina pecunia donat.

Adora pecuniam, qui deos adoras:
10 cur struis armaria, cur libros honoras?
Longas fac Parisius vel Athenis moras:
si nichil attuleris, ibis, Homere, foras.

Disputet philosophus vacuo cratere,
sciat, quia minus est scire quam habere;
15 nam si pauper fueris, foras expellere,
ipse licet venias musis comitatus, Homere.

Sciat artes aliquis, sit auctorum plenus,
quid prodest si vixerit pauper et egenus?
Illinc cogit nuditas vacuumque penus,
20 hinc usura vorax avidumque in tempore fenus.

Illud est, cur odiens studium repellam
paupertatem fugiens vitamque misellam;
quis ferret vigilias frigidamque cellam?
tutius est iacuisse thoro, tenuisse puellam.

25 Idcirco divitias forsan non amatis,
ut eternam postmodum vitam capiatis.
Heü mentes perdite! numquid ignoratis,
quod semper multum nocuit differre paratis?

Semper habet comitem paupertas merorem,
perdit fructum Veneris et amoris florem, 30
quia iuxta nobilem versificatorem
non habet unde suum paupertas pascat amorem.

Sit pauper de nobili genere gigantum,
sciat quantum currat sol et Saturnus quantum,
per se solus habeat totum fame cantum: 35
gloria quantalibet quid erit si gloria tantum?

Audi, qui de Socrate disputas et scribis:
miser, vaca potius potibus et cibis;
quod si dives fieri noles vel nequibis,
inter utrumque tene, medio tutissimus ibis. 40
Walter of Châtillon (*fl. 1170*)

PART SEVEN

GHOSTS AND MARVELS

GHOST stories seem to require little introduction or justification. Then, as now, they could chill the blood, and, no doubt, chill it agreeably. But they went further than this. For they represented not just a shadowy 'something after death', but a conviction of woe beyond all experience, though not beyond human imagining. So most of these stories serve a double purpose: a warning to be taken to heart, while there is yet time; and one more illustration of the power of the Most High.

They correspond then, at the opposite pole, to the miracle stories in which the lives of the saints abound. But where the saints have won heaven, and in their lifetime already drew on its resources, these have won perdition, and return to tell us of it, from a world where Satan and his evil spirits are as real as God and his angels. No wonder William of Malmesbury can add at the conclusion of one of his stories, *Haec pro utilitate legentium me inseruisse non piguit.*

WILLIAM OF MALMESBURY (*c.* 1080–*c.* 1143)

67 § 1 *The Witch of Berkeley*

Hisdem diebus simile huic in Anglia contigit, non superno miraculo, sed inferno praestigio; quod cum retulero, non vacillabit fides historiae etsi mentes auditorum sint incredulae. Ego illud a tali viro audivi, qui se vidisse
5 iuraret, cui erubescerem non credere. Mulier in Berkeleia mansitabat, maleficiis, ut post patuit, insueta, auguriorum veterum non inscia, gulae patrona, petulantiae arbitra, flagitiis non ponens modum, quod esset adhuc citra senium, vicino licet pede pulsans senectutis aditum. Haec

cum quadam die convivaretur, cornicula quam in deliciis 10
habebat vocalius solito nescio quid cornicata est: quo
audito, dominae cultellus de manu excidit, simul et vultus
expalluit; et, producto gemitu, 'Hodie', ait, 'ad ultimum
sulcum meum pervenit aratrum; hodie audiam et accipiam
grande incommodum.' Cum dicto nuntius miseriarum 15
intravit: percunctatus quid ita vultuosus adventaret,
'Affero', inquit, 'tibi ex villa illa', et nominavit locum,
'filii obitum et totius familiae ex subita ruina interitum.'
Hoc dolore femina pectus saucia continuo decubuit;
sentiensque morbum perrepere ad vitalia, superstites 20
liberos, monachum et monacham, pernicibus invitavit
epistolis. Advenientes voce singultiente alloquitur: 'Ego,
filii, quodam meo miserabili fato daemonicis semper
artibus inservii; ego vitiorum omnium sentina, ego illece-
brarum magistra fui. Erat tamen, inter haec mala, spes 25
vestrae religionis quae miseram palparet animam; de me
desperata, in vobis reclinabar; vos proponebam pro-
pugnatores adversus daemones, tutores contra saevissimos
hostes. Nunc igitur, quia ad finem vitae accessi, et illos
habebo exactores in poena quos habui suasores in culpa, 30
rogo vos per materna ubera, si qua fides, si qua pietas, ut
mea saltem temptetis alleviare tormenta: et de anima
quidem sententiam prolatam non revocabitis, corpus vero
forsitan hoc modo servabitis. Insuite me corio cervino,
deinde in sarcophago lapideo supinate, operculum plumbo 35
et ferro constringite; super haec lapidem tribus catenis
ferreis, magni scilicet ponderis, circumdate: psalmicines
quinquaginta sint noctibus, eiusdemque numeri missae
diebus, qui adversariorum excursus feroces levigent. Ita,
si tribus noctibus secure iacuero, quarta die infodite 40
matrem vestram humo; quanquam verear ne fugiat terra
sinibus me recipere et fovere suis, quae totiens gravata est
malitiis meis.' Factum est ut praeceperat, illis magno

studio incumbentibus. Sed, proh nefas! nil lacrymae valuere piae, nil vota, nil preces; tanta erat mulierculae malitia, tanta diaboli violentia. Primis enim duabus noctibus, cum chori clericorum psalmos circa corpus concreparent, singuli daemones ostium ecclesiae, immani obice clausum, levi negotio defringentes, extremas catenas diruperunt; media, quae operosius elaborata erat, illibata duravit. Tertia nocte, circa gallicinium, strepitu advenientium hostium omne monasterium a fundamentis moveri visum: unus, ceteris et vultu terribilior et statura eminentior, ianuas maiori vi concussas in fragmenta deiecit. Deriguere clerici metu, 'steteruntque comae et vox faucibus haesit.' Ille arroganti, ut videbatur, gestu ad sarcophagum accessit, inclamatoque nomine, ut surgeret imperavit: qua respondente quod nequiret pro vinculis, 'Solveris', inquit, 'et malo tuo'; statimque catenam, quae ceterorum ferociam eluserat, nullo conamine ut stuppeum vinculum dirupit. Operculum etiam tumbae pede depulit: apprehensamque manu, palam omnibus, ab ecclesia extraxit: ubi prae foribus equus, niger et superbus, hinniens videbatur, uncis ferreis per totum tergum protuberantibus; super quos misera imposita, mox ab oculis intuentium, cum toto sodalitio disparuit. Audiebantur tamen clamores per quatuor fere miliaria miserabiles suppetias orantis.

De Gestis Regum Anglorum, Book II, § 204

§ 2 *The Two Clerks of Nantes*

Erant in urbe illa duo clerici, nondum patientibus annis, presbyteri; id officium magis precario quam bonae vitae merito ab episcopo loci exegerant: denique alterius miserandus exitus superstitem instruxit quam fuerint antea in inferni lapsum ambo praecipites. Ceterum quod ad scientiam litterarum tendit ita edocti, ut aut parum aut nihil ipsis deberent artibus; a reptantibus infantiae rudimentis adeo iocundis amicitiae officiis aemuli, ut, iuxta Comici dictum, 'Manibus pedibusque conando, periculum etiam, si necesse esset, capitis pro invicem facerent'. Quare die quadam liberiorem animum a curis forinsecis nacti, in secreto conclavi huiusmodi sententias fudere: Pluribus se annis nunc litteris, nunc seculi lucris, mentes exercuisse, nec satiasse, magis ad distortum quam ad rectum intentas: inter haec, illum acerbum diem sensim appropinquare qui societatis suae inextricabile in vita vinculum dirumperet; unde praeveniendum mature, ut fides, quae conglutinarat viventes, primo mortuum comitaretur ad manes. Paciscuntur ergo ut quisquis eorum ante obiret, superstiti, vel dormienti vel vigilanti, appareret infra triginta proculdubio dies: si fiat, edocturus quod, secundum Platonicos, mors spiritum non extinguat, sed ad principium sui Deum tanquam e carcere emittat; sin minus, Epicureorum sectae concedendum, qui opinantur animam corpore solutam in aërem evanescere, in auras effluere. Ita data acceptaque fide, cotidianis colloquiis sacramentum frequentabant. Nec multum in medio, et ecce, mors repentine imminens indignantem halitum uni eorum violenter extraxit. Remansit alter, et serio de socii sponsione cogitans, et iam iamque affuturum praestolans cassa opinione triginta diebus ventos pavit; quibus elapsis, cum desperans aliis negotiis avocasset otium, astitit subito vigilanti, et quiddam operis molienti, vultu, qualis solet esse morientium anima fugiente, exsanguis. Tum tacentem vivum prior mortuus compellans, 'Agnoscis me?' inquit: 'Agnosco', respondit; 'et non tantum de insolita tua turbor praesentia, quantum de diuturna miror absentia.' At ille, ubi tarditatem adventus

excusavit, tandem ait, 'Tandem, expeditis morarum
nexibus, venio: sed adventus iste tibi, si voles, amice, erit commodus, mihi omnino infructuosus; quippe qui, pronuntiata et acclamata sententia, sempiternis sim deputatus suppliciis.' Cumque vivus, ad ereptionem mortui, omnia sua monasteriis et egenis expensurum, seque dies et noctes ieiuniis et orationibus continuaturum, promitteret, 'Fixum est', inquit, 'quod dixi, quia sine poenitentia sunt iudicia Dei, quibus in sulphuream voraginem inferni demersus sum: ibi "dum rotat astra polus, dum pulsat littora pontus," pro criminibus meis volvar; inflexibilis sententiae manet rigor, aeterna et innumera poenarum genera comminiscens, totus modo mundus valitura remedia exquirat. Et ut aliquam experiaris ex meis innumerabilibus poenis,' protendit manum sanioso ulcere stillantem, et 'en,' ait, 'unam ex minimis, videturne tibi levis?' Cum levem sibi videri referret, ille, curvatis in volam digitis, tres guttas defluentis tabi super eum iaculatus est; quarum duae tempora, una frontem contingentes, cutem et carnem sicut ignito cauterio penetrarunt, foramen nucis capax efficientes. Illo magnitudinem doloris clamore testante, 'Hoc', inquit mortuus, 'erit in te quantum vixeris, et poenarum mearum grave documentum, et, nisi neglexeris, salutis tuae singulare monimentum. Quapropter dum licet, dum nutat ira, dum pendula Deus opperitur clementia, muta habitum, muta animum Redonis monachus effectus apud sanctum Melanium.' Ad haec verba vivo respondere nolente, alter eum oculi vigore perstringens, 'Si dubitas', inquit, 'converti, miser, lege litteras istas'; et simul cum dicto manum expandit tetricis notis inscriptam, in quibus Sathanas et omne inferorum satellitium gratias omni ecclesiastico coetui de Tartaro emittebant, quod cum ipsi in nullo suis voluptatibus deessent, tum tantum numerum subditarum

animarum paterentur ad inferna descendere praedicationis incuria, quantum nunquam retroacta viderunt secula. His dictis loquentis aspectus disparuit; et audiens, omnibus suis per ecclesias et egenos distributis, sanctum Melanium adiit, omnes audientes et videntes de subita conversione admonens ut dicerent 'Haec est mutatio dexterae Excelsi.'

Ista pro utilitate legentium me inseruisse non piguit; nunc de Willelmo loquar.

De Gestis Regum Anglorum, Book III, § 237

69 § 3 *Buried Treasure*

Gerbert of Aurillac (*c.* 945–1003) was an outstanding scholar at a moment when learning was still only on the brink of a great revival. He went from a Benedictine monastery in France to study mathematics and astronomy in Spain, where the Arabs were far ahead of the rest of Europe; then made a great name for himself in the cathedral school of Rheims, before becoming archbishop there, and finally pope as Sylvester II (999–1003). After his death legend quickly gathered round him: he had sold his soul to the devil, it was said, and all his successes were due to black magic. William of Malmesbury admits that this is a common charge among the vulgar against literati, but is inclined to believe it in this instance—and in any case the stories about him are too good to omit. But the charge would have been hardly possible a century later, when scholars in increasing numbers—an Englishman, Adelard of Bath, among them—were setting out for Spain to recover the lost treasures of Greek and Arab science.

Erat iuxta Romam in campo Martio statua, aerea an ferrea incertum mihi, dexterae manus indicem digitum extentum habens, scriptum quoque in capite, 'Hic percute.' Quod superioris aevi homines ita intelligendum rati quasi ibi thesaurum invenirent, multis securium ictibus innocentem statuam laniaverant. Sed illorum

Gerbertus redarguit errorem, longe aliter ambiguitate absoluta: namque meridie, sole in centro existente, notans quo protenderetur umbra digiti, ibi palum figit; mox superveniente nocte, solo cubiculario laternam portante comitatus, eo contendit. Ibi terra solitis artibus dehiscens latum ingredientibus patefecit introitum: conspicantur ingentem regiam, aureos parietes, aurea lacunaria, aurea omnia; milites aureos aureis tesseris quasi animum oblectantes; regem metallicum cum regina discumbentem, apposita obsonia, astantes ministros, pateras multi ponderis et pretii, ubi naturam vincebat opus. In interiori parte domus carbunculus, lapis inprimis nobilis et parvus inventu, tenebras noctis fugabat. In contrario angulo stabat puer, arcum tenens extento nervo et arundine intenta. Ita in omnibus, cum oculos spectantium ars pretiosa raptaret, nihil erat quod posset tangi etsi posset videri; continuo enim ut quis manum ad contingendum aptaret, videbantur omnes illae imagines prosilire, et impetum in praesumptorem facere. Quo timore pressus Gerbertus ambitum suum fregit: sed non abstinuit cubicularius quin mirabilis artificii cultellum, quem mensae impositum videret, abriperet; arbitratus scilicet in tanta praeda parvum latrocinium posse latere. Verum mox omnibus imaginibus cum fremitu exsurgentibus, puer quoque, emissa arundine in carbunculum, tenebras induxit; et, nisi ille monitu domini cultellum reiicere accelerasset, graves ambo poenas dedissent. Sic insatiata cupiditatis voragine, laterna gressus ducente, discessum. Talia illum adversis praestigiis machinatum fuisse, constans vulgi opinio est.

De Gestis Regum Anglorum, Book II, 169

70   *Warning to Slanderers*

Iohannes bonus monachus apud sanctum Albanum et Elemosinarius eiusdem loci propter sanctitatem suam licenciatus fuit ut posset trahere moram ad orandum in ecclesia post congregacionem quandocunque sibi placuit. Qui narravit fratri Galfrido de Neketone quod quadam nocte quando venit de ecclesia post orationem et transivit per medium claustrum et venit ad ostium capituli ita fuit perterritus quod non audebat transire et retraxit se; postea signavit se signo sancte crucis et voluit transire et iterum territus retraxit se. Tandem armatus lorica fidei cogitavit penes se quod diabolus nichil sibi nocere posset nisi Deus hoc iuste permitteret et audenter capitulum intravit. Ingressus autem capitulum vidit quemdam horribilem quasi diabolum sedere in loco ubi abbas sedere consuevit. Et tandem adiuravit eum ut diceret ei quare ibi sedit. Qui respondit quod nescivit causam. Qui iterum adiuratus respondit, 'Modo scio causam,' et sic incepit blasfemare creatorem et maledicere horam in qua creatus est. Et statim descendit et sedit in terra et extraxit linguam suam de ore suo quasi fulvi coloris, scilicet, blodiam. Et postea extraxit de manubio suo magnum cultellum quasi falcheon et scidit linguam suam in minutissimas partes quam iterum redintegratam retraxit in os suum. Et postea eam extraxit nigram quam iterum sicut prius in minutissimas partes scidit, quam secundo redintegratam iterum retraxit in os suum. Et postea extraxit eam quasi ignei coloris et iterum in minutissimas partes eodem cultello scidit et iterum redintegratam in os suum retraxit. Postquam autem viderat dictus Iohannes monachus adiuravit eum ut diceret ei quis esset et quid ista significarent. Qui respondit ei, 'Ego fui monachus in loco isto

quem bene noscis, in quo regnabant ista tria vicia,
scilicet, detractio, mendacium et contencio. Et licet
particeps sim omnium penarum inferni, tamen propter
35 ista tria vicia singulariter istam triplicem sustineo penam
et in eternum sustinebo: fulvam, propter detractionem
que minuit famam confratrum erga abbatem meum
seminando discordias: nigram, propter mendacium quod
simpliciter destruit famam aliorum: igneam, propter
40 contencionem qua animos aliorum ad inpacienciam
provocavi.' Et postea dixit quod ideo ibi tunc venit ut
ille manifestaret aliis quantum Deus detestatur illa tria
vicia. Et statim surrexit et exiit capitulum et rediit in
cimiterium. Et dictus monachus, scilicet, Iohannes de
45 Damis manifeste et vigilans non per sopnum vidit qualiter
corpora mortuorum usque ad humeros surrexerunt de
terra contra ipsum et dixerunt anglice, 'Wite a way and
glyde a way, thou forweried thyng, for wyth us in the blyss
of heven ne has thou na parte'.

Anon., fourteenth century, from the Ingilby MS.

COMMENTARY

ABBREVIATIONS

The following abbreviations are used in the Commentary:

BOOKS

AV   Authorized Version (King James Version)
DNB   *Dictionary of National Biography*
MLV   *The Oxford Book of Medieval Latin Verse*, ed. F. J. E. Raby
NEB   The New English Bible
ODCC *The Oxford Dictionary of the Christian Church*
NT   New Testament
OT   Old Testament
RSV   Revised Standard Version
Vulg.   Vulgate

Where shortened titles are used in the Commentary, full details will be found in the Bibliography.

Note that Psalm references are given in the Vulgate numeration, where the Latin is concerned, followed by the Hebrew/English in parentheses, if this differs.

LANGUAGE

AS   Anglo-Saxon
CL   Classical Latin
EL   Ecclesiastical (or Christian) Latin
LL   Late Latin
ML   Medieval Latin
VL   Vulgar Latin
LN   Notes on Language (pp. xix–xxvi)

1 *Trust in God: Psalm 90 (91)*

For the Psalms Jerome made three versions between 384 and 400. The first two were largely revisions of existing ones, and were translated from the Septuagint, a Greek translation so called because it was said to have been made by seventy scholars, probably at Alexandria, in the third–second centuries B.C. The third version was made direct from the Hebrew, but the second had already established itself, and was retained in the Vulgate.

The Greek (and Latin) versions combine Psalms 9 and 10, and so the numeration remains one behind that of the Hebrew text and all other versions, from Psalms 10 to 147 inclusive. (A recent large-scale revision of the Roman Psalter follows the Hebrew numbering, but it is not incorporated in the Vulgate.) Both numerations will be given throughout the book: that of the Vulgate first, as the source of the quotation, followed by the Hebrew/English in parentheses.

Something of the musical character of Jerome's version is due to the polysyllabic Latin. Compare 'Confiteantur tibi, Domine, omnia opera tua, et sancti tui benedicant tibi' with the monosyllabic 'Let all thy works praise thee, O Lord, and thy saints bless thee.' But Jerome himself was artist as well as scholar, as he shows, for example, by his skilful use of word-order. So he dramatizes the parallelism of the Psalms by means of inversion: e.g. in vv. 7, 10, 13, 14; and in vv. 14–16 he avoids monotony by ringing the changes on all four conjugations.

v. 3 *a verbo aspero*: 'from the harsh word' (of calumny and slander).

v. 6 'Plague and Pestilence are personified as destroying angels.' These phrases with their atmosphere of mystery and horror are aptly used by M. R. James in one of his ghost stories.

v. 9 This is the literal translation of the Heb. and Gk. texts, but they seem to be corrupt, and the RSV amends to 'Because you have made the Lord your refuge, the Most High your habitation, no evil shall...'.

vv. 14–end: God is represented as replying to the Psalmist.

vv. 15, 16 *ipso, illi* are variants on *eum*, etc. (see LN 7*b*): but they may be used here to bear additional rhythmical stress.

2 *Wisdom: Proverbs 8. 22–36*

This passage illustrates the Hebrew concept of wisdom as a divine attribute, the creative activity of God himself, which he bestows on men that he may draw them to him. By contrast it suggests the different perspectives of Greek wisdom; broadly speaking man-centred, once their earlier religion faded, and reaching outwards towards the confines of knowledge, whether God, or the impersonal laws of the universe, or the dark unknown; a speculative human wisdom that came under fire from St. Paul, and was rejected by St.

Bernard in the name of Heavenly wisdom.[1] Yet this same Greek philosophy was to play a key part, at different levels in different periods, in shaping the Christian world-picture, while remaining subsidiary to the over-all range and authority of the Scriptures.[2]

The picture too of creation given here is different from anything in classical literature, with a richness and simplicity, a repetition and amplification (as in the Psalms) which together make up its own rhetoric; ending with the supreme antithesis-in-action of life and death.

The language is closely moulded to the thought, with its short paratactic clauses and its expressive word-order, closer than classical Latin to modern English, yet retaining a flexibility which we have lost.

v. 24 *abyssi*: 'depths' (Gk.).

v. 25 *parturiebar*: 'I was brought forth'.

3 *St. Jerome: Cicero or Christ?*

For the full text see *Select Letters of St. Jerome*, ed. with an English translation by F. A. Wright (Loeb Classical Library), 1933.

Eustochium and her mother Paula were members of a devout circle in Rome. They followed Jerome to Bethlehem, and presided in turn over the convent there. The letter runs to fifty-two pages—a tract rather than a letter—packed with argument and exhortation in favour of virginity, and with warnings against the allurements of the world. Among these allurements is pagan literature: *Quae enim communicatio luci ad tenebras? . . . quid facit cum psalterio Horatius? cum evangeliis Maro? cum apostolo Cicero?* This leads him to recount his own experience ten years earlier.

1 *ante annos plurimos*: 'many years before'; for CL *plurimis ante annis*.
3 *castrassem*: metaphorical; 'had cut myself off from'—an allusion to Matt. 19. 12: *sunt eunuchi qui seipsos castraverunt propter regnum caelorum* ('there are others who have themselves renounced marriage . . .' NEB). For this early monasticism, see introduction to No. **10,** and H. Waddell, *The Desert Fathers*, 1936.

[1] Quid ergo docuerunt Apostoli? . . . non Platonem legere, non Aristotelis versutias inversare, non semper discere, et numquam ad veritatis scientiam pervenire. Docuerunt vivere.
[2] See introduction to Part Four: The World of Learning; and No. **39.**

COMMENTARY

4 *militaturus*: St. Paul's metaphor (Eph. 6. 10–15) had already become a semi-technical term for the monastic life.

9 *Plautus*: the Roman comic poet (*c*. 254–184 B.C.), twenty of whose plays survive (largely adapted from Greek comedy).

10 *memet*: -*met* is an emphasizing suffix added to personal pronouns. *coepissem*: subj. expressing indef. frequency: a Gk. constr. which became common in LL.

10–11 *sermo... incultus*: Augustine had the same experience: (Scriptura) *visa est mihi indigna, quam Tullianae dignitati compararem. tumor enim meus refugiebat modum eius, et acies mea non penetrabat interiora eius* (*Confessions*, III. 5).

13 *antiquus serpens*: i.e. the Devil.   *illuderet*: for subjunctive see LN 7*e* (v).   *quadragesima*: Lent (cf. Fr. *carême*).

15 *sit*: 'may be'; potential subj.

18–19 *tantum...pectusculo*: 'in my feeble breast, which was all but cold'. For the diminutive see LN 4, and cf. the emperor Hadrian's address to his soul: *Animula vagula blandula* ....

24–25 *ubi thesaurus* ... Matt. 6. 2.   27 *In inferno* ... Ps. 6. 5.

33 *gentilium*: 'pagan', see LN 5*b*.

34–35 *tanto constrictus articulo*: 'in the stress of that dread hour' (F. A. W.).

36 *deiurare*: 'swear'.

37 *codices*: the *codex*, or book, had begun to take the place of the *volumen* or roll, by the third century. (The splendid *Codex Sinaiticus* in the British Museum, one of the earliest manuscripts of the Greek Bible, was written in the fourth century.)

Did he keep his oath? Rufinus, his contemporary and one-time friend (they were parted by a theological quarrel, and each defended himself and attacked the other in an *Apologia*) maintains that there is not a page which does not show him *Ciceronianus* still; adding that his own monks had copied classical manuscripts for Jerome, and that Jerome had taught small boys in Bethlehem to read Virgil and the Comic poets. Jerome claims that he quoted from memory, but he does not refute the other charges; and defends himself elsewhere on much the same lines as does Augustine (see No. **39**). Then what is left of the dream? A tension, and an anxiety, which pressed heavily on some; but most, including Jerome himself, resolved them not by an 'either–or', but by a 'both–and'. (See introduction to Part Four, and Nos. **39** and **42**.)

4 *Wars, and Rumours of Wars*

12. The first half of the letter does not concern us. Jerome then turns to the siege of Rome by Alaric the Goth. After being reduced to starvation in 408, the Romans bought the enemy off; but in 410 the city fell, and for three days was given over to plunder. In one sense it was only a single incident in the swamping of the West by barbarian invaders, but it struck a shattering blow at the prestige of Rome, and provoked, among other things, St. Augustine's *De Civitate Dei*.

1 *Iebus*: the Canaanite name for Jerusalem: cf. 'Jebusites' in OT.

5 *dictantis*: 'as I write (compose) this letter'.

9 *recipit utero*: rhetoric at its worst.

10 *Nocte Moab* . . . Isa. 15. 1.   *Deus, venerunt* . . . Ps. 78. 1–3 (79. 1–3).

12–13 *posuerunt in . . . custodiam*: 'they have turned . . . into an orchard'.

18 ff. *Quis cladem* . . . : *Aeneid* II. 361–5 and 369 (Aeneas is describing the last hours of Troy). Jerome quotes from memory, and telescopes two lines together.

19 *explicet . . . possit*: potential subj.

22 *plurima . . . imago*: 'every shape . . .'.

5 *St. Augustine: The Confessions: Introduction*

(N.B. An occasional sentence has been simplified by omitting a few words, where the sense is unaffected; and in these instances the omissions are not indicated.)

The title *Confessions* has a double meaning. Alongside the familiar one of acknowledging one's faults is the equally prominent meaning in the Vulgate of acknowledging the glory of God: e.g., *Confitemini Domino, quoniam bonus*: 'Give thanks unto the Lord . . .'; *Confitebor tibi*

170 COMMENTARY

in cithara . . . 'Upon the harp will I praise thee . . .'. It is this second meaning which is uppermost in Augustine's mind. (Hence the title given to certain saints who, without being, for example, Martyrs, or Doctors of the Church, proclaimed God in their lives, e.g. Edward the Confessor.)

He strikes the keynote straight away in his quotations from the Psalms (the whole work is steeped in them, with some 350 citations); while the concluding lines *fecisti nos* . . . give the central theme of the book.

1–2 Ps. 144. 3 (145. 3), and 146. 5 (147. 5).

3 *mortalitatem suam*: his mortality is seen as the proof of his sin, i.e. as the direct consequence of his pride, and subsequent fall.

5 *testimonium quia*: reported statement: see LN 7*e* (i).
superbis resistis: Jas. 4. 6; one of the key-texts of Augustine's thought, which he quotes five times in the *Confessions* (the equally important second half, *humilibus autem dat gratiam*, is omitted here). It is central to the OT; e.g. *initium omnis peccati est superbia* (Ecclus. 10. 15), as well as being the heart of the Christian paradox; and in all discussions of the 'deadly sins' from Augustine onwards pride stands first. It is equally the starting-point of his *City of God*, where pride, or self-love, is at once the inspiration of Roman conquests, and the rock on which human communities are wrecked.

6 *Childhood and Schooldays*

4 *istam*: 'this'; see LN 7*b*.

13 *ridebantur*: the subject is *plagae meae*, l. 15.

18 *nec*: '*but* not'.

21–22 *quo referrem* (id) *quod*: 'what use I was to make of . . .'.

23 *copiosae inopiae*, etc.: the rhetorical figure of speech known as 'oxymoron'—'pointedly foolish'—where a paradox is driven home by an apparent contradiction in terms. Cf. Horace's *splendide mendax*, and Tennyson's 'faultily faultless' (of Launcelot).

27 *adamaveram*: 'love deeply': *ad-* intensifies.

28 *grammatici*: schoolmasters who teach literature, as opposed to those concerned with elementary education.

COMMENTARY 171

31 *et hoc*: 'this too' (along with his other perversities).

33 *fiebat*: the subject is the noun clause '*ut et legam*': 'I began to acquire . . . the power to read'.

35 *tenere*: 'remember'.

43–45 'bread of my soul, and power wedded to (and fertilizing) my mind and inmost thoughts'.

7 *Adolescence*

2–3 A difficult sentence: 'I did not restrict myself (*modus*) to a relationship between minds, following the sunlit path of friendship'. *luminosus* is contrasted with *nebulae*, etc. Compare Milton's *Comus*, 463 ff.

> . . . but when lust
> By unchaste looks, loose gestures, and foul talk,
> But most by lewd and lavish act of sin,
> Lets in defilement to the inward parts,
> The soul grows clotted by contagion,
> Imbodies and imbrutes, till she quite lose
> The divine property of her first being.

(Milton is in turn drawing on Plato.) For a modern treatment see C. S. Lewis's *Four Loves*, chs. 4 and 5.

7 *utrumque*: i.e. 'dilectio' and 'libido'.

14 *et tacebas*: cf. the closing lines of Browning's *Porphyria's Lover*, where he has just murdered his mistress:

> And all night long we have not stirred,
> And yet God has not said a word!

16 *sterilia*: because they produced only a barren harvest of sorrow.

8 *Conversion*

Here begins the climax of his conversion: the fruit in fact of years of thought and prayer, of hesitation and rebellion. Augustine's psychology of the will—*duae voluntates meae confligebant inter se*—recalls St. Paul's analysis in Rom. 7. 18 ff., and is much more subtle and convincing than the earlier simplification of Socrates: Virtue is knowledge.

COMMENTARY

Augustine knew where virtue lay for him, but he would not, or could not, bring himself to act. Cf. also Ovid (Medea is speaking): *video meliora proboque, deteriora sequor*.

3 *donec abrumperetur*: 'in the hope that it might be broken'.

9 *modo*: 'now'.

10 *faciebam*: cf. colloquial English, 'I almost made it'.

15–16 *deterius inolitum . . . melius insolitum*: an elaborate assonance, characteristic of Augustine at his most rhetorical. For *deterius inolitum* cf. Virgil, *Aeneid*, VI. 736–8.

20 *vanitantium*: an adaptation of the phrase in Eccles. 1. 2: 'Vanity of vanities . . .'. *vanitare* (LL) = 'to speak idly or falsely', then 'to praise falsely': hence Fr. *vanter* (boast), Engl. *vaunt*. Here perhaps 'the deceptions of self-deceivers'.

21 *succutiebant*: 'plucked softly'; cf. *subrideo*, 'smile'.

30 *transilire*: an allusion perhaps to Ps. 18. 29: 'By my God have I leapt over a wall'.

30–31 *consuetudo violenta*: 'the strong force of habit'.

35 *effunderem*: sc. my tears.

40 'gave rein to'. Virgil uses the same metaphor.

43 *usquequo*: 'how long?' He combines Ps. 6. 3 and Ps. 78. 5, 8 (79. 5, 8).

46 *quamdiu cras et cras*: a reminiscence of the satirist, Persius (A.D. 34–62). Cf.

> Tomorrow and tomorrow and tomorrow
> Creeps in this petty pace from day to day . . . (*Macbeth*).

51 *Tolle lege*: commentators have not been able to identify the game.

52 *utrumnam*: 'whether'.

57–59 *audieram . . . quod . . . admonitus fuerit*: reported statement: see LN 7e (i).

57 *de Antonio*: St. Antony of Egypt (*c.* 251–356) retired into the desert to become a hermit, and there attracted so many disciples that he exercised great influence on the early development of monasticism. This practice of opening some book of the Bible at random, and

treating as an oracle the first passage that met one's eye, has a long history. It was applied also to Virgil, who throughout the Middle Ages enjoyed a halo of Christian sanctity: e.g. Charles I consulted the 'sortes Vergilianae' in the Bodleian Library at Oxford, and drew verses prophesying his destruction and death.

59 ff. Matt. 19. 21.

63 *codicem apostoli*: i.e. St. Paul's Epistle(s). The passage is Rom. 13. 13–14.

65 *capitulum*: 'chapter, section, or verse' (LL) (for later meanings, see note on No. **14**, l. 28).

9 *Looking Back*

A remarkable passage—one of the many asides where Augustine turns to his Creator with a fresh outburst of gratitude. Not merely do 'the deaf hear and the blind see', but he represents God's mastery over him metaphorically in terms of all the five senses. *vocasti et clamasti et rupisti*: a rhetorical figure of speech known as the tricolon— a device used consciously or unconsciously to heighten the emotion as well as build up the meaning. Cf. Lincoln's speech at Gettysburg: 'But in a larger sense, we cannot dedicate, we cannot consecrate, we cannot hallow this ground' (the threefold repetition there is entirely emotional).

8 *gustavi*: Ps. 33. 9 (34. 8): 'O taste and see . . . '.

8–9 *exarsi in pacem*: 'I burned to possess'.

10 The Rule *of St. Benedict: from the Prologue*

The Rule contains seventy-three chapters of varying length, and is divided into daily portions for reading aloud in such a way that the whole Rule is read three times in the year. (A long chapter may be spread over six days: ch. 34, on the Cellarer, given here in full, is spread over two days.)

1 *Dominici*: from this adj. comes *dies Dominica*: It. *domenica*, Fr. *dimanche*.

processerit: 'emerges, proves to be'.

5-6 *non . . . refugias*: 'you should not . . .' jussive subj. *Non*: see LN 7d (ii). *angusto*: Matt. 7. 13: *Intrate per angustam portam*.

7 *conversationis*: something of a technical term, occurring ten times in the Rule, and combining the two meanings of conversion, and the religious (i.e. monastic) way of life. In the latter sense, but without the monastic overtones which dominate it in ML, it was retained by the AV, e.g. 'our conversation is in heaven' (Phil. 3. 20).

8 *dilatato corde*: met., 'swelling with joy': an echo of Ps. 118. 32 (119. 32): *viam mandatorum tuorum cucurri, cum dilatasti cor meum*.

11 *The Abbot*

As his name implies, the abbot (Heb. *Abba* = father) is the head of the community and claims their absolute obedience, since he represents Christ to them. St. Benedict devotes a long chapter to him (ch. 2) besides this shorter one, emphasizing equally his powers and responsibilities, since he will have to answer for his monks at the Day of Judgement. He was normally elected by the community, and for life, though at certain times and in certain areas in the Middle Ages he might be imposed by king or noble, or be himself the secular landowner-protector of the monastery. (Three notable portraits of abbots emerge in this book: that of St. Anselm (see Nos. **13, 14, 15, 41**), of Samson of Bury (see Nos. **37, 38**), and the self-portrait of St. Bernard (see Nos. **16, 17, 24**).

2 *suscepit*: indic. in reported question: LN 7e (ii).

2 Luke 16. 2. A *villicus* was steward or bailiff of a 'villa', which might range from a small farm to a large estate.

3 *prodesse . . . praeesse*: a favourite antithesis of St. Augustine.

4 *doctum lege divina*, etc.: Matt. 13. 52: 'so that he may have a treasure of knowledge . . .' (McCann).

6 *superexaltet . . .* adapted from Jas. 2. 13.

7 An important principle: hate the sin, but love the sinner.

8-9 *ne quid nimis*: a proverbial expression going back to early Greece ($\mu\eta\delta\grave{\epsilon}\nu$ $\ddot{\alpha}\gamma\alpha\nu$), and introduced into Latin as early as Terence (d. 159 B.C.).

10 *suspectus sit*: trans., probably due to confusion with *suspicor* (dep.).

11 *calamum*: quoted in Matt. 12. 20 from Isa. 42. 3.

COMMENTARY 175

13 *amputet*: tech. term—'prune, lop off'.

15f. *turbulentus*: 'restless'; *nimius*: 'overbearing'; *zelotypus* (Gk.): 'jealous'.

18 *opera* (1 fem.): normally 'effort, exertion', used concretely for 'task'.

19 *discernat* (and *discretio* below) implies good judgement—i.e. prudence, one of the four cardinal virtues of Gk. philosophy.

20 *si greges* . . . Gen. 33. 13.

23 *ut sit* . . . 'so that there may be something for . . . to long for . . .'; generic subj.

25 *dum*+fut. perf. for *cum*: see LN 7e (v). *quod*: relative (sc. *audivit*).

27-28 Matt. 24. 45-47.

12 *The Cellarer*

The cellarer is the only official St. Benedict recognizes, after the abbot and prior. He had complete control of all the material resources of the community. In later centuries, when monasteries grew to be rich and powerful corporations, his responsibilities were divided among a number of officials, or 'obedientiaries' (see n. on No. **37**, l. 17), while he himself had sub-cellarers to assist him; but he remained an important figure, on whose sound administration the prosperity of the house depended. (For a portrait of a cellarer, see St. Bernard's lament on the death of his brother, Gerard: No. **24**.)

2 *sobrius* . . . *edax*: since he would have access to all the monastic stores.

5 *sine iussionem*: see LN 7a.

10f. *memor* (adj.) is treated as an active pres. participle and governs acc. *quia*: introduces a reported statement. 1 Tim. 3. 13: 'Those who serve well (as deacons) gain a good standing for themselves'.

12 These responsibilities were later taken over by the Infirmarer, the Magister Scholae, the Guestmaster, and Almoner. *infantum*: children 'offered' (*oblati*) to the monastery in their tender years, to be brought up as monks. Bede was so offered at the age of seven, as was Eadmer, the biographer of Anselm. For Anselm's comments on their education, see No. **41**.

13 *sciens* . . . *quia* . . . reported statement.

15 *ac si*: sc. *essent*: 'as if they were . . .'.   *conspiciat*: 'look on, regard'.

17 *stirpator* = *exstirpator* (LL): 'waster'.   *mensurate*: adv. 'with measure' (LL).

20 *cui*: refers to the cellarer: 'if he has nothing else to offer'.

21 *sermo bonus* . . . Ecclus. 18. 17 (Apocrypha).

23 f. *a quibus* . . . *compressed*: 'let him not presume (to deal with matters . . .)'.

25 f. *annonam*: came to be used for supplies in general, (soldiers') rations.   *aliquo* for *ullo*: see LN 7*b*.   *typho* (Gk.): 'conceit', 'pride'. *scandalizentur* (Gk.): used in Septuagint and NT: lit. 'cause to stumble'; so 'give offence to'.

26–27 Matt. 18. 6.   28 *solatia*: 'aids', i.e. assistants: sub-cellarers.

29 ff. The pattern of monastic life is to be an orderly and peaceful one at all times.

31 *ut nemo*: for CL *ne quis*: see LN 7*d* (ii).

13 *Faith seeks Understanding*

The (Greek) title *Proslogion* means an address (to God), as contrasted with his *Monologion*, or Soliloquy. The central idea, and the original title, is *Fides quaerens intellectum*. The opening chapter serves as prelude to the argument (there are twenty-six chapters in all). The style is Augustinian in both form and spirit; in, for example, the whole conception of a dialogue with God; in his dramatic use of questions (Augustine has fifteen in the first two chapters of the *Confessions*); in the repetition of keywords and ideas; and in his exploitation of two favourite devices, antithesis and assonance. Latin, with its compound verbs, such as *spero—despero*, *aspiro—respiro—suspiro*, lends itself readily to the latter. They may be decried as verbal jingles, but they are at once antithetical and a musical device, and as such found a home in medieval Latin verse.

The background of the argument here—the shattering consequences for human nature of Adam's Fall—is set out in full in Augustine's *De Civitate Dei*, XIII. 13 ff., and XIV.

The opening paragraph consists of ten appeals, leading up to the climax of a double assertion.

COMMENTARY

1 *homuncio*: for diminutives see LN 4. Here pity seems to be uppermost. Cf. G. M. Hopkins: 'Soul, self; come, poor Jackself...'.

4 *vaca*: + dat., 'have leisure for, devote yourself to'.

5 *intra*... an adaptation of Matt. 6. 6.   6 *iuvent*: generic subj.

8-9 An adaptation of Ps. 26. 8 (27. 8).

11 *quaerat ... inveniat*: indirect delib. subj.

14 *lucem inaccessibilem*: 1 Tim. 6. 16.

17 *qua facie*: 'by what features (shall I recognize you)?'

20 *exsul*: since the Fall all men are exiles from Paradise, and to a real extent from God. The notion is developed below.

26 *refecisti*: the only hint in this ch. of the Redemption.

27-28 *ad te ... factus sum*: cf. Augustine, *Confessions*, I. 1: *Fecisti nos ad te. feci ... factus sum*: 'I have not done what I was made for': cf. Fulke Greville:

> O wearisome condition of humanity!
> Born under one law, to another bound.

38 *quo ... careremus*: sc. *id* as antecedent of *quo*: 'what was to prove so grievous a loss to us'.

41 *unde ... quo*: supply suitable nouns; e.g., 'from what (bliss) ... into what (a bleak world)'.   *quo obruti*: instrumental abl.

47-48 Ps. 6. 4 (6. 3), followed by Ps. 12. 1 (13. 1).

56-57 *amaricatum ... indulca*: 'made bitter ... sweeten' (LL).

61-62 *vel ... vel*: 'even' (CL), not 'either ... or'.

63-64 *doceas ... ostendas*: suggested humbly as a faint possibility; so pres. subj.

64-66 *quaeram te desiderando*, etc. Cf. *Confessions*, I. 1: 'quaeram te, domine, invocans te et invocem te credens in te'.

69 *abolita ... offuscata fumo*: the first metaphor is that of the image on a coin being gradually worn away; the second, where it is clouded over, is probably suggested by Augustine (see No. 7, l. 5).

72-73 *nullatenus ... aliquatenus*: 'in no wise ... in some measure'.

178   COMMENTARY

75 *credo, ut intelligam*: an echo and adaptation of Augustine's *credite, ut intelligatis*.

14 *Monastic Life under Difficulties*

Eadmer's *Life of Anselm* is 'the first intimate portrait of a saint in our history, by an observant pupil and an ardent disciple' (R. W. Southern). (For his edition of the Life, see the Bibliography. Suggestions adopted from his translation are marked R. W. S.) For a short note on Eadmer, see introduction to Part Three.

4 *in prioratu . . . positus*: 'in his position as prior and abbot' (of Bec).

5 *iocunde*: LL form of *iucunde*.   *solebat*, etc.: indic. in reported questions, although subj. is used in the sentence above.

7 *suae*: his (Anselm's) reward: cf. ll. 13–14, 'to the loss of his own reward'. St. Benedict laid immense emphasis on the responsibility of the abbot for his flock.

11 *proximo*: 'his neighbour' (Vulg.).

12 *adeo* intensifies *quemquam . . . velle*: 'nor indeed . . .'.

15 *suorum hominum*: the tenants on his manors.

17–18 *circumquaque detonantes*: 'thundering all round him'.

24–25 *salva . . . innocentia*: abl. absolute.   *omnibus*: neuter.

27 *institutio vitae*: 'their rule of life'.

28 *quod*: object of *innotuit* (trans. in LL): 'he made this plain'.   *quadam vice*: 'once', 'on one occasion' (LL).   *capitulo*: an important word with three basic meanings:

1. A 'little chapter': i.e. a few lines from the Scriptures or (in monasteries) the Rule, which were read each morning after Prime to the assembled monks, after which they proceeded to discuss the business of the day;

2. The assembly of monks (or cathedral clergy) to hear this read: the 'Chapter'—as here;

3. The place where they assembled: the Chapter-house, normally opening off the cloister, where the business of the community as a whole was conducted.

29 *de huiusmodi*: sc. *rebus*.   34 *sibi* for *ei*: see LN 7*b*.

37 *saeculares*: 'men of the world'.   38 *causarum*: 'legal disputes'.

40-41 *meum huiuscemodi esse*: 'my being in this state'; subject of *procreet*. For the ML treatment of the infinitive, see LN 7*d* (vi).

41-42 *ad quod verbum*: 'at these words', 'when he reached this point'.

42 *licet . . . coeperit*: 'although . . .'.

43-44 Job 19. 21.   45 *conversatione*: 'companionship' (R. W. S.).

45-46 a play on the two compounds: *respirabat . . . suspirabat*.

48-49 *loco pueri*: 'as a boy'.

51 *cathedrae*: 'the bishop's throne': hence *ecclesia cathedralis*—'cathedral'.

52-54 Ps. 132. 1 (133. 1): 'Behold how good and how pleasant it is for brethren to dwell together in unity!'

54-55 *esset . . . reputaret*: imperfect for pluperfect subj. (so also below).

55 ff. The archbishop's manors were widely scattered over Kent, Sussex, and East Anglia. *pro more terrae*: 'the customs of England'.

61 *oppido*: 'to the town'.   62 *praepositis*: 'his reeves'.

63 *quem interpellarent*: dependent delib. subj., 'none to appeal to'.

67 *iis duntaxat exceptis*: 'apart of course from those . . .'.

70 *siquidem*: 'indeed'; see LN 7*e* (vii).   *involutos . . . evolvi*: 'entangled . . . disentangle'.

72-73 *morum discretione*: i.e. distinguishing (and so solving) some moral problem.

74-75 *datis (eis) quibus opus habebant*: *quibus* (abl.) gov. by *opus*: 'what they needed'. (*opus habeo* v. rare.)

77 *quosque* for CL *quoslibet*.   *ea . . . ea*: abl. (the former governed by *indigentes*, the latter instrumental).

78 *pro posse*: see LN 7*d* (vi).

15 *St. Anselm and the Hare*

1-2 *Heisam*: Hayes near Windsor. *villam*: 'manor'. *pueri quos nutriebat*: not the schoolboys of No. **41**, who were the *oblati* of a monastery, but those of his household. As a feudal lord of high standing he had a considerable retinue. (As late as 1490 Thomas More at the age of 12 was put by his father into the household of Archbishop Morton for two years as a page, to learn good manners.)

4 *quem ... sedebat*: used transitively.

5 *sibi sub se*: *sibi* refers to *bestiam*, *se* to the archbishop.

8 *haud grato obsequio*: 'restrained against their will' (R. W. S.).

9 *in aliquo*: for CL *ullo modo*: see LN 7*b*.

10 *sumus*: shows that Eadmer was there.

11 *quasi pro capta*: 'thinking it was as good as caught'.

12 *laetitiae frena relaxare*: 'giving their delight free rein'.

15 *Hoc plane est*: 'It is just the same for...'.

16 *inimici sui*, etc.: these devils can be seen in many medieval sculptures trying to drag souls down to Hell.

18 *assunt = adsunt*.

25 *persequi ... interdicens*: indirect command. See LN 7*e* (iii).

16 *Come to Clairvaux!*

Henry Murdac (d. 1153) was a native of the north of England who at the time of this letter (*c.* 1125) held preferment under Thurstan, archbishop of York, and was a teacher of repute. He had evidently written to Bernard, laying bare his own uncertainties, prompted perhaps by the departure of two of his own pupils to Clairvaux. He himself answered the summons ... and in 1143 was sent back by Bernard for election as abbot of Fountains, founded ten years earlier. 'The new abbot was by temperament a consuming fire, and temperament and circumstances alike were to stimulate his combative spirit in Yorkshire.' Four years later William, archbishop of York, was deposed by Eugenius III, Murdac's fellow monk at Clairvaux, and Murdac was elected in his place. (For the full story, see Knowles, *Monastic Order*, pp. 239, 255-7, and *DNB*.)

Apart from direct quotations Bernard's letters echo the Scriptures at every turn, adapting phrases to his purpose, and converting the future of OT prophecy into its present fulfilment in Clairvaux.

2 *supra petram*: Ps. 39. 3 (40. 2).   3 *quid horum*: Rom. 8. 35.

COMMENTARY 181

4 *et* (*quid dicam*): *et* throws the clause into relief: 'if only . . .'.

5 *oculus . . . non vidit*: Isa. 64. 4, quoted by St. Paul, 1 Cor. 2. 9. (Bernard, quoting from memory, combines the two.)

7 *putas . . . intelligis*: Acts 8. 30. Colloquial Latin, cf. No. **8**, l. 31.

8 *propheticae lectionis*: picks up *legis* above. *lectio*: 'reading' (CL) later extends to 'writings' or 'text' (as here), a 'lesson' from Scripture, lecture, etc. ('Lecture' appears to be the meaning in l. 38.)

10 i.e. 'why look for words (in the OT) in the presence of the Word?' (John 1. 14).

11–12 *de latibulo Prophetarum*: i.e. from the obscurities of the Prophets to the clear vision of the Apostles (*Piscatorum*).

13 *de monte . . . condenso*: 'thickly wooded'. *sponsus* . . . Ps. 18. 6 (19. 5).

15 *aures audiendi*: gerund: 'ears to hear': Matt. 11. 15.

16 *qui sitit*: John 7. 37. 16–17 *venite . . . vos*: Matt. 11. 28.

19 *tenebrosa aqua* . . . Ps. 17. 12 (18. 11) i.e. 'Murdac's book-learning contrasted with supernatural enlightenment' (Knowles).

20 *haurias*: potential subj.

22 ff. *de adipe frumenti*: Ps. 80. 17 (81. 16). Jerusalem represents the Church in general, but Bernard claims it in particular for Clairvaux (see *Ep*. 64). Murdac was gnawing the dry crusts of the OT, in comparison with the NT; or (additionally) 'the dry outer crust of Scripture, in the company of "lettered" (i.e. literally-minded) Jews; the monks of Clairvaux were filled with the fat of its inner spiritual meaning as they listened to their abbot preaching. *Lectio divina* in the Cistercian sense, i.e. the Scripture lived and experienced as well as read, is contrasted with the intellectual study of Scripture in the schools' (B. Smalley, *The Study of the Bible in the Middle Ages*, p. 173 and n. 4).

23 *suas* refers to *litteratoribus*. *litterator*, 'teacher', can be used contemptuously as 'dabbler', 'hack'.

25 An allusion to Murdac's school, where he was *magister*.

27 *pectoris vasculum*: 'the vessel of your heart'. *unctioni*: oil had great importance for the Jews, for practical purposes, as a symbol of richness

COMMENTARY

and gladness ('oil of joy'), and for the anointing and consecration of priests and kings: a symbolism taken over by the Church in christening, ordination, and the coronation of kings. (Keep 'unction', used metaphorically here of the Holy Spirit.)

28 *calidos panes*: a verb is understood from *supponere* above: 'How gladly would I set before you'.

30–31 *suis pauperibus*: describes literally the poverty and simplicity of early Cistercians.   *quos . . . Christus frangit*: echoes Luke 24. 35; *cognoverunt eum in fractione panis*.

32 ff. 'B. was not a nature-mystic, nor does he refer to "sermons in stones"—the simpler truer thoughts to which natural beauty gives rise—but to the Spirit of God who will instruct the soul in solitude and desert places' (Knowles).

34–35 *mel de petra, oleumque . . .* Deut. 32. 13. (The Promised Land of the Jews is seen as forerunner and symbol of the Church by St. Paul and the Fathers.)

35 ff. Joel 3. 18 and Amos 9. 13: *in die illa stillabunt montes*—a prophecy now fulfilled at Clairvaux. The *colles* and *valles*, besides their scriptural background, may suggest to him those of Burgundy, and many Cistercian sites—e.g. Rievaulx in Yorkshire.

40 i.e. two former pupils at York. This William is possibly to be identified with William, first abbot of Rievaulx, founded 1132. *idipsum*: sc. some verb; e.g. *orant*.

41 *quod . . . scitis*: *quod* introduces reported statement: sc. *desideramus* (from *desideremus*) 'you know *that* we long to see you, and why . . .'.

64 *vel*: contrasts *sequi* with *praeisse*: 'at any rate'.

17 *Jerusalem Found*

Nothing more is known about Philip, a prebendary of Lincoln, who on his way to Jerusalem as a pilgrim called at Clairvaux, and found there all he was looking for. Alexander 'the Magnificent' (d. 1148) was a considerable figure. Norman by birth, and nephew of the great Roger, bishop of Salisbury and Henry I's chief minister, he quickly rose to high place as bishop of Lincoln (1124); a great feudal lord, building castles as well as monasteries, and vaulting his own cathedral

COMMENTARY 183

in stone. Involved in the troubles of Stephen's reign (1135–54), he was imprisoned and deprived of his castles; but he came to terms with Stephen and managed to die in his bed.

1 *Ierosolymam*: sc. as a pilgrim; but Bernard immediately takes it in a metaphorical sense as Clairvaux (see introduction to Part One, and n. on l. 18 below). From l. 6 ff. the Vulgate form *Ierusalem* is used.

3 *hoc mare magnum*: 'the sea of this world': a familiar metaphor from Augustine onwards. Cf. No. **18,** l. 35 'mare enim saeculum est; naves, ecclesiae'.

5 *Stantes sunt*: adapted from Ps. 121. 2 (122. 2), one of the pilgrim songs sung by the Jews on their way to Jerusalem for one of the great feasts. (For *stantes sunt* see LN 7*d* (v).)

6 ff. Ps. 131 (132). 6, 7. The original refers to the Ark. Bernard, by substituting a masc. pronoun (*quem*) for the fem. of the original, converts the reference to Christ, and the *campis silvae* to the woods round Clairvaux.

8 *sanctam civitatem*: i.e. the heavenly Jerusalem: Rev. 21. 2, 10.

9–10 f. Eph. 2. 19.

12 *conversatio*: Phil. 3. 20. AV keeps 'conversation' to represent 'our (Christian) way of life'; but the Gk. original is 'citizenship', an idea which fits the context closely. (See n. on No. **10,** l. 7.)

15 ff. Gal. 4. 25, 26.

18 ff. While the 'Jerusalem that is above' is only to be reached in heaven, yet it has its forerunner here in the Church in general, and more particularly in Clairvaux, which has turned away from the admixture of worldliness which disfigures the Church. (Take *ei . . . sociata* together.)

20–22 Ps. 131 (132). 14, 13—once again adapted to suit Philip.

23 *visio . . . expectatio*: 'Jerusalem', (Hebrew) 'abode of peace', has an alternative trans. 'vision of peace', used from Augustine onwards of the Church in heaven. (See *MLV*, note on No. **63.**)

26 *beneplacito*: 'good pleasure' (EL).

27–28 Prov. 10. 1. *quod . . . sit*: reported statement.

28 *paternitatem*: 'your fatherly goodness'. Abstract nouns came to be used for dignitaries, and have persisted into modern English: 'your worship', 'your grace', etc.

29 *quatenus*: introduces reported command.

30 *praebenda*: the share of cathedral revenues to which a member of the chapter was entitled, the holder being called a 'prebendary'. (Philip has perhaps raised a loan on his future revenues in order to pay the expenses of his pilgrimage.)   *quod . . . constituit*: 'the arrangements he has made'.

32 *praevaricator pacti*: 'one who breaks his word': an EL extension of CL usage.

33 *munus contriti cordis*: combines Matt. 5. 24 and Ps. 50. 19 (51. 17).

38 ff. The last paragraph gives one some idea of the personal fearlessness of Bernard, and the immense moral authority he claimed—and was accorded—in western Christendom. The same uncompromising spirit is seen in his *De Consideratione*.

38–39 Cf. Acts 15. 28.   *intimante*: 'make known' (LL).

40 *praesumentes*: 'venture' (LL).

42 *pro vobis*: 'instead of' (or 'for your own sake').

43 ff. *ne blandiens*, etc.: the remaining clauses may be final, but are more probably still reported commands: 'not to allow', etc.

47 *praeoccupet*: Wisd. of Sol. 4. 7 (relegated to Apocrypha in AV, but much studied and quoted in the Middle Ages).   *improvidum*: masc., and active in force.

48–50 *pax*, etc.: 1 Thess. 5. 3.

18 *Your Greatness*

2 *personam*: 'what part you play': originally a mask worn by actors, then character in a play, etc.

3 *sacerdos* and *pontifex* are largely interchangeable, but *pontifex* is used for 'the chief priests' in NT, and was, broadly speaking, annexed by the popes as 'chief pontiff'.

3 ff. Eleven titles in ascending order. All bishops were 'heirs of the apostles', but Rome as the see of Peter claimed in a special sense the title of *sedes apostolica*; and bishops visiting Rome were said to come *ad limina apostolorum*. (The plural includes St. Paul, claimed by Rome as their second founder.) 'In your primacy you are (a second) Abel',

COMMENTARY

etc.: i.e. the pope recapitulates in himself some of the type-figures of the OT. (For 'types' see introduction to Part One: The Bible.) Abel was the first shepherd (Gen. 4. 21), Aaron the first priest, Moses the law-giver, Samuel the last of the 'judges' and 'a second Moses'. *gubernatu*: 'in steersmanship you are Noah': the word is skilfully chosen for its literal and metaphorical sense. The latter ('government') common in CL: e.g. *rempublicam gubernari*.

5 *patriarchatu* (Gk.): 'in fatherhood you are Abraham', father of the Chosen People, who were themselves a 'type' of the Church.   *ordine M.*: Ps. 109. 4 (110. 4): 'in priesthood you are Melchisedech': a shadowy figure in OT as priest-king; but used in Heb. 5–7 as forerunner and 'type' of Christ as priest-king.

7 *potestate*: 'in authority'.   *plenitudo potestatis* (see below, l. 22) was a technical phrase for papal supremacy.

unctione Christus: all bishops and kings were anointed (a rite taken over from the OT); but the pope is the personal representative of *Christus* (Gk.), 'the anointed One'. Innocent III was the first to use the title 'Vicar of Christ', but the idea itself is earlier.

7–8 *claves traditae*: Matt. 16. 19.   *oves*: John 21. 15–17.

12 *uni unus*: 'one flock to one shepherd'.

15 *totae*: 'all' (moving towards Romance languages where it replaces *omnes*).

18 *certi regni*: 'some particular kingdom'.

19–20 'There is no exception where there is no distinction'.

21 *canones tuos*: 'the laws defining your position'. *Canon* (Gk.), 'rule' or 'law', was adopted as an ecclesiastical term, with many related uses. Bernard goes on to stress the distinction between the pope and his fellow bishops.

26 *tradere satanae*: a power claimed by St. Paul in 1 Cor. 5. 5 and 1 Tim. 1. 20.

28 ff. A typical allegorical interpretation, such as the Fathers and Bernard, 'the last of the Fathers', loved, seeing a hidden meaning in almost any incident in the Scriptures.

29 *praerogativam*: 'privilege'.

36-37 *ecclesiae*: probably refers to the regional churches which soon developed in Africa, Gaul, etc., each with their own metropolitan and their particular traditions, and which asserted their independence even more strongly in the Middle Ages. (Bede speaks of the *sancta ecclesia gentis Anglorum*).

19 *Your Wretchedness*

3 *haec perizomata* (Gk. n. pl. 'girdle') from Gen. 3. 7; 'Away then with this "apron", inherited (from our father, Adam) and accursed . . .', i.e. realize that you are a fallen man, naked and ashamed. Cf. Lear, speaking to Edgar (Act III, Scene iv): 'Unaccommodated man is no more but such a bare forked animal as thou art. Off, off, you lendings! Come; unbutton here'.

5 *fucus*: 'disguise'.   *male coloratae*: 'tarnished, sham'.

8 *Numquid infulatus?* 'Were you born wearing the tiara . . . or bright with silks, or decked with plumes [possibly the ostrich-feather fans carried by papal attendants], or loaded with gold and silver?'

10 *nubes matutinas*: Hos. 6. 4; 13. 3.

12 *exsuffles*: 'puff away'. The present subj. suggests how hard it is for a pope to discount the pomp which surrounds him.

13 Rev. 3. 17.   15–17 Job 5. 7; 14. 1.

19 *Quid vacat*: 'what is missing for one born . . .'.   *calamitate*: abl. of respect.

20-21 *vere repletus*: 'your cup of wretchedness is indeed full, when to weakness of body . . . is added the inheritance (*tradux*) of original sin and subjection to death'.

22 *salubris copula*: 'it is good to link these two together . . .'.

24-25 'Take a lesson from nature; and, better still, from the author of nature'.

27 *spiraculum*: 'breath' (EL).

28 i.e. 'the word was made flesh' (John 1. 14).

29-30 *tam . . . quam*: i.e. remember your double origin, at once fallen and redeemed.

31 Rom. 12. 16; but Bernard improves on this by adding the middle phrase *humilia de te sentiens*.

20 *Your Perils*

2–3 Matt. 6. 34: ' "Sufficient unto the day is the evil thereof." Would that it were so! But even your nights . . .'.

4–6 *pausationi*: 'pause, respite' (LL). *sufficiat*: generic subj. *dies . . . malitiam*: an adaptation of Ps. 18. 3 (19. 2): 'Day unto day uttereth speech, and night unto night showeth knowledge.'

6–7 *usque . . . non est*: 'so impossible is it'. *bonis*: neut. 'among virtuous occupations'; as, for example, Gregory the Great amidst his unceasing labours yet worked on his commentary on Ezekiel.

7 *vel rara*: 'even occasional . . .'.

10 *sic facias*: sc. *deplorare*. *nec . . . duraveris*: perf. subj. for prohibition.

11 *quolibet* for CL *ullo*. *Duritia*, a growing callousness, is what Bernard fears above all for him.

14 *nec*: 'not even', for *ne . . . quidem*, found in Livy and later writers.

16 *advocatorum*: these were lay 'protectors' of churches or monasteries —often powerful neighbours who exploited church property, and at times paid the sovereign for the privilege of 'defending' them, in spite of various attempts by Church Councils to check the abuse.

21 *instruunt*: sc. *eos* as antecedent of *a quibus*. There follows an elaborate play on *struo* and its compounds.

25 *non est . . . exhorreat*: 'there is no longer anything for her to shudder at'; *or* 'there is no longer any reason for her to shudder' (intr.).

26 *spelunca latronis*: Matt. 21. 13.

21 *Virtue and Vice*

5 *dicuntur . . . virtutes*: 'they are called virtues, because they are a kind of courage, taking up their stand . . .'; an allusion to Eph. 6. 13–14: 'Stand therefore . . .'.

11–12 *victoriam meritum . . . sequitur*: 'victory brings merit'. 'Merit' is a technical term—a credit balance (so to speak) with God, which in a certain sense 'earns' the reward He has promised, though the earning is itself made possible by the freely accepted gift of grace. This 'credit' could become an accumulated capital, built up by prayers and sacrifices on earth—and here monasteries played a vital part, both for the monks themselves and for mankind at large, and in particular for their founders, whose lives might otherwise be heavily 'in the red'. So the average man could hope to draw on this, along with the intercession of the saints in heaven, and his own efforts in carrying out the various 'works of mercy', in order to achieve, God willing, his final salvation.

22 *Avarice*

1 *de ordine nigro*: i.e. the Benedictines, commonly known as Black Monks, to distinguish them from the Cistercians with their white habits. Cf. Blackfriars (Dominicans), Greyfriars (Franciscans), etc.

4 *dispensatores*: sc. the Almoner and Guestmaster.

11 *dapsilis*: 'bountiful'.   14 *grandinata*: 'beaten down by hail'.

16 *pallians*: 'cloaking' (ML), from *pallium*.

21 *portarium*: masc. 'porter'.

22 *clanculo*: dim. of *clam*.   *collegit*: 'welcomed' (Fr. *accueillir*).

23 *pro posse*: 'as best he could': see LN 7*d* (vi).

27 *si venisset Episcopus*: 'even if . . .'. Bishops were generally unwelcome visitors, and monasteries struggled to be exempt from their control.

33–34 *cum esset laicus*: 'though he was a lay-brother' (and therefore illiterate). Lay-brothers did much of the farming and household chores, and often outnumbered the choir-monks in Cistercian houses.

23 *Simplicity*

5 *detractionis*: 'slander'; one of the three vices scourged in No. **70**.

10–11 Matt. 6. 22.   16–17 Matt. 10. 16.   19–20 Matt. 18. 3.

18 *propter vecordiam*: 'because of men's wickedness'.

24 *Wido*: Guido, Guy: cf. *Willelmus, Guillelmus*; *werra, guerra*.

25 *Coloniam* (Cologne, Köln): i.e. *Colonia Agrippinensis*, founded c. A.D. 50 as a settlement for veterans. Its archbishops were immensely powerful from the eleventh to the sixteenth century.

30 Luke 18. 4, the parable of the unjust judge, 'who neither feared God nor regarded man'. *eo quod* . . . there is no real ground for subj. here.

33 *dimisit*: 'left'.

34 *actitaret*: frequentative vbs. are common in VL: see LN 4.

36 *minari*: pass. infin. of ML *minare*: 'drive' (cattle, etc.) (Fr. *mener*); derived from CL *minari*: 'threaten'.

38 *quid facto opus esset*: 'on what must be done'.

39 *castrum*: 'castle'.

40 *merces*: 'his reward'—i.e. the penalty that awaited him.

42 *aërem . . . verberamus*: St. Paul's metaphor of the boxer who 'beats the air' (1 Cor. 9. 26).

42–43 The chief officials have now excused themselves. (For the Cellarer see No. **12**.)

47 *si . . . vellet*: reported question: see LN 7e (viii).

51 *accipias*: jussive subj., a polite form (CL): 'you should accept'.

54 *secundum Iob*: Job 12. 4–5 (English versions do not support this translation).

56 *parvipendens*: 'disregard': *parvi pendo* (gen. of value) became a single word in LL. *exspectate*: 2nd pl. came into use in ML as a polite form of address: cf. Nos. **16**, 40 ff., and **17**, throughout. (But *pransus fueritis*.)

65 *quia . . . manducaret*: reported statement dep. on *considerans*.

78 Job 8. 20: 'does not stretch out his hand to help the wicked, but rather to strike him'.

87 *accensa fuit*: double perfect: see LN 7d (iv).

COMMENTARY

24 *The Death of Gerard* (*1138*)

1 Bernard breaks off suddenly in the middle of his sermon-commentary: 'How long can I conceal my feelings, while . . .'.

3 *Quid mihi* . . . 'What have I to do with this song (of joy)?' The phrase occurs in John 2. 4 and in OT, a Hebraism literally translated into Greek, and thence into Latin.

6 *siquidem*: 'indeed'; see LN 7*e* (vii).

7 *utcumque*: 'in one way or another'.

13 *sacerdotalibus*: 'priestly vestments'.

16 *flerem*: subj. of virtual indirect statement, representing their thoughts.

22 ff. *addictione naturae*: 'the bondage of nature'; *addictus* is one who has been bound over by a judge as servant to his creditor. *universitatis*: 'all mankind'. *conditionis usu*: 'the common experience of our human condition' (Pliny speaks of *condicio mortalium*). The series builds up to a climax in *Domini voluntate*, with its echo of 'Fiat voluntas tua'.

25 *Exeat*: jussive subj., loosely dependent on *necesse est*.

27 *aestiment*: final subj., or perhaps potential. *humanius . . . dulcius*: 'with more kindness . . . gentleness'.

33–34 *frater . . . germanus* are identical in meaning, but the latter being an adj. can be compared. Cf. Terence: *Nunc tu mihi es germanus et corpore et animo.*

34–35 *dolete vicem meam*: 'on my behalf, for my sake' (CL).

38 *Quo*: 'why?' (CL).

41 *posset*: generic subj., 'such as only death . . .'.

47 *feriatus*: 'at leisure'; p.p. of *ferior*, from *feriae*.

50 *agentem*: intr. *manum, lumen*, etc., are in apposition to *te*.

52–53 *oculus simplex*: Matt. 6. 22. (For simplicity as a virtue, see No. **23**.)

57 Distinguish *expers* ('without part in') and *expertus* (*experior*).

58 ff. *Norunt* (contracted form of *noverunt*): 'those endowed with the spirit who knew him, know . . .'. The opposition between *spiritus* and *caro* is a favourite one with St. Paul; the latter representing ordinary

human nature, 'our lower nature'; so *non carnem saperent* (below): Rom. 8. 5. Cf. *Non sapis quae Dei sunt, sed quae sunt hominum* (Mark 8. 33): 'you think as men think, not as God thinks' (NEB). (For the adj. *carnalis*, see l. 77 below.)

57 *quam*: introduces an indirect question.

61–62 *castigando corpus*: mortification of the body by use of a scourge or hair-shirt was extensively practised. (Abbot Samson wore a hair-shirt after learning of the fall of Jerusalem in 1187: see No. **38**.) It derived to some extent from St. Paul, 1 Cor. 9. 27: *castigo corpus meum et in servitudinem redigo*.

62 *districtior*: 'more intent on'. *suspensior*: 'more lofty'.

66 *idipsum*: 'the self-same thing': a common ML compound.

67–68 *litterarum . . . sensum*: 'the understanding which finds out the meaning of . . .'.

73–74 'masons', 'smiths' . . . 'cobblers', 'weavers'. The passage gives one some idea of the immense range of problems involved in constructing a monastery in a remote countryside, and maintaining a community which might run into hundreds. (Rievaulx in Yorkshire within ten years of its foundation in 1131 housed some 300, and twenty years later, under Ailred, rose to 600.)

77 *carnalem*: 'carnal' (AV), 'unspiritual' (NEB), is St. Paul's term in Rom. 7 and 8 for unredeemed human nature. *Nam et ego . . .* Rom. 7. 14. *quis dixerit*: indef., 'someone may call me . . .'.

86 *id miraculi*: partitive gen., an extension of CL *id temporis, aetatis*, etc.

87–88 *ubi est . . . tuus?* 1 Cor. 15. 55. *stimulus*: 'sting'. *iubilus*: 'shout of joy'. CL *iubilum* is perhaps assimilated to *stimulus* to heighten the assonance.

90 *usurparis*: 'taken over', and so 'transformed into'. The whole sentence is highly rhetorical, with its parallel clauses, its rhyme, and its rhythm.

94 *larvalis effigies*: 'ghostly spectre'.

25 *The Day of Judgement*

The author is traditionally Thomas of Celano, an early Franciscan and the first biographer of St. Francis.

1 *dies irae, dies illa*: the opening line is taken verbatim from Zeph. 1. 15 ('That day is a day of wrath'), and at the same time supplies the rhythm for the whole poem: see Verse Notes, 4*b*.

2 *saeclum* for *saeculum*: 'the world' (EL).

3 *David*: e.g. Ps. 101. 27 (102. 26). *Sibylla*: the Christian writer, Lactantius (see No. **39**, l. 32 n.), quoting from Varro, enumerates ten Sibyls; and there was a Jewish-Christian collection of oracles ascribed to them as prophetesses. The Erythraean Sibyl was supposed to have foretold the end of all things. (The choir-stalls at Ulm (*c.* 1470) show eight Sibyls—among them the Cumaean Sibyl who led Virgil's Aeneas through the lower world—alongside prophets and heroines of the OT; and Michelangelo depicted them together with nine prophets on the ceiling of the Sistine chapel.)

13 *Liber scriptus*: the book of life (Rev. 20. 12).

37 sc. Mary Magdalene, traditionally identified with the woman in Luke 23. 40–43.

43–45 Matt. 25. 32 f.   47 *addictis* (abl.) agrees with *maledictis*.

26 *The World to Come*

Hildebert of Lavardin (1056–1133), 'recognized as the first man of letters of his age', studied at Le Mans, and after being head of the cathedral school, became bishop in 1096. He clashed with William Rufus, and was taken off to England for trial and only saved by the king's death, visited Rome, where he saw the ravages of German, Norman, and Saracen troops in support of a rival pope, and was inspired by all its rich associations, classical and Christian, to write his two Roman elegies (see *MLV*, No. 158). In 1125 he was elected archbishop of Tours against his will. He was equally at home in classical elegiacs and the new rhythmical and rhyming verse, but technical mastery takes second place to the deep feeling and personal experience they express. (See Raby, *Christian Latin Poetry*, pp. 265–72; and *Secular Latin Poetry*, vol. i, pp. 317–29.)

This is the second half of a long poem of 203 lines in the form of a prayer addressed to the Trinity. Lines 1–95 are devoted to a subtle exposition of the doctrine, followed by an affirmation of his own faith, and an appeal for mercy. The metre is trochaic (accentual) dimeters, with adisyllabic rhyme throughout—a *tour de force* when sustained for this length (see Verse Notes, 4*b*). N.B. the orthography of this version

COMMENTARY

conceals some of the medieval rhymes; e.g. ll. 1–2, 23–24, 39–40, 41–42.

1 *reus mortis*: sc. the 'guilt' of original sin, which weighed so heavily on many, in spite of the Redemption, and the various means of acquiring 'merit' (see n. on No. 21). Cf. Anselm, *Proslogion*, No. 13.

7 *cataplasma*: a compound of *plasma* (l. 8), a Gk. medical term, 'poultice, plaster': so 'by this sacred medicine (of faith) may your sick creature be healed'.

8 *plasma* (Gk. 3 n.) adopted in EL: 'something formed or moulded', e.g. the clay moulded by the potter (see Rom. 9. 18–21), and so 'a creature fashioned by God'.

9 See Luke 7. 12: 'behold, there was a dead man carried out . . .'. The dead were buried outside the city; so, for example, tombs line the Appian Way for miles outside Rome. From this incident ll. 10–16 move on to the raising of Lazarus (see John 11. 17–44).

11 *vitta*: 'graveclothes'. See Luke 8. 22–24.

25–32 The parable of the barren fig-tree (Luke 13. 6–9), combined with Matt. 3. 10.

34 *officinas*, lit. 'workshops', is used metaphorically in CL: e.g. *officina crudelitatis*, 'torture-chamber'.

40 Mark 9. 43–44.

42 *gehennae* (Heb.) is the Vulgate term trans. in English as 'hell'. (For its history, see *ODCC*.)

ll. 43 to the end are often printed as a separate extract (e.g. *MLV*, No. 159), but they gain immensely from the contrast with all that goes before.

47 i.e. Peter's power to bind and loose: Matt. 16. 19.

49 *lapis vivus*: see 1 Pet. 2. 4–5.

50 The parable of the marriage-feast: Matt. 22. 1–14.

51 'There shall be no night there': Rev. 22. 5.

54 *melos* (Gk.): 'song'.

58 Rom. 8. 29.

COMMENTARY

60 *super petram*: the Church built upon a rock (Matt. 16. 18) is the 'type' of the heavenly city.

68–69 Rev. 21. 19–20.   70 *norunt = noverunt*.

27 *The Conversion of Northumbria: Edwin*

1 *Quibus auditis*: Paulinus has just finished speaking. *se* belongs to *et velle et debere*, and *suscipere* depends on both. The king's Council (Witanagemot), consisting of fighting companions, chief retainers (thanes), and wise men (or 'aldermen'), was an important Germanic institution.

4 *conlaturum*: intr., 'confer'.   *cum illo* for *cum ipso*, or *secum*.

11 *ipsius* for *suorum*.   *Coifi* is nom. sing.

12 *Tu vide*: 'it is for you to examine'.

14 *profiteor quia*: reported statement: see LN 7*e* (i).

15 *huc-usque*: 'hitherto'.   *Nullus* for *nemo*. Coifi's argument is purely mercenary and shallow: 'What have I got out of it?' Cf. *sine fructu utilitatis* below, l. 44.

19–20 *agenda . . . disponunt*: 'arrange to do . . .'.

21 *impensius*: comp. adv., 'more zealously'.

27 ff. A highly involved sentence, which seems to have got out of hand, as fresh clauses and phrases were added. In outline it runs: Our present life, compared with the vast tracts of time unknown to us, is like the brief flight of a sparrow through a lighted hall on a winter's night. *pervolaverit* and *exierit* both depend on *cum* (the repeated *qui cum* seems to be equivalent to *atque*): the fut. perfs. suggest that the whole incident is over in a moment.

29 *caenam* for *cenam*: the vowel change is usually the other way round (e.g. *preceptum* for *praeceptum*); but cf. *caeteri*, *haereditarius*.

30 A central fire burnt in the hall and the smoke escaped through an opening in the roof. The practice continued till the late Middle Ages

42 *maiores natu*: 'aldermen'. Cf. *senatus*, *seigneur*, etc., and see note on *seniores*, No. **35**, l. 19.

44 *Adiecit . . . quia*: reported statement.

54 *ocius*: 'speedily'; comp. adv., often used with positive force. *anathemati*: (Gk. 3 n.) lit. 'a thing accursed', and then (as here) 'perdition': used in the NT, and so passed into EL, along with a new verb coined from it, *anathematizare*, 'to consign to Satan, curse'.

54–55 *con-tradamus*: strengthened form of *trado* 3. *Quid plura?* 'To cut a long story short': a standard CL formula.

55–56 *evangelizanti*: (Gk.) 'preach the gospel'.

59 *septis*: 'the sacred enclosure': perf. part. pass. of *saepio*.

60 ff. *Quis enim . . . destruam?* the 3rd sing. vb. is attracted into 1st sing. to agree with *ipse*. Potential subj.

63 *superstitione vanitatis*: 'vain superstition'.

64 *rogavit . . . dare*: reported command. *equum emissarium*: 'a stallion'.

65 *veniret*: final subj.

69–70 *Nec distulit . . . profanare*: 'did not hesitate to . . .'.

70 *mox ut*: 'as soon as'. *adpropiabat*: ML for *appropinquo*, 1.

72 *iussit sociis*: dative is classical, though accus. is normal usage.

76–77 The river Derwent. Goodmanham, *c*. 20 miles ESE. of York. The parish church is said to stand on the site of the pagan temple.

78 *quas . . . aras*: an echo of Virgil, *Aeneid*, II. 502. (Bede quotes *Aeneid* II again in Book III.)

28 *Oswin and Aidan*

The Irish Church of the sixth–seventh centuries was intensely monastic (on an earlier pattern than the Benedictine Rule), and intensely missionary. Besides the mission of Columba and his followers to Scotland, where they settled at Iona in 561, Columban (*c*. 550–615) went to Gaul in 590, where he founded the famous monastery of Luxeuil, then, when he was driven out, that of Bobbio in north Italy, where he died. Conversely, English and Frankish scholars made their way to Ireland as a home of religion and learning.

Aidan established himself at Lindisfarne, a small island off the coast of Northumberland: i.e. he rejected York, the Roman fortress-city, and chose an island-refuge, following the Celtic way of life: 'not a diocesan centre, but a secluded home of prayer'.

196   COMMENTARY

1 *Donaverat*: sc. Oswin. *antistiti*: CL 'chief priest', was taken over as 'bishop' alongside Gk. *episcopus*.

5 *elimosynam*: (Gk.) 'alms'.   6 *stratus*: 'saddled'.

11 *numquid* (LL) asks a question; *numquid non* = *nonne*.

13–14 *quamvis ... non dares*: 'though you should not have given'.

23 *postulans ut ... placatus esset*: 'begging his forgiveness'.

32 *lingua patria*: Aidan and his chaplain were 'Scots', i.e. Irish, who settled in such large numbers in south Scotland as to give their name to it. The natives were still known as *Picti*.

34 *victurus est*: from *vivo*.   40 *pridie ...* 31 August 651.

41 *saeculo*: (EL) 'this world'; see LN 5*b*. Hence 'secular' as opp. to 'regular' clergy, or 'religious'.

29 *The Synod of Whitby*

Notice how the king both convenes the Synod and settles the matter with unquestioned authority. (The authority of the lay ruler in spiritual, not to say temporal, matters will not go unchallenged in the 450 years between Gregory VII (1073–85) and the Reformation.) 'Synod' (Gk.), Lat. 'Council', was particularly used for ecclesiastical assemblies.

1 *praemissa praefatione*: 'opened the discussion by saying that (*quod*) ...' Everything down to *sequendam* depends on this, and *iussit* is the main vb.

7 *qui*: interrog. adj.

9 *Pascha*: (here neut., but sometimes 1 fem., or indecl.), Hebrew 'Passover', was taken over in Gk. NT and Vulg. to represent the Christian feast of 'Easter' (Fr. *Pâques*, etc.). 'Easter', according to Bede, derives from an AS spring goddess.

12 *cui*: indef. pron., after *ne*.   16–17 *proferre in medium*: 'declare'.

19 *vice mea*: 'in my stead'. Wilfrid has just been ordained by Agilbert.

20 *unum ... sapimus*: 'we are of one mind with the other upholders...', i.e. James and Romanus.

COMMENTARY 197

24 ff. *Pasca . . . celebrari*: acc. and infin., depending on *vidimus*. (This may be true of Wilfrid's experience; but in the fourth and fifth centuries there had been considerable divergences: see *ODCC*.)

32 *praeter hos tantum*: 'except for this handful of Irishmen'. *et his non totis*: the Roman usage had already been adopted in south Ireland. *totis*: for *omnibus* (ML; and hence in Romance languages).

42 *litteris sacris*: sc. the Scriptures.

44–45 *universali . . . ecclesiae*: dat. dependent on *praeferenda*.

47 *virtutibus*: 'mighty works, miracles' (see LN 5*b*).

49 *Tu es Petrus*: this, Wilfrid's proof-text, he cunningly reserves to the end as a knock-out blow.

56 *si*: introduces a direct question; see LN 7*e* (vii).

57 *consentiunt*: strictly speaking should be 2nd pl. *quod*, and *quia* (l. 60), introduce reported statements.

63 *non sit qui reserat*: 'there may be none to open'.

65 *quique*: *quisque* is regularly used in pl. in ML for *omnes*.

30 *William Rufus: The Siege of Mont-Saint-Michel, 1091*

2 *comite*: in ML normally 'count': see LN 5*b*. Here the duke of Normandy.

3 *magnanimitatis* in medieval chronicles generally implies valour, prowess, though it may include nobility of spirit (chivalry).

8 *feminibus*: normal abl. of *femur*.   9 *marcis*: see n. on No. 37, l. 4.

10 *fides loricae*: 'his trusty mail'. *miles*: 'knight'; see LN 5*b*.

13 *Tolle*: 'Unhand me': *tollere* sometimes = *liberare* in ML. An astonishing incident; but it was a family quarrel, and all were Normans—and to kill the king would have been a hideous crime.

16 *ascensorio*: 'someone to mount him'. *sonipedem*: 'steed': see No. 31, l. 27 n.

17 *perstringens*: 'sweeping them with his gaze'.

198 COMMENTARY

19 *non defuit* . . . 'spoke up in his own defence'. *qui non putarem*: causal subj.

21 *per vultum de Luca*: William's favourite oath, after a famous crucifix at Lucca in north Tuscany. *de*: see LN 7*a*.

22 *a modo*: 'from now on': see LN 7*c*. *albo*: 'my pay-roll'.

23 *Macte animi*: 'A noble gesture!' *Macte* is found in voc. only, with abl. or gen., e.g. *Macte virtute*: 'Well done!' *praeconium*: 'tribute'. The highest praise a medieval historian could bestow on a soldier was to compare him with Alexander or Caesar—and Rufus earns both from William of Malmesbury.

35–36 *praetendebant*: 'kept guard'.

38 *Belle scis*. . . .' you have a fine notion of how to . . .' (*scio*+infin., 'know how to' . . .). *actitare*: for frequentative vbs. see LN 4. *guerra*: see LN 5*c* (collateral forms *werra*, *warra* give Engl. war, Ger. *Wehr*).

42 *dimitterem*: delib. subj. (Henry showed himself more ruthless, though not without some humanity, when after defeating Robert in Normandy in 1106 he kept him prisoner till his death in 1134.)

31 *Back to Normandy, 1099*

The Norman kings had a passion for hunting and converted vast areas into royal forests.

3 *quadam silva*: Clarendon, near Salisbury, *c*. 35 miles from the coast.

5 *fratre profecto*: Robert had set out for the First Crusade in 1096, after pledging Normandy to William for 10,000 marks (wrung by William out of the English). For the mark, see n. on No. **37**, l. 4.

6 *expeditus*: 'just as he was', 'without his armour'.

10 *naufragio*: abl. '(even) at the risk of shipwreck'. *pene* = *paene*.

12 *flatus*: gen.

19 Count Helias had been captured in an ambush, and handed over to William.

20 *magister*: used contemptuously: 'My fine fellow'.

20–21 *alta nobilitas*: see note on l. 27. 21 *humilia sapere*: 'be humble-minded (EL): cf. No. **19**, l. 31, and n. on No. **24**, l. 58.

23 *facerem*: 'what I would do': potential subj., although at the same time a reported question. CL would have had *facturus fuerim*.

24 *obuncans*: 'digging his fingers into him'.

27 *pro . . . paciscar*: William is echoing Lucan, *Pharsalia*, II. 515, a highly rhetorical epic on the Civil War between Caesar and Pompey (49–48 B.C.). Caesar had captured an opposing general, but set him free as a proof of his clemency, with the words:

et nihil hac venia, si viceris ipse, paciscor.

Lucan was a favourite author in the Middle Ages, and William quotes him more than any other classical author but Virgil, or borrows his high-flown phrases: e.g. *sonipes, alta nobilitas, ponto, cornipes.*

30 *illiterato*: in spite of a slowly growing literacy among the laity this cleavage ran through society well into the fourteenth century.

34 *conscia virtus*: 'consciousness of his own valour'—a Virgilian phrase. Pythagoras, the Greek philosopher (sixth century B.C.), believed in the transmigration of souls from man to man, or from man to animals, and vice versa. He claimed to remember having taken part in the Trojan War as Euphorbus.

32 *His End, 1100*

4 Berkshire.   *villa*: village; Finchampstead.

11 f. *vidit . . . emittere*: 'he dreamt that he was being bled by a surgeon'. *phlebotomi* (Gk.): lit. 'vein-cutter'. Bleeding was one of the commonest forms of medical treatment both for sick and healthy down to the eighteenth century. It was thought to get rid of excessive 'humours', particularly in spring and autumn, and was a regular routine in monasteries, where monks were given three days off work—*licentia minucionis* (the modern blood-donor gets a cup of sweet tea).

12 *radium*: 'the gush'.   13–14 *interpolare*: 'shut out'.

16 *vigilatum*: sc. *est*: impers. pass., 'all lay awake'.

17 *Aurora*: another of William's poetic flights.

18–19 *filio Hamonis* becomes FitzHamon in Norman English.

20 *quod* introduces a reported statement, with three variations: indic. *venerat* (sc. *Willelmus*); subj. *corroserit*, etc., infin. *tolerasse*, etc.

COMMENTARY

22 *crucifixum*: Engl. 'crucifix' = the figure of Christ on the cross; Latin refers to the figure only; so in l. 24 trans. accordingly.

23 *mordicus*: adv. from *mordeo*: 'in his teeth'.

28 *a secretis*: practically a noun: 'confidential secretary'.

30 *monachiliter*: 'like a monk'. *centum solidos*: see n. on No. **36**, l. 9. A fantastic sum: meant ironically?

33 *suo dispendio*: abl. 'at his own expense', 'to his own cost'.

34–35 *seriis . . . eructuans*: 'finding vent for his ill-digested thoughts and unbridled mind in affairs of state'. *cruditatem*: 'indigestion', is used metaphorically by Augustine, but William stretches the metaphor to breaking-point. *eructuans* (EL): 'utter', 'express'.

42 *Phoebo*: i.e. the sun: a poetic phrase lifted out of its context: the sea is not visible from this part of the forest.

44 *diutile* (LL): 'for a little while'.

47 ff. *facinus . . . parturiens*: 'meditating a noble exploit'. *alias*: 'elsewhere' (normally 'at another time'). *propter*: adv. 'near by'. *impotens*: 'involuntarily'. The whole phrase adds up to 'all unwittingly'. Was it accidentally? Some modern historians suspect a conspiracy; but there is no conclusive evidence.

54 *hausit*: 'perceived', lit. 'drank in': poet., e.g. *auribus/oculis hausit*.

55 *probe evasit*: 'made good his escape'.

56 *coniventibus*: more correct spelling than Engl. 'connive': 'shut one's eyes to', 'wink at'.

68–69 *nonas . . . quarto*, for CL *a.d. quartum Nonas*, i.e. 2 August.

70–71 *si pensa . . . potuisset*: the three *Parcae* (Fates) were said to spin, to measure out, and finally to cut the thread of each man's life. So 'had he been able to live out his allotted span (*pensa*)'.

74 *Pictavis* (loc.): Poitiers, the capital of Poitou.

76 *invadaturus*: 'pledge' (as Duke Robert had already done); from *invădor* 1 (cf. *vadimonium*).

33 The Council of Clermont, November *1095*

3–4 *tam situ . . . nationibus* all qualify *segregata*: i.e. France as a geographical unity, and 'the eldest daughter of the Church'.

COMMENTARY

4 *Ecclesiae* might be either subjective or objective gen., i.e. 'the honour she pays to . . .' *or* 'in which she is held by . . .'.

8 *Iherosolimorum*: n. pl. There are many spellings of Jerusalem (see n. on p. 183. 1). Is this version due to a false analogy with ML *Ihesus*, which itself arose from a misunderstanding of the Gk. abbreviation IHS? (H = the long E of the Gk. alphabet.)

10–11 *gens regni Persarum*: sc. the Seljuk Turks.

12–13 Ps. 77. 8 (78. 8): 'whose heart was not steadfast, whose spirit was not faithful to God'.

17 *mancipaverit*: 'make over'. There follows a description of Turkish atrocities.

22 *verticem capilli*: Ps. 67. 22 (68. 21): 'the hairy scalp'.

25 Charlemagne (769–814), and Louis the Pious (814–40). The conversion of Germany under Boniface (*c*. 720–55) and his companions and successors went forward under the protection of the Frankish kings.

35 ff. Matt. 10. 37; 19. 29.

39 *protrahat*: 'hold back'.   41 *clausura*: abl. 'barrier' (CL).

42 *coangustatur*: 'is made yet smaller'.

44 *in invicem*: 'each other'; see LN 7*c*.   *totius* for CL *omnis*.

52 *umbilicus*: 'navel'. The same metaphor was applied earlier by the Greeks to their religious centre, Delphi.

55 *conversatione*: (EL) 'way of life' (see n. on No. **10**, l. 7).

58 *ancillatur*: 'is subjected to'.   *gentium*: in NT, 'Gentiles' (see LN 5*b*); then simply 'heathen'.

64 *immarcescibili*: 'unfading'.

65 *id genus*: acc., 'of this kind' (CL).

The following three passages (Nos. **34–36**) are from the *Gesta Francorum*. Notes marked (R. H.) are from the edition by Rosalind Hill; those marked (S. R.) are from Steven Runciman, *History of the Crusades* (see Bibliography). N.B. *e* for *ae* (see LN 5*a*): e.g. *prelium*, *merebat*.

34 *Bohemond takes the Cross*

1–2 *Malfi Scafardi Pontis*: Amalfi (S. P. to distinguish it from Melfi in Apulia), an important city south of Naples, rivalling Genoa and Pisa in its trade with the eastern Mediterranean from the ninth to the eleventh century. Nominally a vassal of Byzantium, it had been seized by the Normans, but was at this moment trying to break away.

4 *paganorum*: lit. 'inhabitants of country districts' (*pagi*); then, since the old superstitions lingered there, 'pagans' in Christian usage.

6 *ostensionem*: 'badge'. Take *Christi in via* together.

7 *signum*: 'battle-cry': object of *sonet*. Cf. *sonum*, l. 10.

14 *militum*: 'knights'—its normal meaning in ML. *Rogerius comes*: Roger, count of Sicily, Robert Guiscard's brother and Bohemond's uncle, had gradually wrested Sicily from the Arabs, and was by now the most powerful Norman in the Mediterranean.

16 *quandoque*: 'since'—but oddly constructed with acc. and infin. instead of a finite verb, as representing his thought.

17–18 *in terram suam*: i.e. Taranto (in southern Italy), an important city since Greek and Roman times; Italian naval base in the 1939–45 war.

18 *honestavit sese*: 'set his affairs in order', 'made all preparations' (ML).

20 Tancred, son of the Marquis, was Bohemond's nephew. (Six brothers had set out in 1040 from Normandy to win lands in Italy, and by now they were a powerful—and quarrelsome—clan.) For *Marchisus* see LN 5*c*.

21 Richard assumed the title of prince from Salerno, an old Lombard principality, taken by Robert Guiscard for his capital; seat of a famous medical school, tenth–thirteenth centuries, through which Greek and Arab medicine spread throughout Europe—and in September 1943 one of the two points at which the Allies invaded Italy.

22 ff. *Ansa* and *Canni* probably in south Italy (or Cannes in south France); Sourdeval in Normandy; Boel of Chartres; Aubrey of Cagnano; Humphrey of Monte Scaglioso (both in south Italy).

28 *Bulgaria* was then used for all the north Balkan peninsula.

30 *de Andronopoli*: see LN 7*a*.

31–32 *transfretassent*: subj. expresses their purpose in waiting.

33 ff. Bohemond was anxious to make a good impression; and the army was being provisioned by the emperor—but very shortly they were to begin helping themselves.

39 *Castoria* in west Macedonia, 100 miles or so from the Adriatic, with four-fifths of their march still to come. They reached Constantinople on 9 April 1097.

35 *The Battle of Dorylaeum, 1 July 1097*

1 *civitate*: Nicaea, in north-west Asia Minor.

4 *tenere*: 'they could not see to keep'; infin. used consecutively.

6 ff. Robert, duke of Normandy; Raymond, count of St. Gilles (and Provence); Godfrey of Bouillon; Adhémar, bishop of Le Puy; Hugh the Great, count of Vermandois, brother of the king of France; Robert, count of Flanders.

14 *diabolicum sonum*: probably 'Allah akbar': 'God is great' (R. H.).

18 *fuissent extensa*: for tense see LN 7*d* (iv).

19 *Seniores*: 'Gentlemen' (R. H.); an honourable term of address which has already lost its literal meaning and is on its way to the Romance languages; e.g. *seigneur, sieur* (Engl. sire), *monsieur, signore*, etc.

20 *ecce . . . angustum est*: 'you see what a tight corner we are in'.

22 *citius*: the comp. adv. from *cito* is often used with positive force.
tentoria: the tents were used to form some protection for their flanks, and provide cover for crossbowmen and non-combatants.

28 *Feminae nostrae*: Baldwin of Boulogne was accompanied by his wife and three young children, who probably all died during the crossing of the Taurus range—and he soon married an Armenian heiress. Raymond of St. Gilles brought his wife, and many lesser knights and soldiers must have done the same.

29 *in maximo refugio*: 'were a great support': represents CL predic. dative.

204 COMMENTARY

31 *pugnantes*: agrees with *illos*.

32 *mandavit*: 'sent a message'. The other body was most of a day's march behind them.

35 *quo*: final conj.   43 *pene = paene*.

45 *cooperta de*: see LN 7*a*. *excommunicata generatione*: 'accursed folk' (R. H.).

47 ff. *Estote ... eritis*: 'an interesting example of the way in which the Crusades combined genuine devotion with an eye to mundane advantage' (R. H.).

51 ff. *sapiens, prudens*, etc.: the conventional epithets are used as in Homer, and in the contemporary *Chanson de Roland*.

54 *montanam*: see LN 7*a*.

61 ff. *Agulani*: unknown. *Publicanorum*: 'heretics', deriving from the phrase 'publicans and sinners'. The numbers are unreliable.

69 *tota una die*: see LN 7*e* (viii).

36 *Antioch, June 1098*

1 *castello*: the strongly fortified citadel of Antioch.

2 *sagittando*, etc.: for this use of the gerund see LN 7*d*.

6 *prophani* for *profani*. Gk. *ph* tended to be confused with Latin *f*, and the latter was often substituted for it in the Romance languages (entirely so in Italian: e.g. *filosofia*). Here the reverse process has taken place.

9 ff. *bisantio*: 'bezant', a Byzantine gold or silver coin which circulated widely throughout Europe. *solidis ... denario*: 'shillings ... pence' (cf. £ *s. d.*). The *denarius*, or silver penny, was the basic coin of much of the Middle Ages, issued by kings, nobles, bishops, and cities all over Europe. Its value varied greatly, depending on the weight and purity of the silver, and the circumstances of the moment, but various indications exist: e.g. 'In England *c.* 1136 the allowance for a man's daily ration of food in the king's household seems to have been three halfpence' (R. H.). The *solidus* represented twelve pence.

12 *unam ... uno*: have become indef. articles: see LN 7*b*.

COMMENTARY 205

14 *manducabant*: largely replaced *edo* (hence Fr. *manger*, etc.).

16 *bufalorum*: this is the Indian, or water, buffalo, which had long been domesticated and introduced into the Near East and Mediterranean lands as a farm and draught animal.

19 *deliberanda*: 'deliver'. This compound of *libero* is not found in CL, to avoid confusion with *delibero* (*libra*), 'weigh, deliberate'.

20–21 *viginti sex dies*: 3–28 June 1098.

22 *Wido*: Guido, or Guy, was serving with Alexius as a mercenary. (The name appears in several forms: cf. *Willelmus*, *Guillelmus*, etc.)

31 *et unus . . . non*: 'and none'. Cf. Fr. *personne . . . ne*, and *unquam . . . non* below.

32 *valde mestissimus*: a double superlative (LL can offer *pessimissimus*, etc.).

36–37 *frangentem digitos*: 'wringing his hands'.

40 *speciem*: 'countenance'.

45 *cecidi fracto*: 'fall and break'.

50 *semicano*: 'grey-haired, grizzled'; 'cowardly old fool of a knight' (R. H.).

51 *militia*: 'military exploit'; but used later for 'army'.

52 *turpiter et inhoneste*: his wife Adela, daughter of William the Conqueror, took the same view. She had compelled him to take the Cross; and when he finally reached home, 'furiously ashamed of him . . . she never rested till she had sent him out again to the East to make atonement' (S. R.).

55 *omnes homines* . . . the Christian population was to be evacuated to Europe, 'leaving a cordon of waste land to protect the newly won territory from the Turks' (S. R.). The emperor's retreat was in fact justifiable on his own terms, but it ruined his future relations with the Crusaders.

57 *voluissent noluissent*: 'willy-nilly'.

37 *Who would be an Abbot!*

N.B. For orthography, see LN 6.

St. Edmund (*c.* 840–70), king of East Anglia, was defeated by the Danes and, refusing to share his kingdom with a pagan, he was put to death. Over his tomb another Dane, Cnut, built a monastery which was to rank among the greatest in England and draw pilgrims to the shrine of her national saint, till his fame was overshadowed by St. Thomas of Canterbury.

Early in the twelfth century in the larger monasteries the abbot's growing importance as a feudal lord led to his increasing separation from the community, with his own lodgings and household, including one or two chaplain-secretaries, and his own finances (perhaps a quarter of the whole).

1 Where did Jocelin sleep? In the same room as the abbot, or separated only by a thin partition?

2 Matins, in spite of its name, had been since the early centuries a Night Office said at midnight (or in St. Benedict's Rule about 2 a.m.). The monks came down by a night staircase from the dormitory into the church, then returned to bed till daybreak.

4 i.e. the personal resources of the abbot (see above) as well as his *cura pastoralis* (l. 6) for the community as a whole.

Talem anxietatem: some verb such as *auferat* is understood.

11. *v. vel sex marcas*: the 'mark' was found all over Europe. Originally a weight of silver, in England it represented 160 pence, or 13*s.* 4*d.*, as 'money of account'. (For the 'penny', see n. on No. **36,** ll. 9 ff.)

16 *magister almarii*. In days before the library became an independent department, books were kept in a cupboard in the cloister, in the charge of the Sacrist, who might be assisted by a Library Clerk (*mag. alm.*). (The alternative spelling *armarium* gives Fr. 'armoire'.)

17 *obedienciam*: the different offices that might fall to a monk—e.g. Sacrist, Cellarer, Almoner, etc.—were all grouped under this term, and holders of such offices (who were appointed by the abbot) were known as *Obedientiarii* or *Obedientiales* (see No. **38,** l. 40) or, more generally, as *Officiales*. Abbot Samson had himself held office as subsacrist, guestmaster, master of novices, and master of workmen during two years (1180–2) when the choir was being rebuilt.

19 *annis*: abl. for time how long; see LN 7*e* (viii).

21 *agnoscerem*: probably attracted to mood of *crederet*.

38 *Portrait of Abbot Samson*

3–4 *intuitus . . . auditus*: genitives of description.

7 *paucos*: sc. *capillos* (l. 8).

9 *infra xiiii annos*: i.e. by 1196, when he was 61 years old.

13–14 Jerusalem was captured by Saladin in 1187, after being in Western hands since the First Crusade (1099). Its fall made a tremendous impression on all Europe.

14–15 *cepit* = *coepit*. *femoralibus . . . staminis*: 'drawers of hair-cloth, and a hair-shirt instead of wool': a familiar form of self-inflicted penance.

15 *et carneis*: 'meat-dishes'. The monks normally ate no meat in the refectory, but meat was served at the abbot's table, and to guests.

17 *elemosine*: 'alms'; the food left over was distributed to the poor, who would often be waiting outside (see No. **43**, ll. 18 ff., where a poor Irish chaplain was waiting for alms outside the kitchen of Oseney Abbey).

19 *odio habuit*: predicative dative.

20 *cibi et potus*: objective gen., 'those who grumbled at'.

22 *claustralis*: i.e. before his election as abbot. Monks who held no office were described as *claustrales*.

25 Novices generally waited at table in the refectory. The abbot would normally dine there on feast days.

26 *cogitavi . . . ut ponerem*: 'I thought I would put . . .'.

28 *disco nigerimo*: i.e. blackened pewter. *nigerimo* for CL *nigerrimo*.

30 *arepto*: for *arrepto*? or *abrepto*?

33 *Gallice et Latine*: French was not only important in official circles and for constant cross-Channel travel, but its use was imposed by Ordinals and Statutes in many monasteries and Oxford colleges well into the fourteenth century.

34 *Anglice*: for all his culture Samson was sturdily English, and confirmed the tenancy of one manor to a certain English villein 'in whose faithfulness he had all the greater confidence *quia bonus agricola erat, et quia nesciebat loqui Gallice*' (H. E. B., p. 33). *pulpitum* normally at this period designates a choir-screen between monks or clergy and laity. Here 'pulpit' in later sense.

39 *Spoiling the Egyptians*

(See Exodus 3. 22; 12. 35–36.)

Platonic thought, for all its diversity and range, emphasized the reality of the spiritual, supra-sensible world and the immortality of the soul, with God as the creator and goal of all things, himself the supreme Good, and the rewarder of goodness in a life to come.[1] It had taken on a new lease of life and a greater religious emphasis under the Neoplatonists,[2] Plotinus (*c*. A.D. 205–69) and his successors, and became the dominant philosophy of the later pagan world, serving for many as a rival to Christianity, or as pointer to it. For Augustine it was both. 'Before he rediscovered Christianity, he was to discover Platonism. One day a friend lent him the works of certain Platonists (almost certainly Plotinus and Porphyry) in Latin translation (see *Confessions*, VII. 9, 10, 20, 21). Weary as he was "with wasting time and being wasted by time", he embraced with ardour the vision of a timeless world of immaterial and unchanging Reality. . . . It was a momentous discovery both for him and for the future movement of European thought. This revived Platonism, the last and ripest expression of the Hellenic genius, passed into Augustine's blood, to reappear increasingly diluted with Christianity, but not essentially altered, in his subsequent theological writings. These in turn profoundly modified the whole structure of the Catholic system. It is not, I think, too much to say that Augustine's study of Plotinus is one of the conditions which rendered the Renaissance possible' (E. R. Dodds, *Hibbert Journal* xxvi. 3).

With the fifteenth century and the rediscovery of the originals, both Platonism and Neoplatonism came back on a full tide, radiating out from the 'Academy' of Florence to influence the thought and religion

---

[1] The many affinities between Plato and Christianity are clearly brought out in a series of extracts translated and edited by Adam Fox, *Plato and the Christians*, 1957.

[2] The differences between Platonism and Neoplatonism are considerable, but they cannot be examined here.

COMMENTARY   209

and poetry of Europe—among others in England, Sidney and Spenser,
Vaughan and Traherne, Shelley and Wordsworth.

Only one dialogue, the *Timaeus*, came through the Dark Ages, in
a Latin translation; but this, with its doctrine of Creation, was
immensely influential, offering to eleventh-century thinkers a philosophical account to be harmonized with that of Genesis. But while
Anselm's 'essential philosophical ideas are Platonic, there seems to be
no proof that he had read even the amount of Plato which was accessible in his day, but he had imbibed the elements of Platonic thought
from St. Augustine' (R. W. Southern, *Saint Anselm and his Biographer*,
1963, p. 62).

12 *figmenta*: 'inventions'.

14–15 *duce Christo exiens*: the escape of the Israelites from the bondage
of Egypt was seen by the Fathers as prefiguring Christ's deliverance
of the human race, and is quoted by Dante (*Letter X*) as a typical
example of 'allegory' in the scriptural sense.

19 *instituerunt*: 'invented'. *divinae providentiae, quae ubique infusa est*:
this is not far removed from the Stoic doctrine of the *anima mundi*, the
source of all life and pervading all things: cf. Virgil, *Aeneid*, VI. 726 ff.,
and Cicero, *De Natura Deorum*, II. 58, where, translating from Greek,
he says it can rightly be called *providentia*. Another bridge then from
philosophy to Christianity; but for the philosophers it remained largely
remote and impersonal, even when it appeared as *deorum providentia*, or
is identified by Cleanthes (331–232 B.C.) and M. Aurelius with Zeus
himself.

22 *ad obsequia daemonum*: in late Jewish and Christian as well as pagan
thought, the world abounded with spirits good and evil; cf. Eph. 6. 12:
'we wrestle . . . against the authorities and potentates of this dark
world, against the superhuman forces of evil in the heavens' (NEB).
Christians too identified the pagan deities with these dark forces—
a degradation of the Gk. word *daemon* that came to stay. (Conversely
pagans blamed the Christian God for the disasters of their day: a
charge which Augustine set out to refute at length in his *De Civitate Dei*.)

31 *suffarcinatus*: 'laden'. *Cyprianus*, an African rhetorician, like Augustine, was converted *c*. 246 and elected bishop of Carthage, where he
was martyred in 258.

32–33 *Lactantius* (*c*. 240–*c*. 320), another rhetorician, who was deprived
of his posts by the emperor Diocletian on conversion, though later

appointed by Constantine tutor to his son. Often spoken of as 'the Christian Cicero', he set out to commend Christianity to men of letters in a long work, the *Divinae Institutiones*. *Victorinus*, a fellow rhetorician and African who, like Augustine, taught in Rome with great acclaim. His dramatic conversion (*c*. 350) from Neoplatonism was narrated to Augustine by Simplicianus, the tutor of Ambrose, and helped to push him further along the road (*Confessions*, VIII. 2–5). *Optatus*, an African bishop (*fl*. 370).   St. Hilary of Poitiers (*c*. 315–67), the leading Latin theologian of his day, was another convert from Neoplatonism. His Feast Day (14 January) gives his name to the spring term at Oxford and the Law Courts.

35–36 *eruditus . . . Aegyptiorum*: Acts 7–22.

40 *The Latin Lesson*

(N.B. *e* for *ae*: e.g. *idiote*, *pre*, etc.)

§ 1 2 *recte*: because if they slipped up, either in choir or in refectory, they were liable to be beaten, according to the Rule (ch. 45).   *idiote* (Gk. nom. pl. masc.): 'ignorant, uneducated'.

5 *anilis*: 'old-womanish'.

12 *Professus sum monachus*: the 'monk' merely opens the dialogue, before introducing the other speakers, but one of the boys gives later a fuller account of the monastic day.

13 *synaxes* (Gk.): 'services'; lit. 'assemblies': one of the earliest words borrowed by the Western Church. The seven are the canonical Hours of Lauds, Prime, Terce, Sext, None, Vespers, Compline (excluding the night Office, Nocturns or Matins).   *nimis*: 'fully' (not CL 'too much').

16 *Quid enim*: *enim* heightens the force of the question: 'why, what ...?' He then proceeds to ring the changes on various particles, not always appropriately.

17 ff. *opiliones*: 'shepherds'.   *aucupes*: 'fowlers'.   *salinatores*: 'salters'.

24 *minando*: from ML, *mino*, 'drive' (cattle); Fr. *mener*; from CL *minor*.

27–28 *confirmato . . . aratro*: 'fitting the plough with its ploughshare and blade' (Engl. 'coulter').

After the outdoor workers come the merchant and those indoors.

COMMENTARY 211

§ 2 1 *si indigemus*: *si* introduces a direct question: see LN 7*e* (vii). *aliquo*: neut.

4–5 *nec saltem*: 'not even'.   *ius*: 'broth' (Fr. *jus*).

7 *assare*: 'roast' (LL).   9–10 'Too many cooks spoil the broth'.

13 *illi*: 'those over there' (a fresh group).   14 *erarium*: 'coppersmith'.

'*But how can the farmer, or any of the rest, do without my services?*' argues the smith; and there follows the dispute summarized in the introduction.

22–24 *Primum querite . . .* : Matt. 6. 33.

He then questions one of the boys on how he has spent his day . . . and the colloquy ends with his addressing them all.

28 *mathites* (Gk. 1 m., here treated as 3rd decl.): 'pupils'. The AS gloss for *venusti* is 'winsome'.

30 *inceditis*: one would expect *incedite*. *morigerate*: 'obediently'.

31–32 *campanas*: 'bells'.   *orationem*: 'prayer' (EL); or perhaps used for *oratorium*?

32 *almas*: here used for 'holy'—perhaps by confusion with AS 'halwe', 'holy'.

33–34 *intervenite*: 'intercede'. Much of the teaching or study went on in the cloister.

35 *gimnasium* (Gk.): 'school'.

41 *St. Anselm: Thoughts on Education*

1 *igitur*: 'then'. Eadmer has just observed that Anselm's personality will emerge most clearly if he quotes whenever possible his exact words.

3 *de pueris*: see n. on *oblationem*, l. 20 below.

6 *non cessamus verberantes* is non-classical, but *cessatis . . . verberare*, ll. 7–8 below, is CL.

6–7 *sibi ipsis deteriores*: 'worse than ever'; ? a misunderstanding of CL *se ipsis* (abl. of comparison).

9 *quam bono omine*: lit. 'with what (fine) prospects' (ironical): 'to good purpose' (R. W. S.).

COMMENTARY

11 *inde*: 'what can we do next?' Cf. 'Where do we go from here?'

20 *oblationem*: a technical term. Children were sometimes 'offered' in their earliest years to the monastery, e.g. Bede, and were known as *oblati*: see n. on No. **12**, l. 12.

21 *in tantum*: 'so much' (or 'into so small a space'?).

23 *sibi*: for *eis*, see LN 7*b*.   24 *infra* for *intra*.

29 *alicuius* for CL *ullius*: see LN 7*b*.

30 *boni . . . fidem habeant*: 'have no confidence in any good (intention)'.

33 *semper proni . . .* : ? sc. *sunt*: the sentence as it stands is an anacoluthon.

35 *nullum*: masc., for *neminem*: see LN 7*b*. *depressis superciliis*: lit. 'with lowered brows', i.e. 'suspiciously, askance'. The opposite gives English 'supercilious', 'scornful'.

36-37 *vellem . . . diceretis*: 'I wish you would tell me'.

39 *velletisne essetis?*: 'Would you like to be treated as . . . if you were in their shoes?'

40 *sed esto*: 'But let that be': a concluding formula, leading on to the next simile.

44 ff. The process described is that of relief work—the metal being raised on the inner and hammered on the outer side, and then mounted perhaps on some stronger material (e.g. wood) to form a reliquary, or the cover of a Gospel book.

47 *ornatis moribus*: 'be possessed of', 'have': cf. William of Wykeham's 'Manners makyth man'.

48 *impendatis*: 'bestow'. *levamen* (met.): 'encouragement'.

52 *quisque*: 'all kinds of'. *eo*: abl. governed by *uti*, which itself depends on *valenti*.

55 *cur hoc*: sc. *sit*. *nolo*: 'I need not'.

56 *quia*: introduces reported statement.

58 *sui*: pronoun for possessive adj. *mensura*: 'capacity'.

COMMENTARY   213

60 ff. *concupiscere . . . praebere*, etc.: infins. are treated as abstract nouns, in apposition to *cibo*, though indeclinable. See Matt. 5. 39, Luke 6. 29.

61–62 *odientes*: a ML formation, to supply pres. participle for *odi*.

62 *multa* should, strictly speaking, be abl., in apposition to *cibo*.

65 *advocatione*: 'encouragement'. *supportatione*: 'forbearance.'

66 *vestris* agrees with both *fortibus* and *infirmis*.

42 *A Defence of the Classics*

The original manuscript has not survived, but a fine copy running to 600 folio pages was made by a Flemish scribe in 1444 for William Gray, bishop of Ely.

2 Hortensius was a contemporary of Cicero, and his chief rival at the Bar; and this (lost) dialogue, named after him as one of the speakers, was the first step in Augustine's conversion (see below).

4–5 Only fragments of the *De Republica* were known, chiefly from quotation in Augustine's *De Civitate Dei*, till in 1820 an early palimpsest was discovered in the Vatican containing about a third of the original. (Roger Bacon also complains of this loss, and of his vain search for it.)

8–9 *ne quis . . . scribo*: 'that no one should blame me for . . . copying so many pagan texts'.

10 *vilipendit*: 'despises'.

12 *cesum = caesum*: 'beaten'; see Jerome, *Letter XXII*. 30 (No. 3 in this book).

14 *ornate et eloquenter*: William practised this to the full; for examples see Nos. 30–32. Contrast Abbot Samson,[1] who, at any rate where sermons were concerned, for all his eloquence 'Gallice et Latine, colores rhetoricos et phaleras verborum et exquisitas sentencias . . . dampnabat, . . . ut morum fieret edificacio, non literature ostensio'.

16–17 1 Thess. 5. 21–22.   18 *delectione*: 'choice' (LL).

---

[1] See introduction to No. 37, and *The Chronicle of Jocelin of Brakelond*, ed. H. E. Butler, pp. 40 and 128.

43 *Trouble at Oxford, 1238*

1 *Tunc temporis*: 'at that particular time' (CL).

3 Oseney Abbey was an important house of Augustinian Canons on the outskirts of the city. (At the Dissolution one of its bells, Great Tom, passed to Wolsey's new foundation of Christ Church.)

4 *xenium* (Gk.): lit. 'guest-gift': 'entertainment'.

5 *in poculentis*, etc.: 'consisting of food and drink' (both are adjs.).

7 *suum* for *eius*: see LN 7*b* (cf. Fr. *son*).

8 *transalpinus*: from the English point of view, i.e. Italian.

9 *facetus*: 'courteous' (more commonly 'witty').

12 *credebant . . . ut*: reported statement.

13 *convitiando* (better *conviciando*): 'jeeringly'; gerund used adverbially.

17 *pugnis*: from *pugnus*, 'fist'. *dum*: 'while', but foll. by subj., as it is so often confused with *cum*: see LN 7*e* (v).

19 *capellanus*: the cloak, *capella*, which St. Martin of Tours (*c.* 335–97) divided with a beggar was kept as a precious relic by the Frankish kings and housed in a sanctuary in the palace, attended by *capellani*. The name *capella* then became applied to the sanctuary itself, and in time was extended to any 'chapel', usually attached to a royal or noble household, and served by a 'chaplain'. (St. Martin was venerated all over Europe, and the famous scene depicted everywhere: England keeps the name Martinmas for his feast, 11 November.)

22–23 *aliquid venenosum*: poisoning was greatly feared, and no doubt sometimes employed, but it was often invoked to account for sudden illness and death.

24 *hominum specialissimo*: 'an intimate member of his staff'.

25 *nec exaudivit*: 'hearken to', 'grant'.   26 *lebete*: 'cauldron'.

28 *de confinio Walliae*: 'from the Welsh marches'.

28–29 *Proh pudor*: 'for shame!' *ut quid*: 'why?' (EL). *arcum*: had he brought it, or snatched it from one of the crowd? In 1264 some Oxford scholars who had migrated to Northampton 'did much execution among the king's forces with bows and arrows . . . and on the capture of the town narrowly escaped hanging' (Rashdall, *Universities of Europe in the Middle Ages*.)

COMMENTARY 215

33 *Nabuzardan* (Nebuzar-adan in AV) was captain of the guard to Nebuchadrezzar king of Babylon, who was then persecuting the Jews (Jer. 39. 9)—so a double insult to the pope, and to his legate, who was oppressing 'God's Englishmen'.

37 *capa canonicali*: to leave no doubt about the sanctity of his person. *seratis*: perf. part. pass. of *sero* 1; from *sera*: 'bolt' or 'bar'.

39 *conticinium* (nom.): 'the quiet of evening' (*taceo*).

41 *ducatu*: 'guidance'. Oseney was built on one of the streams into which the Thames divided at Oxford.

43 *ad protectionem alarum*: an echo of Ps. 16. 8 (17. 8): *sub umbra alarum tuarum protege me*. (The rest of the psalm is peculiarly appropriate.)

46 *usurarius*: the condemnation of usury derives from the OT (Exod. 22. 25, etc.), and it was formally condemned by a series of Church Councils. *simonialis* (adj.): 'simoniac'. Simony, the sin of attempting to buy spiritual power or authority, derives from the story of Simon Magus (Acts 8. 9–24). It was a besetting sin of the medieval Church at almost every level, and was perhaps more detested than any other by reformers in every generation. Dante devoted a whole canto of the *Inferno* (Canto XIX) to simony, and exemplified it by three popes of his own age. On the other hand it was precisely one of the vices that papal legates had attempted to root out; and Gerald of Wales, writing *c.* 1210, describes how a legate had deposed three powerful abbots for this and other reasons; and Matthew Paris admits that Otto himself had a high reputation for holiness. (For other references see No. **60**, l. 37 and *passim*, and No. **64**.) *reddituum*: 'revenues, rents' (ML). The papacy exacted tithes, annates, and often payment for 'provisions', i.e. appointments to benefices.

48 *ditat alienos*: they are on firm ground here: English livings were given in a large way to (absentee) relations and friends of the pope and his cardinals. 'When God deprived bishops of sons, the devil gave them nephews': so Alexander III (d. 1181).

51 *cum furor* . . . : Ovid, *Remedium Amoris*, I. 119.

53 Ps. 37. 15 (38. 14): 'in whose mouth are no rebukes'. The whole psalm is a fervent prayer against 'those who seek my life'. The juxtaposition of these two quotations, from Ovid and the Vulgate, is typical of much medieval literature. Cf. No. **48**, 26–27.

57 *anhelus*: 'panting' (CL poet.). *Usque pervenit*: 'without stopping, reached ...'. *usque* normally reinforces preps.

59 *reponens querimoniam*: 'laying a complaint'.

60 *collateralibus*: the personal representative of a ruler was known as *legatus a latere*; so 'members of staff'.

62 *comitem Waranniae*: the earl of Warenne.

64 Odo of Kilkenny, a lawyer.

65–67 *vinculis ... mancipatus*: 'committed to Wallingford Castle'; one of the three royal castles which guarded the Thames valley (the other two were Windsor and Oxford).

67 *contrito laqueo*: another reminiscence from the Psalms, almost second nature in a monastic chronicler: 'the snare is broken, and we have escaped' Ps. 123. 7 (124. 7).

68–69 *interdicto*: a severe ban, just short of excommunication, by which almost all religious rites and sacraments were suspended. (Innocent III had laid an interdict on the whole of England in 1205, followed by excommunication and deposition of the king, till in the end John was forced to submit.)

70 *bigis*: 'carts'.

72–73 *redditibus ... innodati*: 'stripped of their benefices and laid under ecclesiastical ban'.

44 *In Praise of Books*

Notes taken from the edition by E. C. Thomas (see Bibliography) are marked (E. C. T.). For orthography see LN 6.

Many of the ideas, and whole phrases, are taken from Proverbs, Wisdom, Ecclesiasticus: only a certain number of these are noted.

2 He is echoing Aristotle, *Metaphysics*, I. 1.

3–6 Wisd. of Sol. 7. 8, 9. *vilescunt*, etc., a series of inceptive verbs: 'become cheap, muddy, dark, bitter'. *obryzum* (Gk.): 'fine gold'.

8 *virtus, virens, virus*: elaborate assonance.

9–10 *descendens ... luminum*: Jas. 1. 17.

11 *usque celum*: in CL normally *usque ad*. *intellectus*: gen. *celestis*: nom.

15 *operans*: 'one who follows your guidance'.

COMMENTARY 217

15–16 Prov. 8. 15, from a long panegyric of Wisdom put into her mouth by the writer (part of this is given in No. 2 (vv. 22–36)).

17 *elimatis ingeniis*: 'cultivated, polished'.

18 *coëffossis*: strengthened form of *fodio*: 'the thorns of vice being thoroughly rooted out'.

20 *conflassent*: 'would have melted': Isa. 2. 4, Mic. 4. 3.

22 *quo*: 'where have you gone into hiding?' *pre-electe* (voc.): 'chosen before all else'.

24 *posuisti tabernaculum*: a biblical metaphor (Psalms, etc.).

25 *liber vite*: 'the book of life' (Rev. 2. 7; 22. 2), here identified with God himself.

25–27 Luke 11. 8, 9. *improbe*: 'persistently, shamelessly'. *citius*: comp. adv. of *cito*.

27–28 *cherubim ... extendunt*: Exod. 25. 20.

29 Ps. 106. 3 (107. 3): *mari* represents the south.

30 God cannot be completely grasped and understood, but he can be laid hold of (Phil. 3. 12–13). Cf.

> Ah, but a man's reach should exceed his grasp,
> Or what's a heaven for?   (Browning)

31–32 *celestium ... infernorum*: Phil. 2. 10.

33 *politia* (Gk.): 'commonwealth, state'; hence politics, etc.

33–34 *hierarchie celestis ... officia*: 'Dionysius', a Syrian Greek (*c.* 500), in his *Celestial Hierarchies* distinguished nine choirs of angels, who in descending order were mediators between God and man. Translated into Latin by John Scotus Erigena (i.e. the Irishman) in the ninth century, these writings were immensely influential in the West, gaining authority through being attributed to Dionysius the Areopagite, a convert of St. Paul (Acts 17. 34). This attribution was disproved in the sixteenth century, hence he is generally known as 'pseudo-Dionysius' (see C. S. Lewis, *The Discarded Image*, pp. 70 ff.).

42 'the writer's and statesman's skill' ... 'in his single person'. (This play on words, *marte–arte*, by rhyme or assonance, is a favourite device in prose and poetry alike.)

43 Fabricius (*fl.* 280 B.C.), conqueror of Pyrrhus, renowned for his austerity and incorruptibility. Cato (234–149 B.C.), a paragon of

the old Roman virtues (both allusions are taken over from Boethius). For the general sentiment, cf. Horace, *Odes*, IV. 9. 25–28.

49 *pensandum*: this frequentative form of *pendo*, 'weigh up, consider', came to replace commoner verbs of thinking in French and Italian.

53 *cholera*: lit. 'excessive bile', then 'anger' (Fr. *colère*).
sine pannis: on beginning to teach, the newly fledged Master at the university was expected to distribute robes (*panni*) to his relations, to the inmates of his Hall, etc., and to provide a banquet for the Regent Masters who had taught him—altogether a costly business (E. C. T.).

55 *abscondunt*: sc. *se*.

58 *typice* (Gk.): 'figuratively' (Latin *figurate* is used below): 'by what countless images . . .'; see introduction to Part One: The Bible.

60 *sophie fodine*: 'mines of wisdom'; in Prov. 2. 4 the wise man bids his son seek wisdom as silver and 'dig it out' (Vulg.) as treasure.

61 *putei*: see Gen. 26. 18, 19.

63 *eruderavit*: 'cleared' (of rubbish).
nituntur: the pres. tense suggests that the Philistines are always active as enemies of learning. (Matthew Arnold borrowed the term from Heine to denote 'a strong, dogged, unenlightened opponent of the Chosen People . . .', and fastened it on the English middle class. 'Philistinism! We have not the expression in English. Perhaps we have not the word because we have so much of the thing.')

64 *spice*: Matt. 12. 1.   66 *urne auree*: Heb. 9. 4.

67 *petre melliflue*: Deut. 32. 13.

68 *lactis vite*: perhaps an adaptation of the 'spiritual milk' of 1 Pet. 2. 2. *promptuaria*: 'storehouses', Ps. 143.13 (144. 13).

69 *lignum vite . . . fluvius*: Gen. 2. 9, 10; and Rev. 22. 2.

71 *pera David*: 1 Sam. 17. 40.   74 *tela nequissimi*: Eph. 6. 16.

75–76 *lucerne ardentes*: Luke 12. 35.

45 *Student Days at Bologna, c. 1320*

This is a short extract from Petrarch's longest autobiographical letter: a bitter-sweet meditation from one old man to another *de mutatione*

COMMENTARY 219

temporum. A few months later Guido Sette died in the Benedictine monastery he had founded near Portofino, and was buried there.

Bologna, like other great Italian cities, had achieved its independence in the early twelfth century, but this was gradually undermined by endemic strife between the partisans of pope and emperor, and by internal despotisms on the Greek model (*tyrannis*). Finally, in 1506, it was crushed between papal power advancing from the south and the growing aggression of Milan in the north.

The university developed in the twelfth century from a still earlier Law School, and attracted up to 5,000 students from all over Europe (10,000 is quoted for 1262).

4 *iurisconsultos veteres*: 'lawyers of olden days'. Petrarch is thinking of Cicero, and the great Roman lawyers who figure in Cicero's Dialogues. *redivivos*: 'had come to life again'; a LL meaning.

5–6 *tam multis et tam magnis*: there is good CL precedent for these, as against *tot tantisque*, where emphasis is required. (In ML *tot* was commonly replaced by *tanti*: cf. Fr. and It.)

6–7 *una . . . ignorantia*: the word-order throws *una* into relief. *hostis utinam*: sc. *esset*. 'Would it were an enemy . . .' (then men would have recognized its true nature . . .). *at non*: 'at any rate not . . .'.

8 *sic* for *adeo*: 'so completely'.

9 *manum tollere*: 'surrender'.

11 *prescripto cognomine*: 'enjoyed as if by right the title of . . .'.

15 *heret* = *haeret*.

18–19 *ibam cum equevis* . . . cf. Milton's *Lycidas*, ll. 25 ff., and Arnold's *Thyrsis*, looking back to their own student days.

23 *seu* for *vel*. *tanta*: thrown into relief by word-order.

26–28 *ut . . . opus esset*: noun clause, dependent on *fecere*.

46 *The Ascent of Mont Ventoux*

The whole letter, one of his most revealing, runs to *c*. 2,000 words: the present text represents about one third of the original. It appears to be the first example in European literature of a mountain's being climbed for its own sake—though Petrarch, steeped in Livy, adduces

220 COMMENTARY

classical precedents. He was 32 at the time, and it was nine years since he had first caught sight of Laura, and had fallen into the toils—and into other entanglements as well. N.B. *e* for *ae* throughout. Mont Ventoux, a westerly spur of the Basses Alpes, lies about 30 miles north-east of Avignon, and rises to a height of over 6,000 ft., dominating the whole region.

3–4 *Multis ... annis*: abl. for 'time how long': see LN 7*e* (viii).

5 *fato ... versatus sum*: 'I have spent my life ... by the dictates of fate'.

9–10 *euntibus aderant*: 'helped us on our way' (Petrarch had taken his younger brother, Gerard, as companion).

12–13 *ante annos* ... for CL *quinquaginta ante annis*.

18–19 *ut sunt* ... : 'with the natural reluctance of youth ...'.

23–24 *Dimisso ... siquid* ... : 'leaving behind with him any clothes ... that might get in our way'; an abl. abs., with the clause *si quid ... esset* representing a noun.

> Summary. *The directness of Gerard's nature was later to take him into a Carthusian monastery as the shortest route to heaven, while Petrarch never quite resolved the tension between the claims of religion and the world. He is already beginning to interpret the climb allegorically on the two levels of body and soul.*

33 *hostis romani nominis* (objective gen.): sc. Hannibal. Petrarch had a particular passion for Livy, who describes the crossing in Book XXI.

37 *inextimabilis*: ML for *inaestimabilis*: 'indescribable'.
amicum: Giacomo Colonna, younger brother of Petrarch's cardinal patron, and a fellow student at Bologna. They had met again at Avignon, and on Giacomo's appointment as bishop of Lombez in the Pyrenees in 1330, thanks to his high connexions in Rome, he invited Petrarch and two more young men (whom Petrarch nicknamed 'Socrates' and 'Laelius') to spend an unforgettable summer with him there; and the four became lifelong friends.

42 *immutabilis Sapientia*: suggests the double contrast of the folly and the fickleness of men.

45 *Tempus forsan veniet* .... This *recordatio* ultimately took the form of his two collections of letters: *Familiarium Rerum Libri XXIV* (*Fam.*), and the *Epistolae Seniles*. He proposed to complete them by a directly

COMMENTARY 221

autobiographical Postscript, addressed *Posteritati*, but unfortunately did not carry it beyond 1351 (*aet.* 47). (Cf. Newman's remark: 'It has ever been a hobby of mine, though perhaps it is a truism, not a hobby, that the true life of a man is in his letters. . . . Not only for the interest of a biography, but for arriving at the inside of things, the publication of letters is the true method'.)

47 *prefatus illud*: *Confessions*, II. 1. 1. The whole of the following passage is dramatized at length in his *Secretum*: see introduction.

58 *Odero, si potero*: Ovid, *Amores*, III. 11. 35. The whole poem describes the revolt of a lover against his chains; and a later couplet—ll. 39–40—still more closely describes Petrarch's continuing plight:

> Sic ego nec sine te nec tecum vivere possum,
> et videor voti nescius esse mei.

59 *dum* for *cum*: see LN 7e (v).

59–60 *terrenum aliquid saperem*: a reminiscence of Col. 3. 2: '*quae sursum sunt sapite, non quae super terram*'; 'Let your thoughts dwell on that higher realm, not on this earthly life' (NEB).

62 *conditoris*: 'author'.

64 *pugillare*; that can be held in the hand (*pugnus*—fist). Small volumes of pocket-size began to be produced by professional scribes in the thirteenth century, for use in universities.

65 *lecturus . . . occurreret*: Petrarch 'consults' Augustine as Augustine had consulted St. Paul: see No. **8**, ll. 54 ff.

69–70 *ipsumque*: i.e. Gerard. *quod*: introduces reported statement.

70 ff. *Et eunt homines*: *Confessions*, I. 8. 15. This 'Know thyself' theme has a continuous history from early Greece, and was central to Augustine's thought, as later to Bernard's. (See introduction to No. **18**.)

75 *-met*: an emphasizing suffix added to personal pronouns. *ipsum* was sometimes added as well to give yet further emphasis (since demonstratives always tend to lose their force), so leading to It. *medesimo*, Fr. *même*.

76 *gentium*: normally used in Vulgate for Gentiles, hence 'pagan'.

78 *cui magno*: 'compared with its greatness nothing else . . .'.

83 *undosi pectoris motus*: 'surging emotions'. *scrupulosi*: 'stony'.

84 *hospitiolum*: dim. of *hospitium*: 'inn'.

88 *hec tibi raptim*: sc. a quick draft? he can hardly have written a 2,000-word letter in the short interval before supper.

97 *VI Kal. Maias*: for *ante diem sextum Kalendas*, i.e. 26 April. *Malausane* (loc.): Malaucène, the village from which they had set out.

47 *Come to Vaucluse!* (1)

Vaucluse was not only a source of delight to its owner, but a bait to be dangled before each new friend, or to be described in a series of letters spread over a number of years.

Giovanni Colonna was yet another of the great Colonna family, whom Petrarch had met on his first visit to Rome. He suffered from gout, so Petrarch elaborately works out a route for him to come all the way from Tivoli, in the Alban Hills near Rome, by water (this is the concluding paragraph of a long letter). The whole passage is poetic, and 'romantic'—a prose version of some of his Sonnets. It is worth noting the skilful variation of word-order in the long sentence beginning *Videbis*. (These two invitations to Vaucluse suggest a comparison with St. Bernard's invitation to Clairvaux, No. **16**.)

2 *procul ab Italia*: his heart was in Italy, and after a series of visits which gradually became longer he spent the second half of his life there in one city after another, chiefly under the patronage of Milan, Venice, and Padua, to whom he rendered some diplomatic services in return. (He never settled in Florence, in spite of invitations from the city authorities, and from Boccaccio and other admiring friends.)

5 *factum . . . angustius*: '(has become) may prove too slender . . .'.

6–7 *nil . . . expectantem*: this did not prevent him from using all his influence in high quarters to obtain benefices for himself and his friends.

8 *herbivagum . . . fontivagum*: seem to be Petrarch's own coinage, on the analogy of the other two.

11 *curie*: the papal court at Avignon, whose stench at times seemed to reach Vaucluse and was one of the factors which drove him away. He made a series of blistering attacks on its corruptions, half-concealed under the anonymity of his *Epistolae sine nomine*.

15 *nimpharum*: 'streams, springs'; so used poet. in CL. *i* for *y*: see LN 6*d*.

17 *esse*, etc.: the constr. now slips into the acc. and infin., still dependent on *videbis*. *nunc ire*, etc.: the whole passage is close in feeling and expression to Gray's *Elegy*, ll. 98–108 (the two poets had a good deal in common in their scholarship, their love of solitude, and their melancholy); e.g.

> There at the foot of yonder nodding beech
> That wreathes its old fantastic roots so high,
> His listless length at noontide would he stretch,
> And pore upon the brook that babbles by.

19 *que* (*quae*) . . . *est*: a noun clause (commonly introduced by *id quod*) in apposition to *neminem accedere*. *que* agrees with *pars* by attraction.

48 *Come to Vaucluse!* (2)

In the first half of this letter (omitted here) Petrarch moralizes at length on the lessons to be learnt from illness.

1 *inducas*: jussive subj. *quod sciam*: 'so far as I know': generic, or limitative, subj.

3 'Socrates' was Petrarch's nickname for Ludwig van Kempen, a chanter in Cardinal Colonna's chapel, and one of his earliest and closest friends. Petrarch dedicated to him his first collection of letters, *Familiarium Rerum Libri*; and there are long opening and closing letters to him.

5 *Nullus . . . tyrannus minax*, etc.: these conventional enemies of tranquillity figure constantly in Latin verse.

12 *inter . . . optabilis*: the golden mean between poverty and riches is exactly Horace's ideal: e.g. *Odes*, II. 10. 5 ff.

14 *presul*: the bishop of Cavaillon, Philippe de Cabassoles, was a close friend of Petrarch.

22 *certatim . . . Minerve*: 'the hills vie with one another as they bask in the favour of B. and M.' (i.e. with their grapes and olives).

23 A 'parasite' (Gk.) was a diner-out who sponged on his friends and acquaintances; so *p. more*: 'greedily'.

26–27 It is characteristic of Petrarch to put the two comparisons, Christian and pagan, side by side.

31 *qua*: precedes its grammatical antecedent, *copia*.

33 *amicorum*: sc. Petrarch and Socrates; or, more probably, the books themselves.

40 *supra vires*: refers to his recent illness.

43 *Aeneid*, I. 207 (Aeneas heartens his companions after their shipwreck on the shores of Africa).

49 *To M. Tullius Cicero, 16 June 1345*

§ 1 Title: the abbreviation T. for Tullius is illegitimate. S. represents *salutem* (*dat*): a conventional formula in CL and ML.

He is thinking particularly of Cicero's hesitations in the Civil War between Caesar and the senatorial government, 49–44 B.C., when at times Cicero would write to Atticus three times in one day, trying to resolve his dilemma: whether to join Pompey openly, or to remain neutral for the moment.

10 *O preceps ... senex*: the phrase comes from a medieval collection of pseudo-Ciceronian letters.

12 *Ubi* appears to be used for 'Why?'
otium: 'leisure', 'detachment', was the philosopher's traditional ideal, and Petrarch's in particular. He wrote a long treatise *De otio religioso* in 1347, after visiting his brother Gerard in his monastery.

19 *in Antonium*: after Caesar's murder in 44 B.C., Cicero launched a series of violent attacks on his would-be successor, Antony (his *Philippics*), which led directly to his own proscription and death in 43.

21 *Augusto*: sc. Caesar's great-nephew, Octavius (see following line), aged 18, whom he had adopted as his heir; so that officially his style was henceforth C. Iulius Caesar Octavianus; but Brutus uses his former name (Shakespeare calls him 'Octavius Caesar'). The title 'Augustus' was bestowed later, after he had defeated Antony and become master of the Roman world. Cicero was supporting him, thinking that he could play him off against Antony; but Brutus in this letter to Cicero (*Ad Brutum*, I. 16. 7) shows himself far more clearsighted—and in fact Octavian and Antony soon combined with Lepidus in the Triumvirate; and Cicero was one of their first victims.

23 The first *dominum* is Julius Caesar: *dominus* in Republican times had the same overtones as the Gk. *tyrannus*: 'tyrant, despot'.

24 *vicem tuam*: 'on your behalf'.

COMMENTARY   225

26–27 is adapted from a second letter of Brutus, this time to Atticus (*Ad Brutum*, I. 17. 5), in which he says that he has no confidence in Cicero's oratorical skill (*his artibus*) to solve their present problems: deeds, not words, are required.

29 *satius* (comp. of *satis*): 'how much better it would have been ...'.

30–32 *de perpetua ... cogitantem*: from a long letter to Atticus (*Ad Atticum*, X. 8).

32–33 *nullos ... Catilinas*: 'never to have held the consulship' (in 63 B.C.), 'never to have longed for a triumph' (after his provincial governorship of Cilicia in 51–50 B.C.), 'never to have been puffed up by your orations against Catiline' (a would-be revolutionary whom Cicero succeeded in overthrowing during his consulship).

34 *Eternum vale*: because Petrarch did not expect to meet him in the Christian heaven?

35 *Athesis*: now the Adige.

36 *XVI Kalendas Quintiles*: i.e. 16 June. (The Roman year originally began in March; hence the numbering of this and later months. *Quintilis* and *Sextilis* were later re-named after Julius Caesar and Augustus.) Petrarch is using a shortened version of the full formula: *ante diem sextum decimum Kalendas*.

§ 2

The second letter is by way of making amends for the first, as is shown from the start by the more intimate greeting.

4 The line from Terence is quoted by Laelius (hence called *familiaris tuus*) in Cicero's *De Amicitia*.

8 *pace tua dixerim*: a Ciceronian phrase; 'if I may say so'.

10 *ut qui* + causal subj., 'since ...'.

15 *De finibus*: a long work in which Cicero reviewed the three main philosophical schools of his day, and found the arguments of Epicurus illogical, not to say contemptible, though he could still admire his blameless life (see *De Finibus*, II. §§ 80–81).

21 *ducatu*: 'guidance' (EL). *suffragiis*: 'opinions, judgements'.

25 ff. After this glowing tribute to Cicero he is drawn to acknowledge his second main debt, to Virgil. Cf. Dante's *Tu duca, tu signore, tu maestro* (*Inferno*, I. 2. 140). *solutis ... frenatis*: the freedom of prose and the restraints of verse. Cf. *equoribus* and *angustiis* below.

50 *Begone, dull Care!*

The rhythm is trochaic (accentual). N.B. *e* for *ae*.

2 An echo of Horace's *dulce est desipere in loco*: *Odes*, IV. 12. 28.

7–8 'to atone for vices by toiling over . . .' (these two lines have been supplied by an editor to complete the 8-line stanza).

25 sc. the gods of Ovid's *Metamorphoses*, who spent most of their time in pursuing their love-affairs.

27–28 'Let us spend our leisure-hours in pursuit of . . .'.

31 *plateas* passed into all the Romance languages; e.g. *place*, *piazza*, *plaza*.

32 *choreas* combines the idea of dance and song. This is the original meaning of 'carols', popular all over Europe—some of them in dialogue form, with the girls answering the men (at times in the *Carmina Burana* 'answering the Latin stanzas of the clerks with the German ones, while everyone would sing the refrains'). (See P. Dronke, op. cit., vol. i, p. 302.)

51 *The Archpoet's Confession* (*MLV*, *No. 183*)

See Raby, *Secular Latin Poetry*, vol. ii, pp. 180–9; Waddell, *The Wandering Scholars*, pp. 152–60; and *Medieval Latin Lyrics*, pp. 170–83, 338–40.

The Archpoet, as he styles himself—otherwise he is nameless—is one of the masters of twelfth-century rhythmical and rhyming verse. Of knightly birth from the German Rhineland (*fl. c.* 1160), he chose learning and *la vie de Bohème*; and like many other artists in other centuries, proud and poor, he had to look to a powerful patron for a living. This was Rainald (Reginald), archbishop of Cologne and arch-chancellor of the emperor Frederick Barbarossa, to whom he shamelessly unburdens himself, and appeals for charity, with equal readiness.

There are nineteen stanzas (76 lines) in the whole poem, represented here by stanzas 1–5, 10–15. The metre is the 'Goliardic' stanza: see Verse Notes, 4c.

3 Man, along with Nature as a whole, was thought to be compounded of the four elements of earth, air, fire, and water (these in turn deriving from the four 'contraries' of hot, cold, moist, and dry), and

COMMENTARY 227

their relative proportions determined the differing 'temperament' or 'humour' of each individual. The theory goes back to Aristotle, and persisted into the seventeenth century (see C. S. Lewis, *The Discarded Image*, pp. 94–96, 169–73). The 'light elements' were air and fire: cf. Shakespeare, *Henry V*, III. vii. 22 (of the Dauphin's horse): 'He is pure air and fire; and the dull elements of earth and water never appear in him'; and *Julius Caesar*, v. v. 73.

5–6 'the wise man ... built his house upon a rock': Matt. 7. 24.

13 plays on the two meanings of 'serious' and 'burdensome'.

14 *dulciorque favis*: a favourite comparison in the OT.

15 *suavis* is usually trisyllabic in ML: cf. It. *soave*.

17 *via lata*: 'Broad is the way that leadeth to destruction': Matt. 7. 13.

20 *curam gero cutis*: a proverbial expression in CL, 'to take good care of oneself' (e.g. Horace, *Ep.* I. 2. 29), which gains double force from the Christian contrast of *mortuus in anima*.

22 It seems to have been common enough to drink or gamble away the clothes on one's back (cf. the phrase 'I'd put my shirt on it'); and the picture recurs in other drinking-songs: e.g.

> Quidam ludunt, quidam bibunt,
> quidam indiscrete vivunt;
> sed in ludo qui morantur,
> ex his quidam denudantur,
> quidam ibi vestiuntur,
> quidam saccis induuntur:
> ibi nullus timet mortem,
> sed pro Baccho mittunt sortem.   (*Carmina Burana*)

28 *requiem aeternam* (*dona eis, Domine*): the opening words of the Introit of the Mass for the dead; hence known as a 'Requiem'.

32 *huic* is scanned as disyllabic (ML).

36 *praesulis*: 'bishop'. *praesul*, CL 'president', etc., was adopted along with *antistes* as a Latin equivalent of the commoner Gk. *episcopus*. *pincerna* (Gk.): 'cup-bearer, butler', who carefully waters the wine. (But the satirists, such as Bernard of Cluny, give a very different picture of the drinking habits of bishops.)

42 *dominici regulam mandati*: see John 8. 7.

(The remaining stanzas are concerned with his repentance, though it is a defiant repentance as far as the archbishop's staff is concerned, and end with an appeal to his patron.)

52 *A Drinking Song*

One of many parodies of hymns. The opening line is taken from a sixth-century hymn for the morning Office of Prime, but stanzas two to five abandon the traditional iambic rhythm for more lively (accentual) trochees.

12 'Let none be backward . . .'.

17–20 parody the last clause of the Athanasian Creed: 'Haec est fides catholica, quam nisi quisque fideliter firmiterque crediderit, salvus esse non poterit.' (Medieval poets and parodists had a genius for spotting the hidden rhythm of some prose passage, and exploiting it in their verse: e.g. 'Propter Sion non tacebo' (No. **65**), and 'Dies irae, dies illa' (No. **25**).)   22 *salutatio*: 'salvation' (EL).

24 one of the many verse equivalents of the prose 'per omnia saecula saeculorum', 'world without end'.

53 *The Debate between Wine and Water*

For the poetic debate, see Raby, *Secular Latin Poetry*, vol. ii, pp. 282–308. It has a long history, going back in Latin to Virgil's *Eclogues*, which in turn derive from Greek. It was practised by the Carolingians, e.g. in the Debate between Winter and Spring (*MLV*, No. 75), and there are many later examples, including rival versions of the present theme. The whole conception too of debate or *disputatio* played an essential part in the schools and universities, whether doctors were maintaining a thesis against students or students against each other or, as candidates for a degree, holding their own against all comers. Hence the length of this poem (156 lines), as the writer is carried away by his knowledge of Scripture and his own ingenuity. See *Carmina Medii Aevi*, ed. F. Novati, Florence, 1883.

The metre is the favourite Goliardic stanza: see Verse Notes 4*c*. N.B. e for ae, e.g., *celum, quedam, cepisset* (*coepisset*).

1 *Cum . . . tumultum*: 'When confusion reigned supreme'. (The phrasing looks like a reminiscence of Wisd. of Sol. 18. 14: 'Cum enim quietum silentium contineret omnia, et nox in suo cursu medium iter haberet.')

5 *in carne gravi*: the familiar conception of *corpus aggravat animam*.

6–7 echoes 2 Cor. 12. 2: 'scio hominem in Christo ... (sive in corpore, nescio, sive extra corpus, nescio, Deus scit) raptum usque ad tertium caelum ... et audivit arcana verba ....' Jewish tradition deriving from Babylon distinguished seven or (as here) three heavens: that of our atmosphere, that of the stars, and that of God himself (the notion passed into Stoic thought, and is found in Cicero's *Dream of Scipio*).

7 *auscultavi*: can imply 'overheard'.

8 *in concilio fratrum*: 'among my assembled brethren'—implying that the writer is a 'religious'.

9 *siquidem*: 'indeed'; see LN 7e (vii).

11–12 *Thetis*: the sea-nymph (mother of Achilles), used in CL poetry for 'the sea', here represents water. *Lyeus* (Lyaeus), one of the Gk. titles of Dionysus/Bacchus, 'releasing' (men from their cares); then used poetically for 'wine'. *actor fit et reus*: 'plaintiff and defendant'.

14 See John 4. 7.

15–16 See Ps. 109. 7 (110. 7): *de torrente in via bibet: propterea exaltabit caput.*

17 *aquaticus ... Nazareus*: 'your water-drinking Nazarite's: a body of Israelites specially consecrated to God, who took vows to drink no wine, and to let their hair grow. The most famous was Samson: see Num. 6. 1–4, and Judges 13. 5, 16. 17. (Wine is here replying to Water's citation in the previous stanza.)

20 See 1 Tim. 5. 25.   21 Naaman the leper: see Kings 5.

22 *male sane*: *male* can negative an adj. in CL, *male fidus*; and cf. Fr. *malsain*.

25 The good Samaritan: Luke 10. 30 ff. *cesus = caesus*: 'beaten'. Ps. 1. 3.

29 ff. *temporaneum*: 'in due season' (LL). *lignum*: 'tree' (poet. and LL). Prov. 25. 25: 'As cold water to a thirsty soul, so is good tidings from a far country'; but the poet, by converting *bonus nuntius* into the dative, and translating as 'messenger', telescopes the two ideas together. The heavenly host, catching the familiar words *Gloria in excelsis Deo*, continues with the second line *et in terra pax*, etc. (adapting it to the metre); and the poet himself awakening carries it down to the concluding words *in gloria Dei patris*.

COMMENTARY

43 *flamen* 3 n., lit. 'breeze, wind', used for *spiritum sanctum* (*spiritus, animus, anima,* and Gk. *pneuma* all spring from the same primitive conception that breath *is* life). Cf. Genesis 2. 7: *formavit Dominus Deus hominem de limo terrae, et inspiravit in faciem eius spiraculum vitae, et factus est homo in animam viventem.*

54 *Phyllis and Flora*

The complete text is printed in *The Oxford Book of Medieval Latin Verse*, first edition, ed. S. Gaselee, 1928: the revised edition, 1959, contains 108 lines (*MLV*, No. 209).

The subject is a favourite one in the twelfth–thirteenth centuries: the rival merits of clerk and knight *in castris Cupidinis*; and since the clerk wields the pen, and has all the lore of Ovid at his command, he naturally comes off best—at any rate on paper. The whole poem runs to over 300 lines, so that the poet can afford to set the scene in a leisurely fashion, and give thirty stanzas to the 'contention', while the second half (omitted here) is a brilliant description of their journey to the 'Paradise of Love'. Here Cupid, surrounded by flowers and music, with nymphs and satyrs in attendance, bids Nature and Experience give judgement. The verdict is a foregone conclusion:

> Secundum scientiam et secundum morem
> ad amorem clericum dicunt aptiorem.

The metre is the Goliardic stanza: see Verse Notes, 4*c*. N.B. *e* for *ae*: e.g. *celo, terre* (gen. sing.), *equis*.

Stanzas 1–6, 8–18

3 *dum fugaret*: see LN 7*e* (v). *nuntius Aurore*: sc. Lucifer, the day-star.

5 *spatiatum*: supine after a vb. of motion.

15 *parum impares*: 'just a little unequal' (not CL).

27–28 *in sese redit*: 'turned to her own thoughts'. *ledit* = *laedit*.

32 'but their passion was hidden by bashfulness'.

37 *Ille . . . more* (i.e. *morae*): 'Long did they talk together'.

41 *mea cura*: 'my beloved'. By calling her lover Paris, she casts herself for the role of Helen.

44 *Dionei laris*: 'Love's abode'. *Dioneus*: adj. from *Dione* = *Venus*.

48 *mendicum*: the riches of the sleek and learned clerk (as compared with the lean and hungry knight) are described in detail below.

COMMENTARY

49 *Alcibiades*: the gifted, unprincipled Athenian gallant who came to an untimely end in 405 B.C., a figure familiar to the Latinist from the *Lives* of Cornelius Nepos.

52 *iura*: 'lover's vows'.

55 *ecce* governing an acc. was familiar from Plautus and Terence.

56 *Epicuro*: Epicurus himself (341–270 B.C.), though proclaiming pleasure as man's highest good, was far from being an 'epicure' in the popular sense of the word; but his followers soon got a bad name for self-indulgence, and Horace refers to himself half-mockingly as *Epicuri de grege porcus*. So l. 58: 'Your clerk is nothing but an Epicure'. Cf.

> Alte clamat Epicurus:
> venter satur est securus;
> venter deus meus erit,
> talem deum gula querit,
> cuius templum est coquina,
> in qua redolent divina.   (*Carmina Burana*)

64 'that the vows of a knight are very different from those of your clerk'.

68 *amor et iuventus* are the subject, *cibus ... militis* the predicate.

Stanzas 22–25

72 *patere*: imperative of *patior*.   *parum*: 'briefly'.

73 *amici mei*: possessive gen.

74 *quod* introduces a consec. clause (LN 7e (vi)); 'that he has no designs on / never spares a thought for / another's possessions' (so too in l. 78 below).

75 *Ceres* and *Lyaeus* (Bacchus) are used in CL verse for corn and wine; and these, along with oil and honey, are traditional symbols of plenty in the OT.

78 *aliqua* for *ulla* (LN 7b).   79–80 sc. the winged Cupid.

84 'since his mistress loves him unfeignedly'.

Stanzas 30–32

91 Bucephalus was the horse of Alexander the Great; Ganymede, a Trojan prince who was carried off to heaven to be Jupiter's cup-bearer—so 'the squire who attends my Lord'.

55 *In Praise of his Mistress* (*MLV*, *No. 226*)

The poem comes from the Manuscript of Ripoll, a monastery in north Spain which felt the influence of France, and where 'towards the end of the 12th century . . . some clever young monastic poet inserted a group of love poems in the blank folios of a MS. dedicated to other ends'. (Are they his own poems? Do they spring direct from experience, or are they a flight of fancy, an exercise in the school of Ovid and his own contemporaries?) The whole collection is discussed in Raby, *Secular Latin Poetry*, vol. ii, pp. 236-47.

For the metre, see Verse Notes 4*b*. Four stanzas are omitted.

31 Cato (95-46 B.C.) was a stern, unbending Stoic who supported the Republican cause against Caesar in the Civil War, and on the fall of Utica committed suicide rather than submit. He was immortalized by Lucan in his *victrix causa deis placuit, sed victa Catoni*. (The thought is 'All power to Cato . . . but even he . . . '.)

56 *Love's Companion* (*MLV*, *No. 214*)

For the metre see Verse Notes, 4*b*. N.B. *e* for *ae*: e.g. *Helene*, *que*.

14 *quod* introduces a consec. clause: see LN 7*e* (vi). *nec*: with force of *ne . . . quidem*, here qualifies *presumendum*.

16 *mei mali* rather awkwardly defines *causam*: 'and so to my sorrow . . .'.

21 'nor does she return my love'.

57 *Love and Reason* (*MLV*, *No. 232*)

The poem is found in the 'Arundel Collection' (see Raby, *Secular Latin Poetry*, vol. ii, pp. 247, 252), a fourteenth-century British Museum MS. (Arundel 384) containing twenty-eight songs—religious, satirical, and amatory—probably dating from the latter half of the twelfth century. Its fluid and subtly varied structure derives ultimately from the Sequence (see Verse Notes, 4*d*), and equally calls for music.

1-3 'poised in the balance . . .'. *trutine* (gen.) 'scales'.

8 *langueo*: came into the medieval vocabulary of love from Song of Sol. 2. 5: 'quia amore langueo': 'for I am sick of love' (AV). The Latin is used as a refrain in a fifteenth-century English carol; and Engl. 'lovesick' came to stay. Cf. also Sheridan's Miss Lydia Languish.

17 *Dione* = Venus.

23 *anchore* (gen.) acquired an 'h' in ML (cf. *charus*, *charitas*, Fr. *cher*).

31 *sub libra*: it is difficult to see the force of *sub*.

38 *labellula*: a double diminutive; 'those darling lips'.

40 *naris*: nom. sing., occasionally used in verse, but most commonly in pl.

48 'she [sc. *ratio*] thinks to comfort me with . . .'.

58 *Reluctant Celibates*

Clerical celibacy seems to many, as to this contemporary writer, one of the stumbling-blocks of medieval Christianity, and perhaps calls for some account of its theory and practice. It was of comparatively slow and erratic growth in the West, as far as the secular clergy were concerned. It was imposed on them from sub-deacon upwards by various Councils from the fourth century onwards, but was frequently ignored, particularly among the rural clergy; and marriage was sometimes tolerated, sometimes upheld, as, for example, by the Council of Winchester in 1076, presided over by Lanfranc, monk and archbishop, and backed by William the Conqueror.[1] But the same century saw a wave of reform, radiating out from Cluny; and Gregory VII (1073–85) and his successors reinforced the old prohibitions, culminating in the Fourth Lateran Council of 1215, under the formidable Innocent III. It could still be debated, however, whether the ban was enjoined by the law of God or the law of the Church, and St. Thomas Aquinas upheld the latter. Meanwhile concubinage and a good deal of licence persisted; and could be defended, as here, or treated scathingly, or jestingly, by preacher and story-teller: Boccaccio and others exploit them to the full, while Rabelais, under the banner of 'Fais ce que voudras', was to banish abstinence from the abbey of Thélème.

Yet above the dust of the controversy soared the ideal of a dedicated virginity. It is a concept deeply rooted in history, both in primitive religions (though not in Judaism) and in Pythagorean and Platonic philosophy, where an exaltation of the soul is balanced by a contempt

[1] Ailred of Rievaulx (1109–67) was the son of an hereditary priest of Hexham.

for the body. It gathered fresh strength among Neoplatonists and others in the later and wearier Graeco-Roman world;[1] while for Christians it was reinforced by certain texts in the New Testament, by the teaching of the Fathers,[2] and by the general foreshortening of human life when seen against the background of the Second Coming and of eternity.

It was positive as well as negative—its purpose *terrena despicere et amare caelestia*: in fact it was sometimes known as the *angelica vita*, i.e. a life on earth already anticipating the 'new life' where 'men and women do not marry, but are like angels in heaven'.[3] For some, above all in the monastic order, it offered rich fulfilment here and now, besides the promise of a hundredfold to come, in the conception of a mystical marriage of the soul with God, foreshadowed for them in the Song of Songs, and in the new Jerusalem of the Apocalypse. But its demands were too high for the vast numbers that, for one reason or another, were drawn into the clerkly or religious life; and the resulting tensions emerge in the wry humour of this poem—and conversely in a mass of anti-feminist literature.[4]

The following are stanzas 8, 9, 11, 13, 14, 16, 17, 19 of a seventy-six-line poem. The metre is the Goliardic stanza: see Verse Notes 4*c*.

1 *Innocentius*: sc. Innocent III (1198–1216), the most powerful and far-reaching in his aims of all medieval popes.

2, 3, 5 e.g. Gen. 1. 28; 2. 24.

6 *prohibet*: there is certainly no prohibition, but there are some discouragements: e.g. Matt. 19. 12; Luke 14. 26; and 1 Cor. 7. 1, 8, 32–34.

8 *ratio*: reason, expressed in and reinforced by the art of logic, was enthroned alongside the authority of revelation and the Church with a new and wide-ranging vigour from the eleventh century onwards; and there was often no obvious or easy reconciliation.

11–12 *per locum a simili*: 'by argument from analogy'.   Take *omnes . . . qui . . . credunt* together.   *iura*: 'the laws of God'.

---

[1] See E. R. Dodds, *Pagan and Christian in an Age of Anxiety*, Cambridge, 1965.   [2] e.g. St. Jerome (see notes on No. 3).
[3] Rev. 21. 5; Matt. 22. 30.
[4] See introduction to Part Six: Satire and Complaint, and Nos. 62 and 63.

COMMENTARY 235

13 *Zacharias*, father of John the Baptist: see Luke 1.

18 The golden calf of Exod. 32. 4 and Deut. 9. 16.

19 *Levi dedit infulam*: Deut. 10. 8. The classical *infula* is often taken over in Christian literature as a symbol of priestly consecration.

20 *gignerant*: correct usage would require *genuerint*: does the writer deliberately use a solecism for the sake of rhythm and rhyme?

21–22 See 2 Cor. 12. 2–4.

24 1 Cor. 7. 2: *unusquisque suam uxorem habeat*.

25 *dogmata* (Gk. 3 n. pl.): 'doctrines', 'decrees' (already adopted in former sense by Cicero).

32 *cum sua suavi*: 'with his darling'; an ML usage easily derived from *suavium* (a kiss): cf. too Plautus: *cor meum, spes mea, mel meum, suavitudo, cibus, gaudium* (*suavis* is regularly trisyllabic in ML, as in It. *soave*).

59 *A Cursing Song*

A *jeu d'esprit* which cheerfully intertwines (as does so much medieval literature and art) classical and Christian motifs.

2 A sudden and unprepared death, 'unhousel'd, disappointed, unanel'd', was a disaster to be dreaded. Cf. the Roman Litany: *A subitanea et improvisa morte libera nos, Domine*; Tourneur's 'O take me not in sleep' (*The Revenger's Tragedy*, II. 4); and Hamlet on his father's murder:

> He took my father grossly, full of bread,
> With all his crimes broad blown ... (III. iii. 80)

4 Beyond Lethe, the river of 'forgetfulness', lay the Elysian fields, the abode of the blest: see *Aeneid*, VI. 705 ff. and n. on l. 16 below.

7 *de libro ... vite*: see Rev. 3. 5; 22. 19; etc.

8 *Aeacus* was one of the judges in the lower world.

11 *Cerberus*: see *Aeneid*, VI. 417 ff.

12 *Erinys* (Gk.): one of the Furies who punished the wicked.

13–20 *excommunicatus sit*, etc.: all these phrases can be paralleled in the lengthy and terrifying formulas of excommunication used from the early Middle Ages onwards: e.g. 'maledictus sit in via et in agro, maledictus sit in domo et extra domum, maledictus sit dormiendo et vigilando . . . nullam societatem habeat Christianorum . . .' together with the saving clause: 'nisi resipuerit et ad satisfactionem venerit', and the concluding formula: 'Fiat, fiat! Amen.' (See *Die Gesetze der Angelsachsen*, ed. F. Liebermann, vol. i, pp. 432–41.)

16 *Tartareis*: adj. from *Tartarus* (*Tartara*), one of the many Gk. names for the lower world which stressed all the gloom and suffering, as contrasted with Elysium: e.g.

> Hac iter Elysium nobis; at laeva malorum
> exercet poenas, et ad impia Tartara mittit.
>
> (*Aeneid*, VI. 542–3)

18 *presulis examen*: the bishop's examination, and hence 'sentence'.

19 *peccamen*: one of the many semi-abstract nouns coined in LL.

20 *anathema*: 'accursed': see n. on No. **27**, l. 54.

60 *Money Talks*

The *Speculum Stultorum* (the Mirror of Fools) is a long satire of some 4,000 lines, directed against the monks, ecclesiastics, scholars, and rulers of the age by Nigel de Longchamps, himself a monk and Precentor of Christchurch, Canterbury, from *c.* 1170 (the year of Becket's murder). This passage does not do justice to the comedy and rich variety of the whole, 'a true satire in the Roman sense, that is to say a farrago, a mixture'. It enjoyed great popularity, particularly in the fourteenth and fifteenth centuries, as is shown by forty surviving manuscripts scattered over Europe. The text is edited with introduction and notes by J. H. Mozley and R. H. Raymo (University of California Press, 1960). See also Raby, *Secular Latin Poetry*, vol. ii, pp. 94–98.

The repetition of key-words and phrases (*Munera . . . Munera si cessent*) is characteristic of Roman rhetoric, and of Ovid in particular. But while Ovid and the classical poets skilfully limit its use and introduce variations to avoid monotony (e.g. *Tristia*, IV. 6), medieval poets with tireless ingenuity tend to ignore all restraints. (They inherited something of this from Late Latin rhetoric, as practised by Augustine and others.)

1 *Munera*: lit. 'gifts', has throughout the passage the larger connotation of money, and the specific one of bribery and corruption: a recognized usage in the OT, e.g. Exod. 23. 8; 1 Sam. 8. 3; and line 12 below.

COMMENTARY 237

5 Cf. *Carmina Burana*, 42. 31–32:
> Tullium ne timeas, si velit causari:
> Nummus eloquentia gaudet singulari. (J. H. M.)

10 *pensa*: 'payments'.

12 *excaecant oculos*: from Deut. 16. 19, on judges: 'Thou shalt not respect persons, neither take a gift (*munera*): *quia munera excaecant oculos sapientium*.' The previous line is also to be taken metaphorically.

13 *omnia vincit amor*: Virgil, *Eclogue* X. 69.

14 *eum*: sc. *amorem*.   16 *reprobos*: 'the wicked' (LL).

17–18 *recepta* agrees with *munera* (subject); *dona* is in apposition to *damna*. *procis* is dative of agent.

20 *apices*: 'the highest honours'.

22 *proxima causa*: 'the immediate cause'.

27 *primatum pallia*: a band of white woollen material worn round the shoulders by the pope, and bestowed by him on archbishops as a symbol of their authority. It was sometimes sent, sometimes the archbishop sent representatives to receive it, or went to Rome himself to be invested with it. (It still appears in some episcopal coats of arms.)

28 *constabunt levius*: 'will cost less and be bought in a cheaper market'. Cf. *meilleur marché*.

29 *cornua longa*: 'the tall mitres ... will carry less weight (in the realm)'.

The tradition of Benedictine monks as kings' counsellors was an old and honourable one, e.g. 'The wisdom and statesmanship (of St. Dunstan, 909–88) enabled him to be the counsellor and friend of successive kings and one of the creators of a united England' (D. Knowles). Lanfranc (1005–89) as archbishop of Canterbury was the Conqueror's right hand from 1070 till his death. Suger (1081–1151), abbot of St. Denis, was the adviser of Louis VI and Louis VII, and regent of the kingdom during the Second Crusade. By the mid-twelfth century, however, the pattern was changing.

32 ff. *limina sacra ... teret*: 'will frequent his monastery church'. By the twelfth century Cluny had attracted so many gifts that she had become immensely rich, and drew down on herself the indignation of St. Bernard. The whole Cistercian movement in fact was a protest

238   COMMENTARY

against monastic wealth—till the Cistercians in turn became as wealthy as their predecessors.

37 Judas Iscariot, and Simon Magus, who attempted to buy spiritual power (Acts 8. 9–24): hence simony. (See n. on No. **43**, l. 46.)

39–40 *in quorum manibus*: the whole couplet is a close adaptation of Ps. 25. 10 (26. 10): *Ne perdas cum impiis, Deus, animam meam . . . in quorum manibus iniquitates sunt: dextera eorum repleta est muneribus.* (It breaks the sequence here, and is transferred by Mozley to an earlier passage.)

44 *loculos*: 'coffers', 'money-bags'.

61 *Money is King*

The full version (*c.* 50 lines) occurs in various forms in the *Carmina Burana* and in English manuscripts. Lines 2–37 all begin with *Nummus* in one case or another (see n. on No. **60**). The metre is the Leonine hexameter: see Verse Notes, 3. Punctuation presents a problem. In the latest edition of the *Carmina Burana* each line is end-stopped. A compromise has been attempted here.

Similar satires are found in thirteenth- to fourteenth-century French and English, where *Nummus* appears as *Dan Denier* (*Dan* = *Dominus*: cf. Dan Chaucer) or as Sir Peni: e.g.

>   Thare strife was, Peni makes pese. . . .
>   That sire is set on high dese
>   And served with mani riche mese
>   At the high burde . . . .[1]   (Cf. ll. 7 and 20 ff.)

5 *nigrorum . . . priorum*: priors of the Black Monks, i.e. Benedictines.

6 *consiliorum*: 'councils'.

8 *deponere dites* (i.e. *divites*): echoes Luke 1. 52–53.

9 *de stercore* . . . Ps. 112. 7 (113. 7). *ad plenum* (neut.): 'filling him with good things'; suggested by *esurientes implevit bonis* (Luke 1. 53).

20 *mensa . . . densa*: 'loaded table'.

22 *Francorum . . . atque marinum* ('from overseas') suggests that the satire is English in origin.

26 Recalls the Pharisees who 'love the salutations in the market-places'.

---

[1] See *Latin Poems attributed to Walter Mapes*, ed. T. Wright, 1841, pp. 357–62.

27 *virtutes*: 'mighty works, miracles'; see LN 5*b*.

29 Mark 7. 37; Isa. 35. 6.

30 *prioribus*: 'than what has gone before'.

62 *O Most Pernicious Woman!* (1)

For the *De Vita Monachorum* see *Anglo-Latin Satirical Poets*, ed. T. Wright. The poem runs to *c*. 800 lines, and is chiefly concerned with the perils that beset the monk.

> Vita quid est praesens? temptatio, pugna molesta;
> hic acies semper, semper et hostis adest.

Among these perils woman occupies *c*. 120 lines; and after the threat to the monastic life:

> Femina, mors animae, monachis accedere numquam
> audeat; a sacro sit procul ipsa viro,

the writer turns his weapons against marriage.

> Et forsan dices felices esse maritos,
> et casti laudes foedera coniugii.
> crede mihi, frater, miser est quicumque maritus.
> vis dicam quantum triste fit illud onus?

There follows a long catalogue of the woes of marriage. Nor can the married, even in the next life, look for the hundredfold, or sixtyfold, promised in the Gospel (Matt. 13. 23), but must be content with the third place, and thirtyfold. (The same conclusion is reached in Langland's *Vision of Piers Plowman*, *c*. 1370, and seems to have been a commonplace of medieval preaching.) The general attitude, and much of the material, can be found in St. Jerome: e.g., writing to a widow and counselling her against a second marriage, he asks: *Quid facit in facie Christianae purpurissus et cerussa* (rouge and white lead)? *quorum alterum ruborem genarum labiorumque mentitur, alterum candorem oris et colli: ignes iuvenum, fomenta libidinum, impudicae mentis indicia. . . . Qua fiducia erigit ad caelum vultus quos conditor non agnoscat?* (*Letter* LIV. 7).

1 *dulce malum*: 'delicious poison': the phrase is Ovid's (as is much of the poet's technique): *usque adeo dulce puella malum est* (*Am*. 11. 9. 36), and is so striking that Nigel de Longchamps borrowed it for his *Speculum Stultorum* (l. 2609): *Munera, dulce malum*.

240   COMMENTARY

5 ff. 'I have heard of your paintings too, well enough; God hath given you one face, and you make yourselves another: you jig, you amble, and you lisp . . .' (*Hamlet*, III. i).

7 *pingit acu*: 'makes herself up': lit. 'embroiders'.

10 *charus* (ML) = *carus*; see LN 6*c*.

11 *ieiunat mense* (i.e. *mensae*, Dat.): 'abstains from . . .' (LL).

13 *rustica* was regularly used as a term of abuse; cf. *agrestis*, and Engl. 'boorish'. A white-faced fragility was fashionable again in the eighteenth century. Bosoms have been in and out of fashion since fashion began.

20 seems to echo ll. 5 and 18 above. *suo . . . movere loco*: 'to displace'.

23 'What postures she adopts': *frangit* implies something unnatural and artificial.

32 *letifer hostis*: sc. Satan.

35 '*omnis caro faenum*': 'all flesh is grass': Isa. 40. 6.

63 *O Most Pernicious Woman!* (2)

For the Leonine hexameter see Verse Notes, 3. N.B. *e* for *ae*: e.g. *Ve, que*.

1 'Woe (unto the man) who . . .'.

3 *insensati*: 'fools': 'parted from your riches': perhaps suggesting that, like the Prodigal Son, they have wasted their substance with riotous living.

7 *quidquam veri*: 'any secret'.

8 *Maronis . . . Nasonis*: i.e. P. Vergilius Maro and P. Ovidius Naso.

11 *artes* amplifies *scelerum partes*: 'crime and cunning'.

12 For Samson and Delilah see Judges 16. *Salomonem*: a general tilt at his polygamy.

13 *Heliam*: Elias/Elijah, after slaying the prophets of Baal, was driven out of the land by Jezebel: see 1 Kings 19. 1–3. *vita . . . Uriam*: a monstrous charge! For Uriah and Bathsheba see 2 Sam. 11.

15: Eve.

COMMENTARY 241

64 *The Gospel according to the Mark of Silver*

There are twenty-six quotations or allusions in about as many lines. Only some of them will be indicated here.

1–2 *Initium . . . secundum*: *In illo tempore*: these two formulae are regularly used to introduce the Gospel at Mass.

2 *Cum venerit* . . . Matt. 25. 31.

3–4 *Amice . . . venisti?* Matt. 26. 50.

4 *si perseveraverit* . . . Luke 11. 8.

7–8 *Miseremini* . . . a parody of Job 19. 21. *hostiarii* for *ostiarii*: an initial aspirate is not infrequently introduced in ML; e.g. *habundanter*.

9 *Ego vero egenus* . . . Ps. 69. 6 (70. 5).

11 f. *paupertas tua* . . . Acts 8. 20, where St. Peter rounds on Simon Magus. *Vade retro* . . . parodies Mark 8. 33; *quoniam non sapis quae Dei sunt, sed quae sunt hominum. nummi* is probably gen. sing., and *sapiunt* intrans., 'you are not on the side of money'.

14 *donec dederis* . . . Matt. 5. 26.

16 *abiit et vendidit* . . . Matt. 13. 46.

18 *Et hoc quid est . . . ?* John 6. 9. *tantos* for *tot* (ML).

20 *non habens consolationem*: unlike the rich, 'who have received their consolation' (Luke 6. 24).

21 *incrassatus . . . dilatatus*: Deut. 32. 15, speaking of Israel who 'waxed fat, grew thick, and became sleek' (an ominous passage, since it continues 'Then he forsook God who made him').

22 *qui propter seditionem* . . . like Barabbas (Mark 15. 7).

23–24 *At illi* . . . Matt. 20. 10.

26 *infirmatus est* . . . Phil. 2. 27.

27 *sibi* for *ei*: see LN 7*b*. *electuarium*: a medicine compounded of a powder mixed with honey or syrup.

29–30 *Videte ne aliquis* . . . Eph. 5. 6.

30–31 *Exemplum enim* . . . John 13. 15, with the ingenious substitution of *capio* and *capiatis* for *facio* and *faciatis*.

65 *The Roman Curia*

For Walter of Châtillon (*fl.* 1170) see Raby, *Secular Latin Poetry*, vol. ii, pp. 190–204. 'A scholar at odds with the world', he smarted under all the wrongs that poverty and wit could endure at the hands of riches and entrenched authority. Born at Lille, he studied in Paris, and became head of the cathedral school of Laon. He spent some time in England in the chancery of Henry II, where a brilliant circle was gathered round Theobald, archbishop of Canterbury (1139–62). After the murder of Becket in 1170 he left England, studied canon law in Bologna and visited Rome, then settled down at Châtillon to teach and write. Steeped in the classics, he chose the new rhythms, with an uncanny skill for incorporating in them the apt quotation, whether from Juvenal, Horace, Ovid, or the Scriptures. For the rhythm, see Verse Notes, 4*b* (iii). The whole poem runs to 180 lines, or 30 stanzas, of which 12 are given here: Nos. 1–5, 9, 13, 18, 19, 24, 25, 30. N.B. *e* for *ae*.

1 Lines 1 and 5 come straight from Isa. 62. 1 and are skilfully fitted in to the metrical scheme—or perhaps determine it. (Altogether there are *c.* 20 allusions to or quotations from Scripture, and *c.* 10 from the classics.)

Sion (Jerusalem) commonly represents the Church as a whole.

3–4 Isa. 45. 8.

8 *princeps*: 'she that was princess': *princeps provinciarum facta est sub tributo.* Lam. 1. 1.

13 ff. The sea metaphor is worked out with great elaboration, using all the resources of Gk. mythology: e.g. Scylla and Charybdis, who beset the Straits of Messina (*profundi . . . Siculi*): the one human from the waist upwards, but encircled by yelping dogs who snatched at sailors, the other a whirlpool which sucked them down (Virgil, *Aeneid*, III. 420–8, Ovid, *Met.* XIV. 59–67, etc.).

16 *bitalassus* (Gk.): a (dangerous) place where two seas meet; from Acts 27. 41, describing St. Paul's shipwreck on Malta.

17 Crassus, the Roman millionaire who invaded Parthia and perished at Carrhae (53 B.C.), was put to death, according to medieval legend, by having molten gold poured into his mouth. Here he stands for the insatiable greed of Roman officials.

22 *galearum*: 'galleys' (ML, deriv. uncertain).

COMMENTARY

25 The *Sirtes* (Syrtes) were dangerous sandbanks off the coast of North Africa, where Aeneas' fleet was wrecked (*Aeneid*, I. 110 ff.). They seem here to be identified with the Sirens (see l. 37 below), half-human and half-birds, who lured sailors to their doom by the beauty of their song.

Stanzas 6–8

The 'two seas meet' in Franco, the chamberlain, where the winds clash and precious cargoes are sunk, swallowed up in his maw.

33 *advocati curie*: lay 'protectors' of various monasteries, etc., who made a rich living out of their protégés (see St. Bernard's comments, No. **20,** ll. 14 ff.).

39 *bizantium*: see n. on No. **36,** l. 9.

41–42 'With a sudden burst of avarice they lay low your purse'. (*parcitas* does duty for *avaritia* for the sake of the rhyme.)

Stanzas 14–17

Like Sirens they beguile you: 'I know you well, brother, you come from France, a special favourite of the Holy See.' Softly they flatter, and instil their venom—then make your purse disgorge.

44–45 'By an unheard-of abuse of power they sell the patrimony of Christ'; i.e. the privileges of the Church.

47–48: Matt. 7. 15.   50–51: Matt. 16. 19.

53–54 *nox . . . scientiam*: Ps. 18, 2 (19. 2), 'night unto night showeth knowledge': i.e. the blind lead the blind—a brilliant twist given to a familiar text; and once again it fits exactly into the rhythm.

Stanzas 20–23

At the helm sits a monstrous figure, chief of the pirates, Pilate. Not Thetis but Sister Money-bags is goddess of this sea. While your purse is full, you will feast with the pirates, but once it is empty, wind and wave will assail you, and farewell your barque!

58–60 An adaptation of Juvenal X. 22: *cantabit vacuus coram latrone viator*: 'the traveller with empty pockets will laugh in the face of the robber'.

64 *ere* (i.e. *aere*): 'money'.

Stanzas 26–29

There are only two harbours where you can repair your shattered vessel: one is Peter of Pavia, the other my good friend Alexander (God bring him to

Paradise!). *He cares for scholars—but he too, like Elisha, has a Gehazi by his side (see 2 Kings 5. 20–27).*

71–72 Adapted from Ps. 140. 3 (141. 3): *Pone, Domine, custodiam ori meo.*

66 *The Poor Scholar*

The following ten stanzas (nos. 5–9, 12, 14, 17, 19, 20) come from a twenty-stanza poem, *Missus sum in vineam* . . . (*MLV*, No. 198), on the wrongs of the poor scholar. The first three lines of each stanza are in the 'Goliardic' measure (see Verse Notes, 4*c*), while the fourth is a quotation, or 'authority', usually a hexameter or pentameter from the classics, which sums up the argument and drives it home. N.B. *e* for *ae*: e.g. *querens, hec, perdite.*

3 *mimum*: here used for 'poet', 'satirist' (CL 'actor'; 'farce').

4 Horace, *Epist.* I. 1. 53.

5 *sinodis* for *synodis* (Gk. 2 f.): an ecclesiastical assembly: e.g. the Synod of Whitby, 664. *confidendo*: gerund used adverbially (ML).

7 'enthrones bishops, and makes the names of the rich resound'.

8 Horace, *Epist.* I. 6. 37: 'birth and beauty'. For Horace's *regina Pecunia*, cf. the twelfth-century *In terra summus rex est hoc tempore Nummus* (No. **61**).

10 *armaria*: 'libraries': the normal meaning in ML (lit. 'cupboards'); cf. No. **37**, l. 16).

11 *Parisius* used as locative in ML. 'Study as long as you like . . .'. Ovid, *Ars Am.* II. 277–80: 'Why woo your mistress with verses?' (he writes);

> Aurea sunt vere nunc saecula, plurimus auro
>   venit honos; auro conciliatur amor.
> Ipse licet venias Musis comitatus, Homere,
>   si nihil attuleris, ibis, Homere, foras.

Walter of Châtillon uses the last couplet in reverse order for ll. 12 and 16.

13 'The philosopher may be content to go without his wine . . .'. *disputet*: concessive subj., but *sciat*: jussive.

COMMENTARY 245

20 Lucan, I. 181, reads *avidumque in tempora fenus*, i.e. 'interest which lays greedy hands on the future' (Lucan is enumerating the causes of the Civil War).

21 *Illud est, cur* . . .: 'That is why . . .'.

24 Ovid, *Heroides*, 3. 117. Cf. Milton, *Lycidas* 64–69:
> Were it not better done as others use,
> To sport with Amaryllis in the shade?

27 *numquid* (CL) became the standard method of asking a question in ML.

28 Lucan, I. 281: Curio is urging Caesar to strike at once: *Tolle moras; semper nocuit differre paratis.* *paratis*: abl. abs.

31 *iuxta*: 'according to' (Ovid): *Remed. Amoris*, 749.

33 'There were giants in those days' (Gen. 6. 4).

35 'all the trumpeting of fame'.

36 Juv. 7. 81.

38 *potibus et cibis* (dat.): 'devote yourself rather to . . .'.

40 Combines two lines of advice from Daedalus to Icarus (Ovid, *Met.* II. 140, 137).

67 *The Witch of Berkeley*

In the story immediately preceding this the body of Gregory VI (d. 1048), who was wrongly suspected of sorcery, was admitted by divine intervention into the church for burial: the present one illustrates the exact opposite.

1 *Hisdem*: ML for *isdem*.   2 *inferno praestigio*: 'devilish trickery'.

3 *fides* . . . : 'the credit of the narrative will not be shaken'.

5 *erubescerem*: generic subj.   *iuraret* is confused with it, or assimilated to it.

6 *mansitabat*: frequentative of *maneo*: 'dwell'.   *insueta*: 'accustomed to' (to be dist. from *insueta*: 'unaccustomed').

7 *petulantiae arbitra*: 'mistress of wantonness'.

COMMENTARY

8–9 *quod esset . . . aditum*: 'thinking she was . . . 'though soon to knock at . . .' (one kicked at a door for admission). Cf. Horace: *Pallida mors aequo pulsat pede pauperum tabernas Regumque turris* (*Odes*, I. 4. 13).

10 *cornicula*: 'her pet jackdaw'; dim. of *cornix*, 'crow', hence *cornicor*: 'croak, chatter'.

16 *percunctatus*: pass. (more commonly dep.).   *vultuosus*: 'with such a strange expression'.

17 *villa*: 'village'.

24 *vitiorum sentina*: 'sink of iniquity'.

26 *religionis*: normally 'monastic life' in ML.   *quae palparet*: 'to comfort . . .'.

27 *desperata*: nom. 'despairing of myself' (CL).

31 *si qua fides*: 'if you have any loyalty and love for me': a Virgilian phrase (William of Malmesbury is full of these poetic echoes).

32 *alleviare* by fourth century begins to replace CL *allevare*.

34 'Sew me up in a deer-skin' (so that the devils don't recognize me).

35 *operculum*: 'lid'.   36 *lapidem*: 'stone coffin'.

37 *psalmicines*: the psalm-singers were to sing the Office of the Dead, of which the opening words are '*Dirige, Domine . . . viam meam*': hence Engl. 'dirge'.

38 *missae*: 'masses'.

39 *levigent* (LL): 'lighten'.   For the *excursus feroces* cf. St. Anselm and the Hare, No. 15.

41 *fugiat . . . recipere*: 'shrink from' (CL poet.).

44 *nil lacrimae . . .* slips unconsciously into hexameter rhythm, as Dickens in emotional passages into blank verse.

47–48 *concreparent*: 'chanting'.

50–51 *illibata*: 'unharmed'.

55 *Deriguere . . . metu*: the sentence begins with a reminiscence of Ovid (*Met.* 7. 115) and ends with Virgil (*Aeneid*, III. 48).

59 *solveris*: fut. pass., '. . . to your cost'.

67 *miliaria*: CL 'milestone', already used for 'mile' in second century.

COMMENTARY 247

68 *The Two Clerks of Nantes*

Notice the style of the whole narrative: elaborate, learned, and horrific. The normal lower age-limit for the priesthood was 30, but it could be very loosely observed, when considerations of rank or wealth supervened.

4–5 *quam . . . praecipites*: 'how near they had both been to the brink of Hell'.

6–7 *ut . . . artibus*: i.e. they were past masters in the arts . . . 'from their earliest infancy'.

9 *Comici*: Terence (*c*. 195–159 B.C.) adapted Greek comedies for the Latin stage. *manibus pedibusque*: a proverbial expression: cf. Engl. 'with might and main'.

10 *pro invicem*: 'for each other'; see LN 7*c*.

14 *nec satiasse* governs *mentes*: 'but had found no satisfaction'.

17 *praeveniendum* sc. *esse*: 'so they must take measures betimes'.

21–23 *si fiat . . .*' to convince him, if this were indeed the case, that . . .'.—For Plato's teaching see No. **39** n.—The 'prison' metaphor was a familiar one: e.g. *Aeneid*, VI. 734.

24 *sin minus*: 'otherwise'; balances *si fiat*.—The views of Epicurus (341–270 B.C.) and his school and those of the Platonists were familiar from Cicero's discussions of them in his *De Finibus* and *De Natura Deorum*—and William of Malmesbury was a passionate Ciceronian (see No. **42**). Cf. *The Tempest*, IV. i. 148:

> These our actors
> Are melted into air, into thin air.

27 *Nec multum . . .*: 'No long time intervened'.

28 *indignantem*: another Virgilian allusion (*Aeneid*, XII. 952).

31 *cassa . . . ventos pavit*: 'occupied himself with vain expectations', a proverbial expression.

32–33 *avocasset otium*: 'had sought distraction in . . .'.

40 *adventus iste*: 'this . . . of mine'; see LN 7*b*.

41–42 *quippe qui . . . sim*: causal subj.

COMMENTARY

48–49 *dum ... pontus*: a reminiscence of Claudian, *In Rufinum* II. 527: *Dum rotet astra polus, feriant dum littora venti.*

51–52 *totus ... exquirat*: 'though the whole world should seek ...'.

54 *en ...* can be followed by acc. since it has the force of *vide*.

58 *cauterio* (Gk.): 'a cautery' (or 'cauterizing iron').

61 *grave ...* : 'grim evidence'.

63–64 *pendula ... clementia*: abl. abs., 'his mercy trembling in the balance'.

64 *muta habitum*: 'change your (secular) dress for a monk's habit'. St. Melanius was a sixth-century bishop of Rennes, the ancient capital of Brittany.

69 *omne*: used as collective noun: 'his whole band'.

70–71 *gratias ... quod*: 'thanked them not only for denying themselves no single pleasure, but for allowing ...'.

74 *incuria*: abl., 'neglect'.

75 *loquentis aspectus*: 'the ghostly speaker'.

78–79 *Haec est ...* Ps. 76. 11 (77. 10) 'This change is wrought by the hand of the most High' (this is not, in fact, the meaning of the original).

69 *Buried Treasure*

8 *absoluta* for *resoluta*. *in centro existente*: 'was in the zenith'. *existere* often used in ML for *esse* (which in any case has no pres. part.).

10 *cubiculario*: chamberlain', 'attendant'. *laternam*: alternative form of *lanternam*.

11 *solitis artibus*: sc. by means of his magic arts.

14 *lacunaria*: 'panelled ceiling'. *tesseris*: 'draughts'.

16 *obsonia* (Gk.): 'dainties'.

18 *carbunculus*: a generic term for any red stone, incl. rubies. *parvus inventu*: 'rarely found'.

COMMENTARY 249

23 *ut quis*: 'whenever anyone'.

26 *ambitum . . . fregit*: 'restrained his greed'.

34 *cupiditatis voragine*: 'boundless avarice'.

70 *Warning to Slanderers*

The full title of this story is *Contra Detractores, Mendaces, et Contenciosos*. It is found among a few miscellaneous items at the beginning of a long fourteenth-century manuscript written at St. Mary's Abbey, York, whose chief contents are two French chronicles, and was transcribed by V. H. Galbraith in his edition of *The Anonimalle Chronicle (1333–1381)* (Manchester University Press, 1927): see p. xlviii. It will be noticed that the Latin is much less elegant and literary than William of Malmesbury's. (For orthography see LN 6.)

2 *Elemosinarius*: Almoner.   5 *Galfrido*: Godfrey.

7 *capituli*: chapter-house.

7–8 *ita . . . quod non audebat*: consecutive; see LN 7e (vi).

10 *lorica fidei*: 1 Thess. 5. 8.

17 *modo* often takes the place of *nunc* in ML (cf. *amodo*: 'from now on').

18 *blasfemare* (Gk.): *f* often takes the place of *ph* in ML. It persists in Ital. (e.g. *filosofia*), and occasionally in Engl. (e.g. *fantasy*).

21 *blodiam*: ML 'blue'—but seems to contradict *fulvi coloris*.   *manubio*: n., 'pocket'.

22 *falcheon*: Engl. and Fr. from ML *falcio* (CL *falx*).

23 *redintegratam*: like Prometheus' liver, it has to grow again, so that the torment may endure for ever.

32 *quem*: antecedent is *monachus*.

33 *contencio*: 'quarrelsomeness'.

41 *ibi venit*: LN 7e (ix).   42 *ille*: sc. Johannes.

45 *sopnum* is in fact the earlier form of *somnum*.

47 ff. *wite a way*: 'go away, vanish' (thirteenth-century).   *forweried*: from *forwear*: 'worn out'.   *ne . . . na*: a double negative, common down to the sixteenth century.

SELECT BIBLIOGRAPHY

(The following list contains a few suggestions from a wide field. Books marked with a * are more suitable for advanced study.)

LANGUAGE

Coulton, C. G., *Europe's Apprenticeship: a survey of Medieval Latin with examples* (Nelson, London, 1940). An introductory survey in general terms, with 126 pp. of examples, translated.

*Löfstedt, E., *Late Latin* (Kegan Paul, Trench, London, 1959). An important linguistic study, trans. from Swedish.

*Mohrmann, C., *Études sur le latin des chrétiens*, 2 vols. (Edizioni di Storia e Letteratura, Rome, 1958). Articles in French, English, German, and Italian, on a wide range of subjects, linguistic and literary, including *The Confessions, The Rule of St. Benedict, The Style of St. Bernard*.

—— *Latin vulgaire, Latin des chrétiens, Latin médiéval* (Klincksieck, Paris, 1955). A lecture, pp. 54.

Strecker, K. M. W., *Introduction to Medieval Latin*, trans. R. B. Palmer (Weidmannsche Verlagsbuchhandlung, Berlin, 1957). A purely linguistic study.

DICTIONARIES

Blaise, A., *Dictionnaire latin-français des auteurs chrétiens* (Brepols, Turnhout, Belgique, 1954). A valuable dictionary, pp. 863; about half the size of Lewis & Short.

Latham, R. E., *Revised Medieval Latin Word-List, from British and Irish Sources* (O.U.P., London, 1965). A much enlarged version of the earlier *Medieval Latin Word-List*, ed. Baxter and Johnson; pp. 524.

Niermeyer, J. F., *Mediae Latinitatis Lexicon Minus* (Brill, Leiden, 1954–64). The last fascicule, No. 12, is not yet published (1967): pp. 1056 to date. Definitions are given in French and English, and are fully analytical.

History

The standard text-books, e.g. *The Shorter Cambridge Medieval History*, by C. W. Previté-Orton (C.U.P., Cambridge, 1952), will supply the factual background. The books mentioned below adopt some particular point of view, or deal with some special aspect of the Middle Ages.

Dawson, C., *Religion and the Rise of Western Culture* (Sheed & Ward, London, 1950).

Haskins, C. H., *The Renaissance of the Twelfth Century* (Harvard, 1927).

Heer, F., *The Medieval World: Europe from 1100–1350*, trans. J. Sondheimer (Weidenfeld & Nicolson, London, 1962). Is chiefly concerned with the intellectual and imaginative life of the age.

Knowles, D., *The Evolution of Medieval Thought* (Longman, London, 1962).

—— *The Historian and Character* (C.U.P., Cambridge, 1962). (Contains essays on twelfth-century humanism, and on St. Bernard.)

—— *The Monastic Order in England, 943–1216*, second edition (C.U.P., Cambridge, 1962). (Though chiefly concerned with this period, it looks back to the beginnings of Benedictine monasticism.)

—— *Saints and Scholars: twenty-five medieval portraits* (C.U.P., Cambridge, 1962). (These are selections from the above and later volumes, and include Bede, Anselm, Samson, and Matthew Paris.)

Leclercq, J., *The Love of Learning and the Desire for God: a study of monastic culture*; trans. C. Misrahi (Mentor Omega Books, N.Y., 1962).

Rashdall, H., *The Universities of Europe in the Middle Ages*; a new edition, ed. F. M. Powicke and A. B. Emden, 3 vols. (Clarendon Press, Oxford, 1936).

Runciman, S., *A History of the Crusades*, 3 vols. (C.U.P., Cambridge, 1951–4) (vol. i covers the First Crusade).

Southern, R. W., *The Making of the Middle Ages* (Hutchinson, London, 1957). Also available as a Grey Arrow paperback. (Is primarily concerned with 'the formation of Western Europe from the late tenth to the early thirteenth century'.)

Literature

*Curtius, E. R., *European Literature and the Latin Middle Ages*, trans. W. R. Trask (Pantheon Books, N.Y., 1953).

*Dronke, P., *Medieval Latin and the Rise of European Love-Lyric*, 2 vols. (Clarendon Press, Oxford, 1965–6). Vol. i: *Problems and Interpretations*; vol. ii: *Texts newly edited from the MSS*.

*Lehmann, P., *Die Parodie im Mittelalter*, second edition (Hiersemann, Stuttgart, 1963). (A critical discussion, followed by 74 pp. of examples.)

Lewis, C. S., *The Discarded Image: an introduction to medieval and renaissance literature* (C.U.P., Cambridge, 1964).

—— *The Allegory of Love: a study in medieval tradition* (O.U.P., London, 1936). Ch. 1 is relevant.

Raby, F. J. E., *A History of Christian-Latin Poetry from the Beginnings to the Close of the Middle Ages*, second edition (Clarendon Press, Oxford, 1953).

—— *A History of Secular Latin Poetry in the Middle Ages*, second edition, 2 vols. (Clarendon Press, Oxford, 1957).

Waddell, H., *The Wandering Scholars*, sixth edition (Constable, London, 1932).

Wright, F. A., and Sinclair, T. A., *A History of Later Latin Literature, from the fourth to the seventeenth century* (Routledge, London, 1931). An introductory survey of a wide field.

Anthologies and Collections

Brittain, F., *The Penguin Book of Latin Verse* (Penguin, London, 1962).

Browne, R. A., *British Latin Selections, A.D. 500–1400*, with introduction, notes, and vocabulary of medieval words (Blackwell, Oxford, 1954).

Carmina Burana, ed. A. Hilka and O. Schumann, 3 vols. (Winter, Heidelberg, 1930–41). This, the most recent critical edition, is not yet completed. A short selection is included in *Carmina Burana, Lieder der Vaganten*, with German verse translations in the original metres by E. Brost (Schneider, Heidelberg, 1961), and the collection is represented in all the anthologies.

Dobiache-Rojdestvensky, O., *Les Poésies des goliards* (Rieder, Paris, 1931). Texts and translations, with some discussion.

Raby, F. J. E., *The Oxford Book of Medieval Latin Verse* (Clarendon Press, Oxford, 1959).

Waddell, H., *Medieval Latin Lyrics* (Constable, London, 1929). Consists of texts and verse translations, for which *The Wandering Scholars* serves as an introduction.

Wright, T., *The Anglo-Latin Satirical Poets and Epigrammatists of the Twelfth Century*, 2 vols. (Rolls Series, London, 1872).

INDIVIDUAL AUTHORS

Some texts, biographies, and critical studies.

Aelfric: *The Colloquy of Aelfric*, ed. G. N. Garmonsway (Methuen, London, 1939). This edition gives both Latin text and AS gloss, but is chiefly concerned with the latter.

Anselm: Southern, R. W., *St. Anselm and his Biographer* (C.U.P., Cambridge, 1963). See also Eadmer, below.

Augustine: Brown, P., *Augustine of Hippo: a biography* (Faber & Faber, London, 1967), pp. 463.

—— Marrou, H. I., *St. Augustine and his influence through the ages*; trans. P. Hepburne-Scott (Longman, London, 1957), pp. 188.

—— *The Confessions*, ed. J. Gibb and W. Montgomery (C.U.P., Cambridge, 1908). A fully annotated edition.

Bede: *Bedae Opera Historica*, ed. with introd. and commentary by A. Plummer (Clarendon Press, Oxford, 1896).

—— *Bede—His Life, Times, and Writings*, ed. A. Hamilton Thompson (O.U.P., Oxford, 1935).

Benedict: *The Rule of St. Benedict*, in Latin and English, ed. and trans. by Justin McCann (Burns and Oates, London, 1952).

Bernard: Leclercq, J., *St. Bernard et l'esprit cistercien* (Éditions du Seuil, Paris, 1966).

Caesarius of Heisterbach: *The Dialogue on Miracles*, trans. by H. von E. Scott and C. C. S. Bland, with introd. by G. G. Coulton, 2 vols. (Routledge, London, 1929).

Eadmer: *The Life of St. Anselm*, edited with introd., notes, and trans. by R. W. Southern (Nelson, London, 1962). See also Anselm, above.

Gesta Francorum: edited with introd., notes, and trans. by Rosalind Hill (Nelson, London, 1962).

Jocelin of Brakelond: *The Chronicle of Jocelin of Brakelond*, trans., with introd. and notes by H. E. Butler (Nelson, London, 1949).

Matthew Paris: *Chronica Majora*, edited by H. R. Luard, 7 vols. (Rolls Series, London, 1872–83).

—— Vaughan, R., *Matthew Paris* (C.U.P., Cambridge, 1958).

Petrarch: *Francesco Petrarcha, Le Familiari (Familiarium Rerum Libri I–XXIV)*, edited by Vittorio Rossi, 4 vols. (Sansoni, Florence, 1933–42). This forms part of the latest critical edition of Petrarch's Latin works, still incomplete.

—— *Francesco Petrarcha, Prose*, edited by G. Martellotti (Ricciardi, ardi, Milan, 1955): contains some of the *Senilium Rerum Libri XVII* as well as earlier letters and other works, with Italian translation.

—— *Francisci Petrarchae Epistolae Selectae*, ed. A. F. Johnson (Clarendon Press, Oxford, 1923). The only English edition; contains 206 pp. of text and 70 pp. of notes.

—— Bishop, M., *Petrarch and his World* (Chatto & Windus, London, 1963).

—— de Nolhac, P., *Pétrarque et l'humanisme*, 2 vols. (Paris, 1907).

—— Whitfield, J. H., *Petrarch and the Renascence* (Blackwell, Oxford, 1943).

Richard de Bury, *Philobiblon*, edited and translated by E. C. Thomas (Kegan Paul, Trench, London, 1888). The same text and translation is edited with foreword and additional notes by M. Maclagan (Blackwell, Oxford, 1960).

—— Riccardo da Bury, *Philobiblon*, edizione critica a cura di A. Altamura (Fiorentino, Naples, 1954). The best edition of the text.

William of Malmesbury, *De Gestis Regum Anglorum*, edited by W. Stubbs, 2 vols. (Rolls Series, London, 1887–9).